MW01277718

"The best thing about being Canadian is that we have no wars here and no fighting like in other places. It is safe here."

--Tal Elbaz, École Guy-Drummond

"Being kind and loyal to people is what being a Canadian is all about."

--Karamvir Singh Dubb, Cardinal-Léger School

"The best thing about being a Canadian is feeling protected in a country where your dreams come true."

--Atefa Jaffari, Cardinal-Léger School

With thanks to the *Gazette*, Montreal, for permission to reprint these quotes.

About the Author

Egyptian-born Cherif Rifaat was educated in a British school in Cairo and holds post-graduate degrees in electronics engineering (Zurich) and business management (McGill). He is fluent in four languages. His business career included work overseas as corporate executive with a multinational company.

Having personally experienced the transition between cultures—as a student, as an expatriate high ranking employee, as an immigrant, and as a naturalized citizen—he is well equipped to tackle questions of cross-cultural transition. Rifaat lives in Montreal with his wife and three children.

Immigrants Adapt, Countries Adopt...Or Not: Fitting Into the Cultural Mosaic

Cherif Rifaat

NEW
CANADIANS
New Canadians Press
Montreal

Published in 2004 by
New Canadians Press Incorporated
Les Éditions Nouveaux Citoyens Inc.
P.O. Box 26, Station Pierrefonds
Montreal, Quebec, Canada H9H 4K8
www.newcanadianspress.com

National Library of Canada Cataloguing in Publication

Main entry under title:
"Immigrants adapt, countries adopt...or not: fitting into the cultural mosaic."

Includes bibliographical references and index.

ISBN 0-9733754-0-X

1. Rifaat, Cherif; 2. Muslims--Cultural assimilation--Canada; 3. Immigrants--Cultural assimilation--Canada; 4. Immigrants--Cultural assimilation--Quebec (Province); 5; Canada--Emigration and immigration. I. Title

First edition published 2004

FC608.I4R53 2003   305.9´0691´0971 C2003-904698-2

Original water-colour paintings (cover) by Fatma Rifaat
Cover design by Lauren Kligman

Printed and bound in Canada

For Heidi, Tarek, Karim and Shereen.

In memory of my parents who gave us so much.

In homage to the fortitude of immigrants everywhere.

Acknowledgements

I am very grateful to a number of people who have been kind enough to assist me in various ways. Early on, political scientist Ms. Heba Ghaleb gave me valuable feedback and helped me find a style for this book that was both scholarly and entertaining. Many thanks to Senator Céline Hervieux-Payette and Helmut Birk for their carefully considered, precise and valuable comments. Andre Dirlik, Professor (retired) of International Relations at St-Jean Military College, and John Zucchi, Professor of History at McGill University, gave me praise, encouragement, and important suggestions. Many thanks to Professor Jack Jedwab, who kindly supplied me with his study "A Profile of Canadian Immigration at Century's End"; to Linda Cardinal, Professor of Political Science at the University of Ottawa, who was kind enough to make critical comments that helped improve the manuscript; to Mr. Albert Meher, former Consul General of Switzerland in Montreal, who sent for and lent me references on the nineteenth-century civil war in Basel, from the Zentralbibliothek in Bern; to Ms. Nevine Kotry, direct descendent of Taher Pasha, who allowed me access to private family documents relating to his story; to Mrs. Asmeralda Alfi, Director of the Bureau of Islamic and Arabic Education (BIAE) for verification of some facts; to Hussein Ryadh, who sent me relevant findings from his internet research; to Abla Sherif, Dean of the School of Media and Design - Algonquin College, who kindly introduced me to author Amy Friedman (Nothing Sacred, Oberon Press, 1992), who gave me good advice. Thanks also to those who read selected parts of the manuscript and gave useful feedback: Barry and Monique Jackson, Jeff and Johanna Klym, Ramesh Mirshandani, Mahmoud Gawad, Stephanie Normandin, Ahmed El Zanfalli, my brothers Mohsen and Aziz, My nephew Karim Hamdi as well as my nephew Sherif, for his research. I extend my compliments to my editor, Judyth Mermelstein for her keen personal interest in the material and her editorial skills. My thanks also to David Bernardi for his fine copy-editing and punctuality.

Foreword

My first impulse is one of gratitude towards Canadians for the marvelous way they have shaped modern Canada, and for allowing me to come and evolve into a happy New Canadian. My journey from a developing country via studies in Europe to my new home in Canada has had its ups and downs, but all is well that ends well. Before embarking on this story, two clarifications are in order.

The first is that, in many cases, there is no one "truth", only differing perspectives. How to tell which are true and which untrue? Deliberate manipulation aside, the question is moot. What is clear, however, is that, my perspectives about individual issues can be quite different from those of many native-born Canadians. Our different attitudes and beliefs are a function of the widely different contexts and circumstances in which they were shaped.

So, this book is about only one truth: these really are my experiences, hopes, anxieties and perspectives. Some Francophones have praised the book but obliquely suggested that I "drop certain parts about Quebec." Some Anglophones found it "interesting" and discreetly suggested there was no need to rake up the past and "bash the British Empire." I declined to follow such advice. A genuine expression of my perspectives may be relevant to both Francophones and Anglophones: they are those of an immigrant at a time when immigration is changing. Surely, a glimpse of how some of us think can be useful.

Secondly, I have written this book in the same way I face life: as a generalist using a multidisciplinary approach. It is not academic literature. I believe living well requires a multidisciplinary approach: decision making theory, behavioral science, history, political science, engineering, ... I try to bring together what I need to tackle a certain problem or define and achieve an objective. In this book I quote authors and scholars prominent in their fields, whose views have influenced my world view and decision making. However, though an expert on group behaviour or a professional historian knows much more than I do within their fields, it has been my observation that not everyone can or needs to apply such an approach. There are different ways to face life and be "successful", however that may be defined. My way is valid, too. With some luck and in spite of painful mistakes, I am satisfied that I have done well for my family and myself. One of my best and most successful decisions was to come to Canada.

Cherif Rifaat
March 8, 2004

CONTENTS

Introduction   1

PART I COMING HOME TO A PLACE I HAD
        NEVER BEEN
Chapter 1: Is Canada a Real Country? No, It's Better!   9
    Sovereign Nation-States: A Modern Way to Distinguish
        Between Humans
    What Is a "Real" Country in Its Purest Form?
    Immigrants and the Old Country: A Parting of Mindsets
    A Warm Welcome to the Real Super-Country of Canada
    Canada the Civilized

Chapter 2: Racism and Highest Respect for the Individual   31
    "Immigrants Are Vital, Study Says"
    Expatriates versus Immigrants
    Respect and Racism in the U.S.
    Respect and Racism in Canada
    Oppression and Revenge

Chapter 3: Growing Up in a Clash of Empires   49
    A Dog-Eat-Dog World
    Comfortably Tailored Memories
    How nationalism Came to My Country of Birth
    Are Conquerors Better Than the Conquered?

Chapter 4: Language Wars, Long Ago and Far Away   61
    Language and My Identity
    Language as a Factor of Class Distinction
    Language and Nationalism
    Language and Violent Conflict

Chapter 5: Civilized and Reasonable beyond Comprehension   77
    Are Injustice and Oppression Timeless and Predictable?
    Democracy Is Amazing
    Democracy, Respect, and Integrity
    The "Avalanche Effect" of Corruption

Part II RELATIONSHIPS, LIKES AND DISLIKES
Chapter 6: Anti-immigrant Currents   95
    Economic Arguments
    Happy Immigrants Make Good Citizens
    Globalization and Unskilled Workers
    Immigrant Children and Language
    "War on Terror"
    The Added Value That Immigrants Bring
    Racism or Business Decision?
    Hey! Who Is Picking on My Part of the Canadian Mosaic?
    Could I Ever Become a Separatist?

Chapter 7: Interethnic Dissonance? Muslims and Jews?   109
Muslims and Jews: A Benign History
My First Palestinian
Leave the Hatreds Behind
The Importance of "Self-Hating" Jews
Islam Is Here to Stay
A Lost Hope for Peace
Can Israel's neighbours ever accept it?

Chapter 8: The U.S. and I: Fluctuating Admiration   127
The Famous Balancing Act
Intermittent Approval
Why Did I Not Choose America?
Should I Have Chosen America?
Canada Suits Me Better After All

Chapter 9: The Burden of Contradictions   141
The "Gap" Revisited
A Hope Reversed
How I Benefit from Injustice

Chapter 10: Tormenting the Weak and Vulnerable   147
How to Attract Hostility and Hatred
Class Struggles: From National to International
Do The Jews "Control America"?
"Wherever I Go, 'They' Try to Manipulate Me"
"The Evildoers Are Solely Responsible for 9-11"
Envy Is Not a Motivator for Murder
Can the War on Terror Be Won?
Can I Hope to Be Wrong about U.S. Intentions?

Chapter 11: To Plague the Inventor   165
What Should North American Muslims Do?
A Nation-State Cannot Defeat a Religious Faith
Learning from the Rich and Powerful

PART III QUEBEC AND IMMIGRANTS: REDUCED MUTUAL AFFINITY

Chapter 12: Coercion and Failure   173
Taboos
Distinct Impositions
Losing New France
Self-Interest versus Collective Interest
Coercion in New France
Coercion in Modern Quebec
Old-stock and Newcomers: Converging Motivators

Chapter 13: How to Alienate Immigrants   193
Three Priorities of Immigrants
Asking the Right Questions

Chapter 14: English Words and Arabic Numbers   197
Knowledge of English Is Very Desirable
One Way Language Laws Can Backfire
French Is Not Equal to English
French Is Endangered But Nonetheless Important
Everyone Wants Arabic Numbers
Why Is French Not Sufficiently attractive?

Chapter 15: Education   207
Immigration Means Adaptation, Which Means Education
Globalization and Our Children's Education
Education and Terrorism
An "Elitist" Perspective?

Chapter 16: Population   221
Needed: More Procreation and Immigration
Grim Statistics
Some Immigrants Prefer Quebec
The Best Immigrants Can Choose
Why We Stayed in Montreal

Chapter 17: Am I a Real Quebecer?   231
Integrating in Quebec: A Special Case
"A Good Quebecer of Egyptian Origin"
Integrating with a Kind and Gentle Majority of a Different Race
Genuine Belonging or Opportunistic and False Integration?

PART IV AN IMMIGRANT'S WISH LIST

Chapter 18: Two Wishes for Canada   241

Chapter 19: A Wish for Montreal   245
Cities Are Economic Motors
A Tale of Two Basels
A Rich Montreal Benefits All

Chapter 20: A Wish List for Quebec   251
A New Revolution
Language Laws and Social Stratification
Piggyback French on English?
A Genie's Anger

Bibliography   262

Index   264

Introduction

Legal immigration can occur only when both the destination country and its potential new citizens believe it will be to their mutual benefit. This book is about the complex process by which I and others became "New Canadians" and by which Canada justifies an immigrant's hopes.

It is neither the chronological memoir that many immigrants write about their lives nor a dispassionate dissection of immigration issues. Instead, it tries to explain what immigration is really like for the immigrant and what he or she will find most attractive, most difficult, and most puzzling.

It inevitably compares Canada to other countries and also to Quebec's "distinct society," which has its own perspective on immigrants. Though the circumstances and background of each immigrant may be unique, the experience of changing countries and cultures makes for a commonality between a great diversity of individual immigrants. This book describes my own perspectives, hopes and anxieties. It uses my personal history and anecdotes from my own immigration experience, but it also tries to put those in their social and historical context. It draws certain conclusions not everyone will agree with, but those conclusions are based on real-life experiences that I and many others have faced.

The book is organized thematically into four parts which, taken together, present my experience of immigration from my initial decision to find a new home in another country, through the process of adaptation and eventual integration, to my becoming a new Canadian who loves his country dearly. It describes the perspective of a "New Canadian," born and raised in a Middle-Eastern former colony of now-defunct European empires, who spent formative years in Europe before settling in North America.

Canada wants immigrants. It accepts 200,000 to 250,000 each year. It considers them an asset, needed to enhance the growth of its population and skilled workforce. Without newcomers, the growth of Canada's workforce in 2002 would have been only about 30% of its actual rate. Meanwhile, immigrants to Canada also expect to benefit from what is often a demanding and stressful venture. In any case, both parties to the arrangement, immigrant and country of destination, must be willing and able. That Canada can really become "home" depends upon Canada's own interest in immigrants, its accommodating social environment and its warm embrace of people from many cultures. Although I am also at home in Quebec, its relationship with many of its immigrants is characterized by mutual ambivalence; I discuss this, too.

Canada's government deals with a plethora of issues—big and small, essential or less so, including "Citizenship and Immigration"— as a matter of impersonal routine. Though not insensitive, the policies are designed to deal with a large mass of anonymous applicants from many parts of the world. For the immigrant, however, immigration is an intensely personal matter. Changing countries is often the major milestone in an immigrant's life, and is the very opposite of routine. The whole process can dominate one's attention and decision-making, draining one's nervous energy for months or years. Errors can be very costly and difficult to correct. The risk of failure and disappointment is ever-present. Crossing cultures entails risks; immigrants are hopeful, dynamic... and worried.

Native-born Canadians may interact with newcomers without being fully aware of their conflicting emotions. My inner thoughts and feelings as an immigrant who crossed cultures twice may help Canadians understand the mindset and priorities common to many immigrants. The two crossings were different in nature. The purpose of the first was to study engineering in Zurich, then return home to an upscale life in my native country, Egypt. The second was the search for a new home. At that point, neither Switzerland nor Egypt seemed able to satisfy my fundamental human need: to belong to a society in which I could be comfortable, happy, and truly myself. Canada seemed promising, and I resolved to try. The outcome was everything that anyone could wish for.

In this book, "Part I: Coming Home to a Place I Had Never Been" deals with some aspects of the immigration process itself. More than any country I know, Canada allows immigrants great leeway in matters of identity. While most countries stereotype individuals by nationality, race, and religion, North America sees them as human beings first. For adults arriving from elsewhere in our harsh and violent world, Canada's benign environment can come as something of a shock. Everywhere I had been, nationalism and language differences were divisive factors and the likely basis for war and violence.

Upon my arrival, I perceived that danger in Canada, as well. The "reasonable" conclusions and "proven facts" immigrants have learned from direct experience elsewhere can be quite out of place in Canada. New Canadians arrive with some values and attitudes which remain for life. Other values change over time or are deliberately discarded in the process of adjustment. I was born and raised in a country fought over and colonized by powerful empires, where outside influences had intruded and merged into the pre-existing local culture. Growing up, I was exposed to a mixture of cultures and lifestyles whose elements could hardly be separated from one other and the "original" local society. My formative years were strongly influenced by Europe and America but I was neither European nor American. I had internalized a picture of the human race that included a set of nasty and largely predictable attributes. When faced with terrorism and the threat of civil war, I could not imagine any country could be as civilized and reasonable as Canada. The rest of Part I describes these considerations and how they influenced my understanding and personal decision-making when I finally came to Canada.

"Part II: Relationships, Likes and Dislikes" deals with my attitudes and opinions during the period of integration when the mindset of being a "New Canadian" slowly emerged. Years later, there is no doubt that I changed as a person: new North American elements affected my perceptions, values, and motivators. But there is also no doubt that many fundamental aspects of the old mindset remain and exert a powerful influence on who I am.

"Chapter 6: Anti-Immigrant Currents" deals specifically with bias, which exists despite running counter to Canadians' generally positive attitudes towards immigrants. There are those who try to make an economic argument against current levels of immigration, disregarding evidence that Canada is a nation of immigrants to begin with and depends on new immigrants for much of its economic success. There are others who confuse refugees with immigrants, to the detriment of both. Others are uneasy about specific groups of immigrants: for example, after 9-11 there has been "targeted disaffection" against Muslims, especially those from the Middle East, like myself. I predict time will show that recent arrivals from easily-identifiable groups are less dangerous than the growing underclass of the native-born disaffected, who are much more difficult to detect.

If the "War on Terrorism" goes on very long, others in the Canadian "cultural mosaic" may become increasingly hostile towards my part of the mosaic, reflecting U.S. attitudes which lead to actions against Muslims in faraway lands, which in turn may generate more terrorism. However, there are also antipathies between other groups within the mosaic which reflect conflicts abroad, whether current or historical. Turks and Armenians? Irish Catholics and Protestants? Everyone in Canada has the right to like or dislike anyone as long as the expression of those feelings stays within the law. "Chapter 7: Interethnic Dissonance? Muslims and Jews?" describes the experiences I've had in Canada in this regard. In Canada, I learned that, above all, old hatreds should be left behind when we come here.

The rest of Part II discusses a number of issues, influenced in part by my having been born and raised in a former colony of a European empire. Some Canadians will disagree with my views on the cruelty of Western imperialism towards the weak and vulnerable in faraway lands. "My country"—which includes "my culture"—is a concept with a powerful grip on us: it helps define our identities and is a source of pride and solace. We are taught as children that "we" are noble and can do no wrong. I have lived in enough countries to conclude that the "truth" is propagated everywhere that "our country is good and its enemies are not." Speeches by the top leadership, formal education, carefully structured reports in the media and slants in the entertainment industry all converge to explain our actions abroad as good and necessary. In the absence of such "guidance" many more among the generally fair-minded public in Western countries might see past and present actions of their leaders as greedy, ruthless and cruel.

The United States receives special attention, as its impact on life in Canada is crucial. As a youngster, like most Egyptians, I admired America because it helped us when we were attacked during the Suez War of 1956. I liked what I "knew" about the U.S. from its movies and comic books. Over the years, my admiration waxed and waned in direct relationship to the differences between America's professed values and its actions. My very negative opinion of the former European empires is obvious, and I am concerned that the U.S. seems to be following in their footsteps. In the "special-interest driven" U.S., powerful groups are trying to ensure that the majority of Americans never come to believe, as most Canadians do, that America is at least partly to blame for 9-11. Clearly, it is important for Canada to balance a good relationship with our American friends against our own moral standards and the need not to attract terrorism by participating in bombings and otherwise tormenting weak and vulnerable people overseas.

Religion is another major theme in this section. I believe Americans are wise to insist that the war against terrorism is not a war against Islam since a nation-state cannot defeat a universal and well-established religious faith. But after 9-11, I found myself asking how it came about that some especially devout Muslims disobey the strict rule of their faith that prohibits attacks on civilian non-combatants. I also discuss why Egyptians and others in the Middle East are convinced that "the Jews control America." I try to explain that, in my view, they do not.

In "Part III: Quebec and Immigrants: Reduced Mutual Affinity," I try to explain important aspects of the immigrant mindset by looking at their relationship with Quebec. Whenever I have done so, I have come up against strict taboos against raising certain subjects. francophone Québécois have rebuffed my attempts to describe the concerns and motivators of immigrants, and how they are at odds with the priorities of their province. I have been accused of being too influenced by the "anglophone media," of not understanding the policies of the Federal Government, of "bashing Quebec." I have no desire to bash Quebec. I am happy to live here and was faced with a dilemma: should I limit myself only to the good things I have to say about my province? No. I can better serve my society, by taking a stand, and explaining frankly the reasons why too few immigrants come to Quebec, and why I think this is a danger. I would be serving no one by repeating acceptable platitudes.

I am well qualified to judge that Quebec falls somewhere between xenophobic Europe and open-minded North America with regard to newcomers. "Chapter 12: Coercion and Failure" examines the interplay between the individual's self-interest and the collective interests of Quebec. Short-sighted coercion by a ruling elite can cause serious long-term harm. A faint echo of the attitudes that helped lose New France still lingers in Quebec.

The rest of Part III deals with certain aspects of life in Quebec and three fundamental priorities of immigrants: the expectation that hard work will earn a good living, the hope of relatively comfortable integration into the society and, for themselves and particularly for their children, optimism about the future of the society they wish to join. Quebec has been receiving and keeping a disproportionately small number of immigrants, as compared to the rest of Canada. There are reasons why Quebec's "distinct" priorities make it less accommodating towards immigrants. Coercive language laws, substantial support for separatism, a declining population, and a majority that sometimes appears to favour its own all conflict with the priorities of most would-be immigrants. Nevertheless, Quebec is gentle and tolerant and has shaped a fine democratic society, appealing to those newcomers whose circumstances enable them to pursue their priorities anyway. My family and I are happy to be real Quebecers, as long as Quebec remains part of Canada.

In "Part IV: An Immigrant's Wish List" I list my personal wishes:

for Canada, good relations with the U.S. while remaining true to itself, maintaining peace and harmony at home regardless of global conflicts;

for Montreal, a chance to thrive in Quebec, without being stifled by the political power of its other regions;

for Quebec, a new "Quiet Revolution" that would stress equality instead of fraternity, an end to policies which try to protect the French language at the expense of the poor, and that the survival of the French language in the Americas be freed from depending on a single race whose numbers are declining from year to year.

"Good" and "bad" are subjective judgments; individual perceptions vary. This is the perspective of a New Canadian who has lived and worked in several countries, who respects Canada above all others while retaining strong feelings for previous homes—Egypt and Switzerland. Native-born Canadians may take for granted some of what I see as wonderful about my new country. Others may not recognize what I see as negative factors. I hope that this book will help Canadians see their own country though an immigrant's eyes and help ease others' transition from immigrant to New Canadian by explaining what I observed and felt along the way.

Part I

Coming Home to a Place I Had Never Been

Chapter 1: Is Canada a Real Country?
No, It's Better!

When I arrived in Canada as a landed immigrant, had I come to a real country?

At first glance, the question seems nonsensical. Of course it is a real country. I did not know much about the land that was to become my new home, but even my boyhood stamp collection contained a few from Canada. Later, still before ever coming here, I heard of Canada's fine reputation as a global peacemaker under Prime Minister Lester Pearson. Why would one even ask such a question? Well, there are a number of very unusual things about Canada.

For one thing, no other country I know would be tolerant enough to let bits of itself break off given a clearly-expressed desire by a sufficiently large portion of its inhabitants. For another, Lucien Bouchard, a former premier of Quebec where I live, once said, "Canada is not a real country," and many people agreed. It is therefore reasonable to give the matter some thought. As a "New Canadian," I first thought his statement a grave insult. Later, it occurred to me that not being a "real country" is not necessarily such a bad thing.

Sovereign Nation-States: A Modern Way to Distinguish Between Humans

The emergence of real countries—modern sovereign nation-states—was due to nationalism. In the 19th and 20th centuries, powerful and often extreme manifestations of nationalism were commonplace. I have gotten caught up in them myself, having been born in Egypt when it was struggling for independence from Britain and nationalism was at a fever pitch. Whereas earlier wars may have been between royal dynasties or based on religious convictions, twentieth-century wars seem to have been driven primarily by the "greed and fear" of sovereign nation-states. Millions died for the sake of their countries in wars ranging from small to momentous.

It is said that the new global economy is diluting the sovereignty of nations. Is the largely blind loyalty of people to their countries slowly becoming a thing of the past? I would hesitate to say yes. Since World War II, nuclear weapons have effectively blocked major wars between big powers. Thus, fear overcame greed. Countries still go to war, but they are always careful to avoid nuclear disaster. Often, wars occur when there is a severe mismatch between the military power of two countries. If a weaker, non-nuclear power refuses to knuckle under peacefully, then the stronger country, whether or not it has nuclear weapons, need not fear to use violence for material or other gain.

The nation-state continues to thrive due to the hold it has over its citizens' hearts and minds; it is the political structure people currently seem to want. Seeing how school children south of the border pledge allegiance, with their hands on their hearts, to their "one Nation under God" is enough to convince me that nationalism and the nation-state will not go away anytime soon. There is no doubt in my mind that the United States of America is a real country. The strong emotional response of entire nations to their soccer teams' performance during World Cup soccer games shows that nationalist fervour is still very widespread. It remains to be seen whether the expanded European Union will weaken these age-old national feelings. I suspect Europeans will continue to love their individual countries even while developing a strong pan-European feeling.

Immigration entails the transfer of adulation from one country to another. Immigrants are more likely to have a global perspective than other Canadians. However, their highest priority is to succeed in their new environment. For a while, concerns with nationalism, politics, and social issues will be secondary. Rather than join anti-globalization marches, they are more likely to work hard all day and then take evening classes. But even they, however, want to belong to their new country and to develop their new, expanded identity.

I, too, want to belong to a country rather than a small, disconnected social class. I had to change countries to satisfy that desire. Group formation and the feeling of belonging are deeply-ingrained evolutionary tools our species uses to survive and grow. The advantages and synergy of living and cooperating with others are obvious. Individuals need to belong to groups and do so at many levels. Beginning with small bands of hunter-gatherers, humankind went on to build enormous, impersonal national agglomerations. The hold that this super-grouping has since had on people is something to marvel at.

"The feeling of affinity, the participation in a common culture and tradition, the awareness of a common destiny, which are the essence of national sentiment and patriotism, are transformed by nationalism into a political mysticism in which the national community and the state become superhuman entities, apart from and superior to their individual entities, entitled to absolute loyalty, and, like the idols of old, deserving the sacrifice of men and goods."[1]

Peoples seeking independence or engaged in war can become obsessed with their nationalist struggle. As a child, I saw such obsession in Egypt before the British finally departed.

In the 1970s, as the manifestation of Quebec nationalism gathered momentum, a separatist said to me during a heated conversation, "Even if sovereignty leads to difficulties with the economy in our new country, we will just tighten our belts till the bad times are over." He believed economic sacrifices were acceptable.

Another time, at the height of the zeal, I asked a Québécoise married to an allophone who said he was a separatist, "What if there is violence and your husband is killed?" (I had not been long in Canada and still had not properly understood the civilized and reasonable nature of this society.)

"That would be terrible but what must be, must be," she answered.

Even countries that exist only in dreams can have a mystical hold on people and are entitled to the sacrifice of "men and goods."

Nationalism evolved from defensive origins to assume a ruthlessly self-centered stance. Originally, nationalism was a humanitarian movement to protect the people from the tyranny of the European aristocracies. The nationalism of the French Revolution grew partly out of the ideas of Jean-Jacques Rousseau. It was also influenced by the ideas of the American War of Independence, essentially a popular revolt. That early, liberating nationalism in France asserted that power must reside with the nation, meaning the people, not a monarch and ruling class. Its cry for "liberty, equality, and fraternity" was meant for all humanity. However, over time, nationalism changed from a liberal humanitarian concept to a narrow ethnocentric one that put the interests of one people above all other peoples. The resulting aggressive, chauvinistic nationalism was far removed from its benign origins. I believe the early "good" nationalism of Rousseau's philosophy degenerated into the "bad" nationalism of chauvinistic nations, especially aggressive imperial states.

---

1 Morgenthau, *Politics Among Nations*, p180.

The way the nation-state has behaved in the nineteenth and twentieth centuries is rarely endearing to any save its own citizens for whom their country can do no wrong. People love their country because it favours them over all others. It strokes their egos by creating a national folklore which attributes any defeats and failures to accidents, betrayals and evil acts of others. It boosts their pride and happiness by glorifying any way in which they may be distinct from others, no matter how trivial. In a stark, rarely-questioned double-standard, each country teaches its people that they are better than everyone else on the planet. It divides all humankind into two categories: its own citizens and all the rest. It is permissible to harm or kill any of the rest if there is something to be gained. Their territories and resources may be seized or controlled if the means to do so are at hand. (No country can exist without the willingness and ability to kill, either directly, by proxy or through alliances; otherwise it would quickly be conquered and perhaps destroyed.) In contrast, the nation's own citizens must be protected, even at great cost. Its territorial boundaries are sacred. These nations had sunk from their noble origins in French-inspired nationalism to become racist and chauvinist empires, viewing others with contempt while enriching themselves at their expense.

Native-born Canadians, relatively sheltered from the widespread abuse countries inflict on each other, often do not share my stark perception. I grew up in a country struggling to rid itself from foreign occupation. All over the world, the vicious behaviour of sovereign nation-states seems to be the rule rather than the exception. Germany made great contributions to humanity in science, music and other fields. Extreme German nationalism—coupled with racism and a desire for increased "purity"—was devastating to other countries and races, especially the Jewish race. The former Ottoman Empire is said to have been tolerant towards a large diversity of subject peoples. Yet Turkey ruthlessly applied whatever force it deemed necessary against others to promote or protect its own interests. France, a civilized and refined country, forcibly occupied Algeria, among other places. During Algeria's war of independence (1954 to 1962), France, which had no business being in Algeria in the first place, refused to let go of its colony and go away. The French sent an army of 500,000 men to prosecute an oppressive war which killed up to a million Algerians. The Algerians, too, in the name of their nationalism, which they had learned from the French, killed many Europeans and other Algerians who were thought to be collaborating with France.

Great Britain, which gave us the fine gift of parliamentary democracy, practiced a ruthless economic imperialism backed by military power throughout its vast empire. In China, it fought two wars to force the Chinese to import British opium from India. Those wars came about because Britain wanted to import profitable Chinese products, such as silk and especially tea. China did not want enough British products to establish a trade balance and demanded payment in gold and silver. The British could not allow that situation to interfere with their enormous potential profits. They learned of a solution from the Portuguese—another small European country that practiced legendary ruthlessness and cruelty against peoples it conquered. The British smuggled opium into China to obtain gold and silver, which they then used to purchase Chinese goods. When the Chinese emperor tried to abolish the opium trade in 1839, the British initiated the First Opium War (1839 to 1842) to prevent him from doing so. Later, another Chinese emperor attempted to limit damage from the rampant opium trade to China's society and economy. That threat to British economic interests resulted in the Second Opium War (1856 to 1860), in which the French joined Britain to defeat China, burn the Emperor's summer palace, and impose harsh treaties that greatly profited the aggressors. The "real country" of Britain behaved in ways similar to the much-reviled Colombian drug cartels today, though with a much higher capacity for violence and injustice through superior military force. Competent, decent and conscientious English teachers taught me much history during my many happy years in a British primary and secondary school. Never once did anyone mention the Opium Wars.

Some Canadians whose ancestors came from former European colonial powers may have "forgotten" the historical injustices committed against weaker peoples. They might wonder why anyone today should be interested in these old wars. As a Canadian from a former abused colony of a European Empire, I try to explain that the memories of foreign occupation are sometimes well entrenched and affect global events even today. In 2003, one and a half centuries after the Opium Wars, they were used by North Korea to justify, to its people and the world, its need for nuclear weapons to deter aggression by powerful states. It is all very well for aggressors to forget and move on. The traumatized, however, have long memories which may influence events decades or generations later.

There are exceptions, of course, and strongly nationalistic countries are not always a menace to others. Norway has been a benign sovereign nation-state. Modern Greece has a clean record. Switzerland is a country I admire. The Swiss are very nationalistic and some would say verge on the xenophobic. But they did not oppress defenseless peoples for material gain. The Swiss are well-armed and ready for war, but only defensive war. With the emergence of the Industrial Age, they stayed home, adopted a strong work ethic, and developed their skills to produce high-quality goods and services. They did not use their technology to oppress pre-industrial societies but to manufacture fine products and to trade. They have a pure form of direct democracy that relies mainly on referenda at municipal, cantonal, and federal levels. No Swiss government can involve Switzerland in any war or foreign conflict without the specific approval of a majority of voters in a referendum. The Swiss people are in firm control of their government. (Over the centuries, they learned the hard way that a referendum which results in a majority trying to coerce a large minority on a matter of importance— such as religious questions—can lead to civil war. They are experts on referenda, and we in Canada can learn a thing or two from their experiences.) At the time of this writing, theirs is a very prosperous country, even though they have voted not to join the European Common Market or the economic Union.

Europeans, like everybody else, dislike being told that other countries behaved better than (or not as badly as) theirs. Sometimes when I bring up Switzerland's exemplary neutrality and lack of imperialism, citizens of countries with blemished records quickly point to Switzerland's mercenaries to say that the history of Switzerland is "bad," too. ("Bad" is an imprecise, broadly applicable adjective useful in denigrating others. Of course the Swiss feel that foreigners who think Switzerland is bad, are themselves bad.) Having looked into the matter, I believe that chapter of Switzerland's history actually demonstrates how the Swiss achieved freedom while other peoples still lived under the yoke of royal and aristocratic masters.

Over the centuries, the reputation of soldiers-of-fortune has waxed and waned: sometimes they are routinely accepted, other times they are seen as base. In modern times, nations expect their people to go to war and risk their lives when duty calls, but they despise those who go to war for someone else for money. In the 14th and 15th centuries, nation-states did not exist. Monarchs, princes, and warlords pressed their subjects into service in their wars, which were centered around the interests of the ruling classes. A king gave his nobles titles, privileges, and populated lands where peasants toiled for the enrichment of the nobles. In exchange, these aristocrats supplied the manpower needed for their lords' wars. The Swiss, however, had defeated their former lords, the Hapsburgs, and were free men. They had developed a kind of phalanx which hitherto-invincible mounted and heavily-armoured knights could not defeat. For a time, they were the best and most feared fighters in Europe. But this was before the Industrial Revolution, when Swiss communities were poor and their young men's choices limited. They could live in idle poverty, toil for a pittance on someone else's land, or build up their assets by offering a service in great demand and at which they were the best. It is a false argument to use the mercenaries in Switzerland's history to taint the Swiss. While commoners and serfs everywhere else fought and died to increase their masters' territorial holdings or otherwise enrich them, the Swiss went to war and enriched themselves directly. The rewards flowed directly into the pockets of those doing the fighting, because the Swiss were free.

That freedom eventually led to neutrality, peace and prosperity for Switzerland and an aversion to plunder through violence. But nation-states are not inclined to teach its citizens that other countries were or are "better" or somehow "less bad." Germans have told me that the Italians are cowardly. (In my student days during a brief stay in Germany, a former SS Panzer commander told me that had the Italians fought like the Japanese, Germany would have won the war.) The Swiss say the British and their cities and hospitals are physically dirty. More than once, French citizens have said to me that the Swiss are avaricious and "have no culture." As part of their national mindset, many Europeans I have talked to routinely find ways to denigrate other countries.

We all belong to the same species. As humans, we share the same behavioural patterns and motivators: we respond to the same circumstances, threats, and opportunities in much the same ways. War is clearly not inevitable. There are circumstances where humans choose not to pursue gains through violence. But despite some fine exceptions, too many countries engage in bad forms of nationalism. Canada tries hard to avoid violence, both within and outside its borders. It is a better place than many so-called real countries.

What Is a "Real" Country in Its Purest Form?

> " ...a nation is an abstraction from a number of individuals who have certain characteristics in common, and it is these characteristics that make them members of the same nation."[2]

Among the important characteristics shared by individuals belonging to a nation are common beliefs. A real country[3] has a clearly-delineated territory. Its borders are somehow divinely ordained and preferably unchanged for a long time. It has a homogeneous population of the same race, religion, culture, and language. If it speaks a language not shared by any other, it is even closer to the pure model. Apparently, the greater its suspicion of foreigners and the more it sees the world as divided between "our national interests" and everyone else's, the more "real" it is. Complications and "imperfections" move countries and nations away from the pure model. The United States has many races and religions and Switzerland has four official languages; they are, therefore, to some degree less "real" countries than, say, Japan.

There is a mutual repulsion between immigrants and the "real" country. For example, an independent Quebec would be closer than Canada is today to the model of a "real" country, but it would not be as "real" a country—in other words, would be more attractive to immigrants—than many other nation-states. This is because, although there are many in Quebec who believe that a sovereign nation-state based on their own race and language is the noblest objective to pursue, they are not a majority. Their numbers and intensity of feeling do not overcome the open-mindedness, tolerance, and relative diversity of most people here. I conclude that the vocal presence of fiercely nationalistic Québécois keeps the social climate in the province closer to that of the nationalistic, homogeneous societies which emerged with the Industrial

---

2 Morgenthau, *Politics Among Nations*, p117.
3 The words "country" and "nation" are often used interchangeably.

Age and whose attitudes towards outsiders range from less-welcoming to downright hostile.

Though a prominent separatist, Yves Michaud became even better known when, in December 2000, he clashed with the then-Premier of Quebec Lucien Bouchard over statements he made regarding Jews and other "ethnics." Mr. Michaud does not seek material benefits, glory, or financial gain for himself. Rather, he believes his efforts are directed to the higher purpose of creating a country for his people—protecting its language and assimilating others within the territory of Quebec. He resents those who stand in the way of his noble and transcendental objective, and he says so. Such is the stern stuff of which "real" countries are made.

Nevertheless, the overall climate in Quebec is more moderate than in many parts of the world. Canada is much more moderate still and, like the U.S., is generous and just in deciding who is a real citizen. Unlike the U.S., however, Canada seems willing to respect the wishes of territories whose people express a desire to leave, provided certain rigorous criteria are met. This makes it even less of a real country. Separatists should rejoice in what Canada is.

Canada is so unusual that people from many other countries do not understand the degree to which it truly becomes home to "New Canadians." Immigrants are people who switch sovereign nation-states, a tricky business at the best of times. They used to belong to one country—with its transcendental psychic hold and demand for adulation and loyalty—but now belong to another. The "feelings of affinity" and the "awareness of a common destiny" must be transferred from one country to another.

Depending on circumstances, the transfer may be incomplete or may not be fully acceptable to the parties involved. Japan and the Japanese are very narrowly-defined geographically, racially, culturally, religiously, and linguistically. There are simply too many factors working against any outsider wishing to become a "real" Japanese. At the time of this writing, one of my sons is living and working in Japan. He is enjoying it tremendously and has developed an admiration for the country and its people. But even if he were to spend the rest of his life in Japan, he would never be fully Japanese. If he were to marry a Japanese woman, their children born in Japan would not be entirely Japanese as the Japanese define themselves. On the other hand, any Japanese coming to Canada can be as Canadian as they want to be. This is so strange and unusual in human affairs that many people in European and Middle-Eastern countries do not understand how it is possible.

We once lived in Rome. In a conversation with an Italian acquaintance, I told him how respected and valued the large Italian community was in Canada. "You know, in Canadian folklore, it is mainly Italian immigrants, with their expertise in construction, who built up Toronto into a teeming modern metropolis."

"I heard something like that," he said, "but I think these Italians you are talking about are not happy. They are nowhere."

"Oh, they are all over Canada—"

"I mean," he interrupted, "that they don't belong there and they really don't belong in Italy either. They are nowhere."

"They are Canadian; I know several and they are doing well and seem quite happy and at home."

"How can they be Canadian if they are Italian?" he asked.

I was not able to explain. His definition of patriotism was narrow, limited to "real" countries, and he could not understand.

My brother, Mo (short for Mohsen), worked for the Government of Canada in Industry, Trade and Commerce. He was Canadian Trade Commissioner and acting Canadian Consul in Kuwait, and was responsible for issuing Canadian visas. People planning trips to Canada, including many well-traveled businessmen, would come into his office. My brother would greet them in Arabic and they would immediately recognize his distinctive Egyptian accent. (Many Egyptians work in Kuwait, where, because of the oil revenues, they can get much higher salaries than back home. Everyone in Kuwait is used to seeing Egyptians in jobs of all kinds.)

Prominent visa applicants would sit in Mo's office, have Arabic coffee and chat amiably for a while. Eventually, either Mo would ask, "What can I do for you?" or someone would say, "When can we see the consul?"

"I am the consul," my brother would say.

Silence.

"So you wish to visit Canada?"

"Yes. I think we are supposed to see the Canadian Consul. Is he available?"

"I am the Canadian Consul."

More silence. Obviously, they had thought Mo was employed by the consulate to assist the "real Canadian Consul." Now there was confusion; they had to be careful not to offend him: given his quiet and confident air, he must be an important bureaucrat who could cause them difficulties and delay or obstruct their visas.

"You are the Canadian Consul?"

"Yes."

"Of Canada?"

"Yes, of course."

"But aren't you Egyptian?"

"I'm a Canadian of Egyptian origin."

More silence as they struggled to digest this.

"There are Canadians of many origins, including Egyptian," Mo would sometimes say helpfully.

On the way out, some applicants would ask other consulate workers how an Egyptian could be the Canadian Consul and whether the visas they were getting were genuine. But they asked discreetly and obliquely so that if word got back to him, he would not take offence and retaliate.

Our cousin Ismail, who also lived in Kuwait for a while, told Mo that once an Egyptian he knew said to him: "The most amazing thing happened. I went to get a visa at the Canadian consulate and was interviewed by the consul. You won't believe this, but he speaks Arabic just like us!"

These conversation illustrate how "real countries" establish a sharp distinction between their own citizens and "les autres."

Immigrants and the Old Country: A Parting of Mindsets

In most countries, the attitude of the citizenry is shaped in a way that makes crossovers from one nationality to another strange and abnormal, not to say undesirable.

As immigrants adapt to their new country, a schism develops between them and the countries they left behind. Once they have crossed over and become Canadian, their minds evolve in ways unrelated to the old country. Meanwhile, the old country also changes and evolves. Those who emigrate often do not keep up fully with the details of the changes back home. Having lived in Canada for some years, immigrants are separated from their original homeland in two ways. First, their knowledge of it becomes obsolete. Then, they also see and learn new things and internalize values to which people back home have not been exposed. To varying degrees, "new Canadians" and their old countries become strangers to each other.

I always enjoy going back to Egypt for a vacation. Particularly in winter, the Red Sea beaches and coral reefs are a wonderful break. Seeing relatives and old friends is a major part of the fun. Every now and then I say something that makes people chuckle in amusement.

"What is so funny?" I ask.

"We haven't heard that expression in twenty years!" comes the answer.

Once I telephoned some very good friends and, believing I was speaking in an impeccable Egyptian dialect, said, "May I speak to Halim Bey,[4] please?"

The female voice assumed a formal tone and asked who was calling. When I said my name, his wife Nellie identified herself and said, "Cherif! You speak completely like a foreigner. How are you?"

"Hi! I'm very well, praise be to God (the usual form.) And how are you and the kids?"

"We are all well, thank you."

"What did I say that made me sound like a foreigner?" I asked.

"It's unbelievable! We absolutely must see you before you leave. Here is Halim right beside me..." I never did find out why I had sounded like a foreigner.

Occasionally, the talk turns to Canada and I brace myself for the inevitable question, which is nothing but trouble. I call it "The Question." Though many understand that some individuals may wish to emigrate, almost always, when the subject of Canada comes up, someone asks a version of the following:

"Why do you prefer living in Canada?"

I have been faced with this question many times and I still don't know how to handle it. Once I said, "You know, as an engineer, I like to live in a high-tech environment."

Unfortunately, they took this to imply that I thought they were backward. Once (I must have been in a reckless and irritable mood), having been asked The Question, I foolishly said, "I wouldn't like living in a military dictatorship."

4 Common honorific title.

There was a cacophony of loud protestations, an uproar in fact. I must have had a short fuse that day—I think due to the "Curse of the Pharaohs"[5]—because I got mad, too, and burst out, "Are you saying it is not a military dictatorship? Or are you saying I should not mind living in a military dictatorship? What is the problem exactly?"

It turns out that the problem was that "A democracy will not work in this country."

A couple of times, a most curious discussion took place which highlighted how our mentalities had drifted apart, and was reminiscent of conversations in *Alice in Wonderland*. On more than one occasion, when someone repeated a common mantra, "Democracy will not work in Egypt," the conversation would go something like this:

"Gosh, so you think extreme religious fundamentalists could take over the country and impose their views here?" I would say.

"Oh no! Not those!"

"But you just said that a democracy would not work in this country."

"Right, but those guys should not come to power. Can you imagine!"

"But the basic definition of a dictatorship is that we cannot select the ruler, nor can we control what he decides to do once in power."

"That's right. Democracy will not work here, because the people don't understand it. There would be chaos."

Curious. "So, therefore, if we have no say as to who comes to power and must accept some form of dictatorship, we will have no say if fundamentalist extremists take over and establish a moderate or very strict—who knows, perhaps completely unreasonable—theocracy and rule as they please..."

"No! No! Not these guys!"

"But if by definition we are not able to select the rulers, then anyone can take over regardless of anybody else's opinion."

"But not this extreme religious fundamentalism. It would not be good for the country. The majority of Egyptians are not like that at all."

Curiouser and curiouser.[6] "But by eliminating, in your mind, certain groups or political movements from the possibility of assuming power, you are engaging in a process of selection. That means it is no longer a dictatorship. Either there is a peaceful, non-violent process by which anyone can take over power in the country, or it becomes a free-for-all and no one can be sure—"

---

5 Abdominal cramps and diarrhea.

6 As a bewildered Alice said after eating the cake that made her grow very tall.

"It's easy for you to come up with these kinds of arguments—you live abroad. You don't seem to realize how terrible these fanatics can be. Some would like to institute a terrible religious dictatorship, worse than the one we have now. If you disagreed with their interpretation of religion, they would consider you to be disagreeing with what God wants. A person like you, Cherif, would be seen as a sell-out to the West. You probably would not want, or be able, to visit here any more."

"I believe you, but that is not my point. You said only a dictatorship will work here. How are you going to select a dictator?"

"What we really want is a good dictatorship."

When we calmed down, I realized the misunderstanding was my fault, not theirs. I have difficulty balancing two concepts. On one hand, I feel any dictatorship is a bad thing and more likely sooner or later to lead to disaster than democracy. On the other, I am regularly reminded that there is a great deal of poverty in Egypt, so democracy means nothing to millions of people who look to the government—any government of any type—to feed them. The dictatorship has so far more-or-less managed to do this. I have been away from Egypt for many years and am far from understanding their practical everyday problems. Still, whenever I visit, I see that the price of dictatorship is high: Egypt is stagnant in most aspects that matter. Apologists for the over half-a-century-old military regime tell me repeatedly that it would be foolish, if not downright irresponsible, to apply some Canadian or Swiss solution to the situation there. Still, I firmly believe that democracy is better—in fact, that it is the only hope. Other countries in the world have managed to move towards democratic governments. Egypt could, too.

I resolved not to try to answer The Question any more. But often that doesn't help either.

"Why are you being evasive? Tell us."

I still don't know what to say. I realize that what some really want to hear is that moving to Canada was a mistake, that Egypt was a better place than Canada, and that I had seen the error of my ways and would be coming home soon.

Fawzi, a courteous limousine driver who drove my family and me during a vacation in Egypt, once said, "Sir, I don't understand why anyone who does not need to go abroad to earn a living would wish to live anywhere other than here."

You see, Egypt is a "real" country. Despite an authoritarian political system, sandstorms, widespread poverty, and whatever other problems they face, it is nevertheless wonderful and the "Mother of All the World." The president of Egypt doesn't have to keep telling Egyptians that theirs is the best country in the world: it is self-evident. By contrast, in that unusual place called Canada, Prime Minister Chrétien and others have said many times in public that Canada is the best country in the world—after all, the United Nations has said so!

There is a subtle but nevertheless powerful effect which contributes to the schism that develops between some New Canadians and those in the old country. To the extent that "a nation is an abstraction from a number of individuals who have certain characteristics in common" (Morgenthau) there is a change in the mental characteristics of an immigrant, as the complex process of changing countries progresses. As my new characteristics of a New Canadian emerged, I gradually approached a mentality of being non-judgmental about different cultural and ethnic attitudes and customs. In my old country—and most countries I know—individuals share strong judgments about many aspects of life and towards others. Firm and rather homogeneous judgmental attitudes sustain the "abstraction" which is their nation.

A conversation which highlights differences in outlook occurred in Cairo with one of my young nieces, Sherein, when she suddenly decided to wear a hijab, or religious head-scarf. The hijab is a sign of modesty and signals to society that a woman lives according to Islamic ethics. That includes the rejection of promiscuity, meaning she will have sex only with her legal husband. In moderate and reasonable Egypt, the decision to wear the hijab or not is up to each woman—unlike Turkey, where it is often forbidden, or some other Muslim countries, where it is mandatory. Even so, during a get-together with my extended family, it emerged that some judged this act approvingly, while others did not. My brother Aziz was mildly disapproving (he lived in Canada for many years) and talked to Sherein at length about how the Koran does not require a hijab, only modesty. He reminded her that many women who do not wear it live a decent, moral life. Sherein came over, sat beside me, and asked my opinion. I said I had none.

"Uncle! How could you have no opinion on something so important?" she asked.

"I do not judge an action such as this."

"What do you mean?"

"It will take me a little while to explain," I said. "Is that OK?"

"Sure, uncle."

"I have lived in the West a long time. I can generalize and say there is an important difference in the way Western people perceive truth versus the way people here do." A few other relatives overheard us and started to pay attention to what I was saying. I continued.

"Our mind 'knows' something to be true through our senses, combined with some rational organization of what our senses communicate to our brain." I pointed out of a window and said, "For example, if we look at that building in the distance, it appears just two inches tall. But through our experience, our innate mind intervenes to tell us that it only appears so tiny because it is far away. We know the truth: it is really a tall building, though our senses show it quite small. Do you agree?"

"Yes," said Sherein, hesitantly.

"This is a very simple example. Imagine how huge and complex the universe is—or even our own society—and what a tiny part of it our senses can perceive. So, though there is a link between what we believe to be the universe and what the universe really is, it is tenuous and not completely reliable. It is as though what we establish in our minds as the truth is actually some kind of imperfect, incomplete, and distorted image of the real universe. Does this make any sense to you?"

"It seems to," she said cautiously.

I took heart and continued. "The difference between a sizable proportion of people here and a sizable proportion in the West is this: many people here—and in other non-Western countries—tend to think what they believe to be true is actually true. In the West, many tend to think that what they believe to be true is only the best result they have been able to achieve so far. For example, they understand that new scientific instruments can expand the range of our senses and give us good reason to modify old 'truths' or replace them entirely. Those in the West usually do not assume that just because they believe something it is therefore the truth. For them, 'facts' are not absolute certainties. We here tend to assume that what we 'know' is in fact the absolute truth. I notice that some people seem to think that simply because they 'know' something, that in itself is proof that it is actually true. Here we feel that our judgment based on our 'certain knowledge' is very solid, and we dislike contradictions. I do not share that attitude and am not inclined to make a judgment on your hijab."

This kind of talk is unusual in Egypt, even in educated circles. Sherein had apparently not been exposed to such ideas and seemed a little shaken intellectually. We continued for a while, exploring some of these concepts. Some relatives were pleased. Others were silent. Although no one objected, even though this was clearly an alien manner of conversation, I thought I detected some discomfort. I am very proud of Sherein for what she said next:

"Uncle, these are new ideas. Thank you. I'll think about all this." She added "So, in conclusion, you don't disagree with my wearing a head-scarf?"

"I support you completely," I said. "I would also support you completely if you decided not to wear it. I support whatever genuinely makes you comfortable, which is the principal truth I am concerned with. I know that it will be the real truth, because I know you are sincere."

She beamed.

Perhaps the very unusual lack of a uniform judgmental attitude among Canadians, is why some have called it "not a real country" (or, referring to Morgenthau, "not a real abstraction"—whatever that means.)

Later I regretted not having remembered or mentioned Ibn Khaldoun, the fourteenth-century Arab historian and philosopher. That omission reminded me of how powerful and ubiquitous the Western influence is. In talking to Sherein, I was thinking only about the West with regards to the "modern" approach. Returning to Montreal, I told my good friend Mahmoud Gawad, who is well-educated and well-read, about the conversation. He was impressed and, like many immigrants, was quite interested in how New Canadians interact with folks back in the old country.

"Check out *The Muqaddimah* of Ibn Khaldoun," he said. "You will find he was thinking about these things centuries before modern Europeans."

I had heard of Ibn Khaldoun, who lived from 1332 to 1406, and had read some passages of his work. Yet, talking to Sherein, I failed to remember the great Arab achievements in philosophy, science, mathematics, and logic. The Muqaddimah[7] is a brilliant philosophy of history—some say a work of genius—which also presents and critiques the ideas of many great Arab philosophers, such as Ibn Rushd (Averroes), al-Farrabi, and Al-Ghazzali. In a section entitled "The Science of Logic," there is a discussion of "the outside existence of a natural universal" and its relationship with our "inner" mental processes. I occasionally accuse Westerners of bad faith for not giving Arab civilization its due; but, alas, here I myself was selling it short. Ironically, Arab science, philosophy, and mathematics fuelled Europe's Renaissance, which led to a scientific and technological revolution. This led to the production of modern weapons, which Europeans, in turn, used to batter the Arab world.

To a certain degree, I have become a misfit in the old country. Egyptians are far too polite and friendly to use the word "traitor," but I wonder whether the thought has crossed some minds. The point is that changing countries is no small matter—it goes against the grain of human behaviour and the desire to belong to and keenly co-operate with one's nation. Changing countries requires strong motivation, courage, and determination. It represents a major event—usually the major event—in any immigrant's life.

A Warm Welcome to the Real Super-Country of Canada

One of the reasons I am so fond of Canada is that it made the transition so very low-key and agreeable: "Welcome to Canada. Become a real Canadian if and when you like, at your own pace." It is a remarkably tolerant and civilized environment. I became a real Canadian gently, by osmosis. There was no pressure to conform to the new or repudiate the old. I feel like a real Canadian, but am also proud to be Egyptian. Ironically, the very fact that I do not have to give up any part of my identity to become a real Canadian increases my affection and feeling of belonging to my new country.

Canada did not say to me: "Choose! You belong either to me or to some other country. To become Canadian, you must cleanse your identity of its old components, love me alone, and reject any feeling of belonging to any other nation." On the contrary, the message was: "Welcome to your new home; be yourself."

---

7 Ibn Khaldoun, *The Muqaddimah*.

How can anyone not love such a "non-country?"

Becoming a real Canadian did not require that I give up any part of who I was. What Canada did was help me grow and expand my identity, enabling me to add a new component to it. Other, "real" countries may frown upon citizens who continue to identify with other sovereign nation-states and may reject such people entirely. Germany is an example of a stern country that will not allow its people to hold any other citizenship. At least in Montreal, where I live and in other large urban centers where immigrants congregate, Canada is like a mother who loves her children unconditionally, regardless of the choices they make in respect to their cultural identity.

I see Canada and the United States as countries of all humanity rather than of a particular ethnic or racial group. In both countries, one is a person and citizen first. Canada has transcended the model of the nation-state based on ethnicity and race. Within its borders it is closer to the original liberal-humanitarian ideas of early nationalism. It attracts good, dynamic people who come and inject capital, fresh ideas, new vigour, and genetic diversity into the society and the economy.

The unusual things about Canada do not disqualify it from being a real country. They merely make it a very special country. For one thing, Canada stands alone in its reluctance to apply coercion. It is rare, if not unique, that a country would allow a part of itself to break off based on a clear mandate from the inhabitants of that area. The overwhelming majority of other nation-states, including some fine democracies, share one characteristic: they are not divisible and will fight fiercely, tooth and nail, over every square meter of their "sacred" territory. The Russian way seems to lie at the other extreme: although many Russians appear to despise and loathe their Chechen "compatriots," Russia uses violence and destruction to coerce Chechnya into remaining in the Federation and its people into being "loyal and loving" citizens. The lives of soldiers, rebels (formerly "bandits" and, after September 11th, "terrorists"), and civilians are all sacrificed as if to the idols of old.

In most countries, only a small proportion of the population is willing and able to undertake such a wrenching change as emigration, as promising as it might look. Some are traumatized when they are uprooted and lose the emotional comfort of living in the country of their birth. Refugees who are persecuted or must flee from violence or imprisonment are a special case, as are the many expatriates who live for years in a foreign country but are not immigrants. Immigration is a matter of circumstance and temperament. Economic considerations are often a motivator. Alienation of some kind from the old country is a major factor. In some cases, a sense of adventure plays a role.

The temperament of immigrants is such that they are often aggressive doers who tend to take action and assume risks to change undesirable circumstances. Still, the change may not be completed successfully. My brother Aziz lived in Ontario and Quebec for many years, became a Canadian citizen and likes Canada "very much." He decided to go back to Egypt with his family when the situation there improved some years after former dictator Gamal Abdel Nasser died and the late Anwar Sadat (also a dictator) came to power.

"I want nice weather all year round," my brother says.

My brother-in-law, Rolf, went back to his native Switzerland after about ten years in Montreal. He had met and married an attractive young Swiss, Marianne, in Montreal. They eventually decided to go back to live in the old country. I know of other immigrants who, though they do not go back, continue to live here with an expatriate mindset rather than an immigrant one. In some cases, the adaptation process is very difficult and oscillates back and forth. Some immigrants move back "home" only to discover that they belong in Canada after all.

Immigration is a difficult, complex and draining process. Immigrants want to arrive in their new country and get on with the demanding task of integrating and adapting, not to mention making a living in an unfamiliar environment. The last thing we want are additional complications and uncertainties on top of our current anxieties. With the many changes in our lives, we want a stable and welcoming environment. The saddest immigrants are those who become estranged from their original homeland, yet for some reason are unable to acquire a feeling of belonging to their new country.

I was looking for a feeling of belonging. I found it in Canada, in the Province of Quebec. The doctrine of Quebec sovereignty threatens my hard-won feeling of belonging to my new pluralistic, diverse, and tolerant home, Canada. Immigrants are a suspicious and cynical lot. Rightly or wrongly, their experiences and instincts tell them that in largely-homogeneous nation-states dominated by one distinct group, unless they are part of the dominant group, they will not really belong. Immigrants understand, if only instinctively, that a separate country of Quebec would be closer to the model of a "real country" than Canada is. Therefore, they tend to settle elsewhere.

In 1996, the year after the second Quebec Referendum made a splash in the media worldwide, the number of landed immigrants in Canada was 226,074, according to Statistics Canada. Quebec, having 24.5% of Canada's population at the time, should have received about 55,400 immigrants according to that percentage. Instead it received only 29,671, or 13%. Quebec separatist gurus promise that when independence is achieved, Quebec will control its own immigration and everything will be fine. Some people who don't understand the immigrant mindset believe them.

Canada the Civilized

Canada is more civilized and free than any other country I know. It bends over backwards to avoid coercion. It can be amazingly kind and gentle. But there is a line that must not be crossed. There is a sacred compact between a country and its citizens. We are and will continue to be loyal to Canada; if need be, we will risk life and limb to protect it. In return, it will take care of real Canadians, who are its lifeblood.

A "real" country will take risks and make sacrifices and face untold dangers to protect its people, especially from foreign threats. There is a solemn covenant between "real" countries and their people: they take care of each other no matter what. If Quebec were to become a foreign country, there would be millions of Canadians in Quebec who would not want to give up their nation. In that case, Canada would do whatever it took—short of initiating violence or the threat of violence—and bear any hardship to protect loyal Canadians wherever they may be located.

Canada's national anthem sings of "true patriot love." It goes without saying that this love must be reciprocated. If its citizens are expected to be full of patriot love and are to stand on guard for Canada, then it must love its people and stand on guard for them. Or are these just empty words, a façade to give Canada the outward trappings of a "real" country without the substance? To allow people who persistently and clearly declare they do not wish to be Canadian to separate is advanced and civilized. It shows that, though Canada is a nation, it is not at all like

Russia and others. But if Canada were simply to abandon its loyal citizens in the process, then former Premier Lucien Bouchard will have been proven right and Canada would not be a real country.

Chapter 2: Racism and Highest Respect for the Individual

"Immigrants Are Vital, Study Says"

The study[1] referred to in this newspaper headline concludes that between 1991 and 1996, immigration accounted for 70% of the growth in Canada's labour force and 50% of its population. The article states that (then) Immigration Minister Elinor Caplan wanted to increase the current planned number of 225,000 immigrants and refugees to 300,000 in future. "She said the increase is necessary to increase Canada's prosperity." In the long run, perhaps over 500,000 newcomers will be needed every year. In her words, "Canada has no other place to turn for growth but to immigration."[2]

Since Canada is vital to me, it is good to hear that I as an immigrant am important to Canada. This was confirmed by the 2001 census, when Statistics Canada demonstrated that our population is aging. There followed a plethora of opinions that ever more immigrants are needed. Since Canadians are having fewer children, attracting newcomers is important for replenishing the work force and ensuring there is a tax base large enough to pay for medical services and support an aging society. Well, my wife Heidi and I have contributed handsomely. While many in Canada have no offspring or just one child, we have three Canadian-born children. Bringing them up well has been the most important thing in our lives. All have university degrees. All are pursuing their education further while engaged in part-time work. Had we not come to Canada, StatsCan would have counted at least five less people in 2002. In addition, my two brothers followed me here with their wives and now have two Canadian children each.

The happiest and most gratifying aspect of the culture shock I received arriving in North America was that I was embraced by a welcoming and accepting environment. Back in my old country, Egyptians are very hospitable and welcome strangers and visitors from abroad effusively. But this traditional warmth and genuinely sincere

---

1 Jedwab, "Immigration at Century's End."*

2 Article in the *Montreal Gazette*, April 28, 2000, by Andrew Duffy, who refers to the study by Jack Jedwab, Director of the Association of Canadian Studies and professor at McGill University.

welcome is reserved for "outsiders" who remain distinctly non-Egyptian even as they are pampered. *Ahlan wa sahlan!* In Europe, where I studied, polite helpfulness is common, but a spontaneous and warm welcome from natives towards outsiders is unusual. In Canada and the U.S., it is different. Within weeks of my arrival, I began to notice that society and individuals immediately welcomed me, not as someone from abroad but as "one of us." They did not make a special effort to make me feel at home; I just naturally was at home, as far as my new country was concerned. This aspect of North American culture showed me early on that my decision to come here was a good one. It increased my stamina and determination during the difficult period of adjustment.

People who move to another country and "cross cultures" invariably go through a difficult period of adjustment to the new environment. The degree of difficulty varies with a number of factors, such as personality, past experience with different cultures, and the degree to which the new country differs from the old.

The first thing that shook me up when I arrived in Canada was the cold. A few days before, I had been standing in light clothing in Bellevueplatz in Zurich amid colourful tulips. Arriving in Canada in mid-March, I disembarked from the aircraft wearing a light overcoat, thin socks, and light shoes. Walking to the terminal 120 feet away was a terrible shock. I had no hat and my head, feet, and ankles suffered most. Today, with experience and proper Canadian outerwear, it would probably be a piece of cake. At the time it was like a physical blow. I had never experienced such cold, not even skiing in the mountains in Switzerland. As I immediately started my job search, there were days when the cold interfered with my activities.

The enormous distances were intimidating. Coming from one of the smallest to the second-largest country in the world entailed errors of judgment in estimating how long it would take to get from here to there. Driving a car and using a map, I underestimated how long it would take to get from one place to another. A few times, I underestimated the walking distance from a subway station to my destination and the cold made me duck for cover in whatever restaurants or stores were at hand. It was only later that I grasped the bright side of this aspect of my new environment: great distances meant a great deal of space. The populations of North America are not compressed within the tight national borders of small countries. Except for Russia, even big European countries are small. Quebec alone is about five times the size of France. In overcrowded Europe, there is furious competition for land and newcomers represent additional competition for space. According to Hitler, Germany's need for Lebensraum was a fundamental reason he started World War II.

Expatriates versus Immigrants

Over my career, I have worked in several countries as an expatriate, or visitor. When I came to Canada it was as an immigrant. Though adapting to local conditions is required in either case, the experiences are not the same. An expatriate is an extension of his or her homeland abroad, whereas an immigrant leaves one homeland to merge with another. An expatriate knows that he or she will be returning home eventually. In the worst case, adjustment to the new environment may not succeed and the whole experience may become unbearable. Deep down, expatriates know that when all else fails they can throw up their hands and request to be sent back home. While I was general manager of the subsidiary of a U.S. multinational corporation overseas, its growth became very rapid and I decided to bring in personnel from our corporate organizations in other countries including the U.S., Britain, and other parts of Europe. It meant raiding the organizations of other general managers so I had to obtain their permission, of course, but there was no choice: hiring locals and training them would have taken too long and valuable opportunities would have been missed. About a dozen experienced company employees were brought in from various locations. Some were brought in for their management experience and others for their specialized technical knowledge. Some had families; others were single. They adjusted at different rates and some began to enjoy their new environment quite quickly. However, two couples did not make it. One Swiss couple soon gave up and went home—the husband was not happy and the wife had become so tense and pined so much for home that she became physically ill. Another wife went home to France with the children while the husband soldiered on for a while; eventually, he too went home.

Immigrants rarely have the option to simply "go home." If they are unhappy, they usually must grit their teeth and keep trying. The motivations for expatriates are different from those of immigrants, and the conditions of the move are different, too.

As an expatriate corporate executive, I moved under the auspices of a large, cash-rich, multinational corporation. There is always a handsome relocation package, replete with all kinds of features to make the move comfortable. There are employees from corporate human resource departments to prepare for the arrival of expatriates. There are lavish expense accounts. Families are put up in the best hotels while every effort is made by the company to find good accommodation. Even though my job description in the new location was different from that in the old, there was a degree of continuity in corporate policy and culture, corporate contacts, and products lines. Years earlier, when I first arrived in Canada as an immigrant, I had a limited amount of cash that had to last until I found a job. Everything about my new job market was completely unfamiliar and uncertain. The pressures were aggravated by the fact that I was making a major change in the type of work I would be doing. I wanted to move from my past work in research in solid-state physics into a job in technical sales and marketing.

There are stresses and anxieties for both expatriates and immigrants. New manners, rules of the road, laws, and even a different sense of humour have to be learned. One has to be careful not to inadvertently offend others. Eating habits have to change. When I first came to Canada, yogurt was virtually unknown. All my life I had loved yogurt; in Canada, my new country, it was not appreciated and no one could tell me where I could buy it. (Conversely, when I went back to temporarily work in Europe and the Middle East, I could not get a decent rib steak. Before coming to Canada, I did not know what a rib steak was.)

> "People who move overseas must face a number of adjustments all at once…, all [simultaneously] competing for the sojourners' attention and energy, neither of which are unlimited. Adjusting to job, community, and country affect the pace—and the outcome—of the expatriates' struggle to make sense out of the culture around them. The impact of these challenges is so direct and immediate that if the problems they pose aren't addressed early on, the resulting stress and anxiety can overwhelm and defeat the sojourners."[3]

---

3 Storti, *Crossing Cultures*, p2.

Please, native-born Canadians, if you run into bewildered, recently-arrived immigrants, be kind to them. You cannot imagine how much happiness a little kindness can bring to stressed and struggling newcomers. francophones who were rude to my recently-arrived friends in Montreal because they spoke no French (and in one case hardly any English) probably don't realize how cruel such an intolerant attitude was. Perhaps they thought they could protect French by pressuring newcomers in this ungracious way, to force them to learn it. If that was the plan, it backfired. Some of these newcomers were already under much stress, and this hostility merely contributed to their decision to leave the province. Ontario benefited when they went there with their capital and their energy. Furthermore, such incidents are not quickly forgotten. Hard-line francophones who behave this way can cause intense dislike for Quebec, and perhaps all francophones, which may last a lifetime.

As an expatriate, in spite of my genuine interest in the history, geography, and culture of my new country, I maintained a certain politely-camouflaged aloofness. Even as I enjoyed my stay and my fine new friends, I was strongly influenced by the knowledge I was there to do a job and would be leaving eventually. Local problems, including threats of war and actual war, were worrisome mainly insofar as they could affect my family, my new friends, and my work. They were not my business and there was nothing I could do about them. As an immigrant, however, I came to Canada to stay forever. I could not be aloof from anything. This culture was to become my culture and the people, my people. National problems worried me and threats of violence disturbed me greatly.

Though immigrants, unlike expatriates, do not have their moves cushioned and eased by a paternalistic corporation, some are fortunate enough to have relatives or friends who had arrived earlier. These can make an enormous difference in reducing stress and anxiety and helping one to understand the new environment. Many newly-arrived immigrants choose a location for no other reason than knowing someone there. Later on, after absorbing the first shock of adjustment, some may move to other parts of Canada (secondary immigration.)

Arriving in Canada in 1968 was one of my life's greatest adventures. Though I ended up in Montreal, I first went to Toronto because I had good friends there who had arrived about a year earlier. The two brothers, Sherif and Amr Alaily, with whom I stayed, had gone to the same English school in Egypt and the same university in Switzerland. Those who have not experienced the loneliness of leaving a familiar environment and moving for good to a strange new country cannot imagine how valuable it is at the start to know someone there. I had some money, a couple of nice suits and some good technical books. With no job and in an unfamiliar environment, I faced uncertainty at every turn. Most immigrants have no choice but to be—or at least act—tough and resourceful.

I will always remember the Alailys' help and generosity. They both had good jobs and shared a modern apartment on Balliol Street. I slept on the couch in their living room.

"Stay with us as long as you like," they said. They helped me set up an intensive job search. They pointed out sources of information, edited my resume and letters and gave me valuable moral support. Whenever they could spare it, they lent me their sporty new car (a Shelby Mustang with an enormous V8 engine) to drive to job interviews so I could arrive in a more relaxed and upbeat mood.

I was completely cut off from my home base, Egypt. At that time, the country was under Gamal Abdel Nasser's socialist government. It was a regime similar to, but milder than, some of the former communist governments of Eastern Europe. An exit visa was required to leave the country. I could not go back even for a visit since, with my engineering education, I would have been classed "an asset to the state" and would not receive permission to leave. Furthermore, I could not rely on receiving any money from my family in case of emergency. There were strict currency controls in place. I was really on my own, except for the fact that my old friends were there also. From Switzerland, I had written my family informing them of my decision to move to Canada. I told them not to worry: I had plenty of money (an exaggeration), spoke the two official languages of Canada, and had a good engineering degree. I did not tell them I was anxious. I think they were.

The experience of arriving in North America also included happy times, of course. In addition to the immediate feeling of being welcome, there was the sense of adventure and the anticipation of meeting new people. There was the excitement of discovering many new things and of seeing firsthand the aspects of North American life one had only heard about or seen in movies. Also helpful during the transition were the timeless, universal things I had learned before, which gave me a sense of continuity, escape from pressure, and inner peace.

The first of these was classical music. I remember sitting on my paternal grandmother's lap at the piano when I was very young while she played melodies from Italian operas with one hand and held me tight with the other. She often sang along. Later, at age seven, I started piano lessons. I have found solace in that instrument ever since.

Another source of escape and relaxation was going to the movies. What I like best are well-made movies with superb, realistic special effects and an occasional healthy dose of sex and violence. Things keep getting better and better. Like millions of others, I have been fascinated by dinosaurs since early childhood and was kind of sorry I had missed them. With the recent advances in special effects I have been able to see "real" dinosaurs in action, even dinosaurs interacting with humans. A good movie is a boost anywhere in the world.

Last, but not least, was sporting activities, which have always had a special place in my life. At school we could throw the javelin and play soccer. My father, a good tennis player who won many trophies, taught me that game at a young age. I am a strong swimmer: during my business trips, when the day is done and before supper, I often swim laps for twenty minutes or half an hour in the swimming pool of the hotel where I'm staying. (I dislike hotels that have no pools.) The next day, I can be fresh and alert and the meetings seem less tedious as the day wears on. In Switzerland, I learned to ski, one of the most exhilarating activities I know. Sports breaks are valuable and help wash away stress and anxiety.

I was fortunate to have been well-equipped to cope with the immigration experience. In any case, the anxiety did not last long after my arrival in Canada, though the stress of making the right decisions in an unfamiliar, uncertain environment continued for quite some time. Within about a month I was hired by a subsidiary of a reputable American multinational corporation. I had used the company's scientific equipment in Europe and knew of its reputation for excellence. I considered myself very lucky. Though I was hired in Toronto, the boss wanted me in the Canadian head office, located (alas, not for much longer) in Montreal, because of my fluency in French. I explained that my French accent was different from that of the Québécois, but that did not seem to matter.

Respect and Racism in the U.S.

Though I had come to Canada and had been hired here, most of my first year in the New World was spent in the United States. Coming from largely-xenophobic Europe, I was struck by the open-armed welcome Americans show newcomers. Based temporarily in Boston, I traveled for the company to Colorado, California, and some Southern states. My knowledge about the U.S. grew, while I remained unfamiliar with Canada. Like countless millions of young people all over the world, I had felt the influence of America from afar. Now, it was an exciting treat to see the culture first hand. My respect and admiration for America and Americans soared. I wondered whether I had made the right decision choosing Canada instead of the U.S. South of the border, I found a professional and human environment of the highest caliber. There was an air of excellence about the place. But it was more than that. I had just left Europe and its relatively narrow-minded attitudes towards "strangers." In Canada, I'd barely had time to glimpse what I could now see in the U.S.: high respect for the individual and his or her abilities. Competence was admired and it was striking to see how Americans value and try to attract and keep "good people." Subsequent experiences confirmed this again and again. When I returned to Canada, the environment in which I found myself was just the same.

One small incident moved me, made me feel welcome in the early days, and helped reassure me about the New World. In Boston, I needed a driver's license. The test, as usual, was in two parts: a written portion followed by a driving test. After a couple of hours off from work to study the booklet, I did the written test. I then went out into a big, noisy hallway and sat down with other applicants to wait for the result. Soon a tall, stern-looking police officer in a blue uniform and impressive paraphernalia, including a huge revolver hanging from his belt, came out of an office and called: "Mr. Tsherif...Is there a Mr...." He hesitated and scrutinized the papers he was holding "...a Mr. Ryeffiat here?"

I was used to people not knowing how to pronounce my name. What now? I wondered. "Rifaat," I said, raising my hand. "Yes, I am here."

His rather stern and forbidding countenance broke into a warm smile. He came towards me, documents in hand, looked around with enthusiasm and said to everybody, "We have an ace here! No errors! Everything 100% right." He came right up to where I was sitting and stood towering over me, smiling. "Great job," he said.

"Thanks very much," I said.

Noticing my foreign ("precise international English") accent, I thought I could see his smile widen and his eyes twinkle as he said, "Have you been here long?"

"No, less than a week."

"Well, I hope you like it here and I wish you luck."

"I do like it, but I can't stay long. I'm on an H3 visa and I have to go back to Canada."

"But you don't," he said. "I'm sure you can change your status. They will let you stay if you want." He said a few more nice things and went off chuckling to himself.

To most people born and raised in North America, this may seem trivial. However, in spite of many friends and good times I had in Europe, I had rarely encountered this attitude there. I suppose for a policeman who deals with traffic violations, acing a driving test is an indication of intelligence. His natural reflex was to extend a friendly welcome, express his pleasure, and do what he could to keep this "good human resource" in the U.S. As a service to his country, he encouraged me to stay and become American. He didn't care if my name was unusual and that he could not pronounce it or that my accent was different. Thanks to that police officer, I immediately began to like the United States. Subsequently, similar events in the U.S. and Canada confirmed that this mindset was integral to the New World. One day I stopped noticing; I was beginning to adapt. That I no longer noticed it, however, does not mean that I stopped appreciating it.

There were also unexpected events that showed me that not everyone was respected. I was befuddled to discover that racism was part of this society as well. While competence was valued highly, I saw contempt for those prejudged to be incompetent. A few months into my stay, I was sent for ten days or so to Duke University Hospital in Durham, North Carolina. My work with medical electronics equipment required special training. One day, I attended a procedure in a "cath lab" (short for catheterization laboratory.) Everyone treated me with friendly respect because I was "the new bio-medical engineer" and because Southerners are mostly friendly people. As the doctor worked, he was surrounded by about ten people, all dressed in light green-blue overalls, head covers, and face masks. Some were assisting him and others, like myself, were just watching. Standing right beside me was a very attractive medical student. In spite of her mask and the fact that only her exceptional blue eyes were visible, I knew she was attractive. I also knew she had a Southern sweetness to her, since we had had a pleasant chat before entering the cath lab. Her long, drawn-out accent was fascinating. I had heard similar speech in American movies such as "Gone with the Wind", but it had not quite registered that there were real people who actually spoke this way. The way she articulated her words created an aura of poise and serenity, and combined with her good looks, she was a real "Southern belle."

We all watched the procedure, which consisted of inserting four catheters into veins in the arms and inner thighs of the patient. Long, thin tubes were slowly pushed in until the tips were positioned in the chambers of the heart. There, devices to measure blood pressure, in conjunction with our equipment, could indicate problems such as defects in the heart valves.

The patient was a young African-American female, about twenty years old, who had a congenital heart defect. Through it all, she moaned and groaned. I was not used to such things and felt uneasy at her ordeal. I leaned over towards the young, attractive medical student till our heads almost touched and in a low whisper asked, "Does it hurt?"

"What?" she whispered back.

"Is this procedure painful?"

"Them kind," she whispered, "they always scream more than it hurts them."

"Oh," was all I could whisper before turning my attention to the doctor and his work.

Most of my knowledge about the U.S. had previously been derived from Hollywood movies. Now I learned there really was discrimination against Blacks in America. It was not just fiction used to make dramatic movies starring actors like Sidney Poitier. Well, I would be going back to Canada in a few months. There, I thought to myself, "African Canadians" had arrived as respectable immigrants and, because there had been no slavery, there were not many Blacks and no discrimination of this kind. I remember thinking how nice it was. I was wrong.

A week off from Boston allowed me to meet my wife-to-be at Dorval International Airport when she arrived from Zurich. Heidi and I were married in the Unitarian Church in Pointe-Claire. It was explained to us that there was no such thing as a civil marriage in Quebec. The Catholic Church performed the lion's share of weddings. Neither of us was Catholic and we were not familiar with any church here. Someone pointed us to the Unitarians, saying that they are open-minded and attach more importance to people's humanity than their individual faiths. (Thanks, Unitarians!) It all seemed a little unusual, but we did not really mind. There was no wedding dress, no long list of guests, no gifts or fancy orchestra or lavish banquet. In fact, we had a hard time rounding up the necessary witnesses. We did not care; we were madly in love and excited about our new life together. We did not know that something called the "Quiet Revolution" had occurred in Quebec.

A few days after we were married, we drove to Boston in a newly-purchased, pre-owned Volkswagen Beetle. As usual, we made mistakes, underestimating the distance between locations on the road map. We settled into our small furnished apartment. Heidi traveled with me to North Carolina and San Francisco, which we both enjoyed tremendously. At the end of our time in Massachusetts, we loaded our belongings into the Beetle and drove back to Canada. We very quickly fell in love with Montreal. It was a glittering, cosmopolitan city and in some ways reminded me of the open, multinational environment in which I had grown up in Cairo. We found the blend of English and French elegant and interesting; it added a dimension of sophistication to everyday living. I noticed that, as if to make me feel right at home, there even appeared to be a dispute over languages. How utterly charming!

Respect and Racism in Canada

Then, an event occurred which I would never forget. As a young engineer bursting with enthusiasm, I plunged with gusto into my high-tech job. The marriage was wonderful, the job great, and the city so much fun. The abnormally high stress due to the adjustment process gradually declined. The manager who was my boss was a cordial

Englishman. He had arrived from Britain six or seven years earlier and also liked living in Montreal. He spoke with a British accent, as my teachers had at the English school I had attended in Cairo, though he seemed to have adapted a bit to North American English. For example, he said "wanna" instead of "want to"—though he said "wanna" with a British accent. I learned much from him. He was competent and professional, and helped me achieve a high level of efficiency and productivity.

My environment at work was richly multicultural, with individuals from many backgrounds and many countries. Once, in a sales meeting with about twenty managers and sales engineers present, all members of our elite sales force, we began talking during a coffee break about who was from where. We then decided to count who among those present had been born in Canada. We discovered that only six were native Canadians. All the others were immigrants like myself, and had come from a number of countries. It was easy to feel at home. I did notice something odd: among those present there was not a single francophone Québécois. I did not give it much thought. Just a coincidence, I supposed. The year was 1970.

One day, a few months later, my boss was interviewing candidates for a new position. As usual, he had placed a newspaper advertisement, evaluated the resumes he had received, and selected the candidates that seemed most promising. The candidates were then interviewed, about half an hour apart. This was an initial screening to select the few best candidates for further interviews. Also as usual, after the first few interviews, he was running late and candidates began having to wait ten or fifteen minutes in the reception area. The receptionist offered them coffee and I chatted with some of these nervous people, trying to make them feel at ease. I gave them literature about the company and was able to form a first impression about them.

In the late afternoon, after the last candidate had gone, I stuck my head into my boss' office. "How did it go?" I asked.

There was a large pile of resumes on his desk. He picked up a smaller pile, the few he had selected, and waved it in the air. "Very well," he said. "We got a few really good ones. I think I'll pass some of these on to other departments if I don't hire them myself."

"Hey, excellent! I bet I know whom you will probably hire."

"Really, now. Who?" He smiled his cordial smile.

"You mean 'whom'," I said.

"No," he said. "I mean: Who do you think will be hired?" We laughed at the grammatical jousting.

One of the candidates I had chatted with was a well-educated and bilingual Québécois de souche.[4] He was very presentable and well-spoken, which was important since the opening was for a field engineer position that required face-to-face interaction with customers. I had not met all the candidates and I was not yet an experienced manager, but this was the one I thought should get the job. I told my boss the name of my preference.

"Oh, no," he said. The smile faded.

"Why not?" I asked.

"He is too 'dees and dose'—he won't do."

"What do you mean, 'dees and dose'?" I asked.

"He doesn't say "these" and "those," came the reply. "He is too French."

Oh-oh. Trouble. Big trouble.

I had not yet heard of the book *White Niggers of America*.[5] In Durham, North Carolina I had observed racism against a Black person. That memory immediately flashed in my mind. The shocking truth was revealed: Canada was apparently no better than the U.S. in matters of racism. Suddenly the language tensions no longer seemed charming. This was not "just" a racist remark; rather, it reflected a mindset that deprived a deserving candidate of a good job. How could this be? The unfairness of it was appalling. Other countries in Europe and the rest of the world generally did not give resident foreigners the same rights as their own citizens—that seemed normal, and foreigners knew the regulations of the countries to which they were going. But this was a matter between two supposedly-equal citizens of the same country. I had never seen such discrimination first hand. Perhaps this is the way it had been in Egypt before independence, when foreigners dominated the economy. Perhaps I had just been too young, naïve, and sheltered to notice. My parents had not said much about interethnic and interracial relationships and had never denigrated other backgrounds. My school

---

4 This expression refers to Québécois who are descended from the original French colonists and, by extension, is used for any natively French-speaking Québécois whose ancestors were predominantly French Catholic and who shares the culture of the majority.

5 Pierre Vallière's book *White Niggers of America* is out of print.

had a very diverse, international student body. As children, my brothers and I had had a Belgian nanny and later a French piano teacher. As true-blue Egyptians, we had always felt slightly superior to foreigners (though we tried politely never to show it), so everything had seemed normal because, as I learned later, a feeling of superiority is intrinsic to practically every distinct group. I also learned that as long as that feeling is kept to oneself, it should not present a problem to maintaining good interethnic and interracial relations. But when that feeling of superiority becomes overt and is acted upon to the detriment of others, trouble and hostile reactions ensue.

This experience embedded itself permanently in my memory and influenced my perception of events in Quebec and Canada later on. Like most immigrants, when I had been here long enough to understand the politics and to take sides, I became an unwavering federalist. Whenever Quebec separatists do or say something to anger me, however, that incident comes back to me and I calm down.

I went back to my cubicle, troubled and pensive. A number of thoughts struck me. Though my manager and the candidate were citizens of the same country, one had recently arrived and the other's roots were probably centuries old. Yet, the newcomer was denying a job to the most competent candidate because he was "too French." This was not good for the company or the economy. In my (admittedly limited) experience in the U.S., the most competent person got the job or the promotion. Yet this same manager who rejected the Québécois had accepted me comfortably because I spoke perfect English. Though in Montreal for only a few months, in English-speaking circles I was "one of the boys," just like in the U.S. I decided not to say anything or bring up the matter with anyone else—I was too new and valued my job. I was afraid of antagonizing my new boss when things were going so well. Besides, we had a genuinely friendly relationship and I felt it would have been an act of betrayal to go over his head and complain to a higher level of management.

In retrospect, do I feel ashamed for having kept quiet? If the answer were yes, I would be judging myself too harshly. After the initial euphoria subsides, most immigrants continue to experience a higher level of stress and anxiety than the general population for months or years, depending on personality and circumstances. Except for wealthy immigrants who can take their time, most of us in the early months or years are scrambling to find work, understand how to communicate and function, prove ourselves, and make sure we can pay for food and lodging. There is little discretionary energy or courage and few mental resources beyond what are needed in the basic struggle to adapt and earn a living. Very few immigrants will take risks with their personal progress or divert their energy into the broad questions of social justice and employment equity. Recent immigrants are not social movers and shakers.

I did manage to do something for the French language when I had the power to do so. About a year after that incident, what we called the "demo bus" drove up from the division in Waltham, Massachusetts. A technician and I drove the bus to Quebec City to demonstrate our medical electronics equipment. A number of prominent cardiologists visited the bus and were impressed by our technological advances and engineering prowess. After having been presented with the features and advantages of the new instruments, my distinguished visitors asked for brochures, and I had plenty to give them, all in English. The director of the Institute of Cardiology in Quebec City was present, a Dr. Morin, if I remember correctly. Along with a few other doctors he later came to me, thanked me for the demonstration, and asked—nay, pleaded—for technical brochures in French, if I had any to give. I had none and was truly embarrassed. They were disappointed but accepted the English brochures, for they were professionals who naturally wanted to keep up to date with technical developments.

Upon returning to the office in Pointe-Claire, I asked my boss and then his boss, both anglophones, for a budget to translate our product literature into French. "No," came the answer. There was no need: everyone of consequence could read English.

"How about just the few newest, most advanced products?" I asked.

"No. There is no money left in the budget for promotion. Besides, it's not necessary."

I called the division in Waltham, where I had established good contacts during my time there. I asked around and finally spoke to an American, George Breed, who spoke good French and who was eager to help. He had an idea. He would contact the European head office, and see what they could do. He called me back two days later.

"We are lucky," he said. "They are about to print some brochures in French and they agreed to put the address of your Quebec office alongside the other addresses in France, Switzerland, and Belgium. But they are almost ready to go to print, so you had better hustle." He gave me the name of the contact in the European head office. I hustled.

A few months later I went back to Quebec City, visited every doctor who had visited our demo bus, and gave them the entire French catalogue, which contained most of the equipment they had seen. The very newest instruments were not in the catalogue because information about them had been released too late to be included in that printing. There is simply no getting around it: professionals who want to be up to date must be able to function in English. When I visited Dr. Morin, I gave him a pile of these product catalogues so he could give them to colleagues I had not met. He got up from his big desk, walked around it, took my hand, and shook it warmly.

"Thank you for doing this for us," he said.

There is no doubt that I did this partly to increase my business. But I also did it because I felt it was unfair not to have French technical literature for my francophone customers. I felt I had atoned in a way on my company's behalf for rejecting that deserving francophone candidate on the basis of language.

Few if any fair-minded people can seriously believe that nothing should have been done or that Canada would be a better country had the linguistic situation not been changed. Since Franco-Quebecers turned things around, anglos have been complaining that they and their language are being discriminated against. There is a fundamental characteristic of our species I recognized at an early age: humans adhere ardently to groups, and whichever group can gain dominance over other groups naturally inclines towards trampling on the rights of *les autres*.

Oppression and Revenge

At an early age, I had learned how injustice and oppression breed revolution and revenge. My best friend in high school, Omar, belonged to a large land-owning family. His father was a pasha, a title given by Egypt's rulers to those whom they favoured, somewhat like aristocratic titles in Europe. His family was one of the richest in Egypt. In the feudal society in Egypt at the time, wealth was equated with land, and Omar's family owned thousands of acres of fertile agricultural land in the lush Nile valley. We lived close to each other. We had a very nice, big apartment while my friend lived in a huge villa built in the style of la belle Époque, with huge reception halls, rooms too numerous to count, and a magnificent garden that looked like a small piece of paradise. Several gardeners took care of the beautiful flowerbeds and magnificent trees, some of them rare and exotic. Since we lived in the same area of the city, every morning of every school day for many years, we took the same school bus. We took it again to come home in the afternoon. Every trip, we sat next to each other and talked about everything under the sun. One Monday morning, we got on the bus and my friend excitedly told me what he had done over the weekend.

"I went with my father to one of our cotton farms to supervise the harvesting. He wants me to learn the business," he said. "It was great fun. When we suspected a peasant was stealing some of the cotton he was picking, we searched him, and if we found any cotton hidden in his clothes, we beat him with a *kharazana*."[6] He chuckled happily. "Quite a few of the sons of dogs tried to steal our cotton, but I think we got them all."

We were about 13 years old; today I am ashamed to confess that at the time I also thought it was all very amusing.

Shortly thereafter, there was a revolution and revenge. All privately-held land was confiscated by the revolutionary government and distributed among the peasants, except for a few hundred acres per family. In addition, all liquid assets belonging to very rich families like Omar's, were "frozen." Money could be withdrawn from bank accounts only by the permission of a commissar. It was not easy to get permission. My friend's family income fell precipitously and they joined the middle class. The magnificent villa—really a small palace—was seized and turned into a school for poor children. The garden—a symbol of the enjoyment of the feudal rich on the backs of the many poor—was neglected and the beautiful plants died.

One day, a few years later, my friend was arrested without charges of any kind and, for no reason except that there were political troubles and the government was worried that he and others like him could hurt the revolution. He later told me that when he asked the arresting

---

6 Long, thin canes that can inflict a painful sting but are not heavy enough to break bones or cause permanent damage.

revolutionary officer what would happen to him, the answer was, "We don't yet know what we are going to do with you lot."

It was unfair and grotesque. My friend did not deserve to be treated like that. It was not his fault he had been born into a wealthy family. Still, I wonder whether that officer or some of his men could have been among the peasants beaten with *kharazanas* years before on Omar's or some other plantation. Oppression breeds oppression. As a result of my observations and experiences, beginning in the region where I grew up, there is a theme which I brought with me when I immigrated to Canada, and which will recur in this book. Powerful groups oppress and abuse weaker ones for gain. Weaker groups try to resist, defeat and overthrow those who oppress them, whether they be local ruling classes or foreigners.

Leaders of the abused poor are often not themselves from poor or less educated classes. Sometimes the weak succeed other times they do not. There appears to be proportionality between the degree of cruelty of the oppressors and the harshness of revenge if the oppressed are able to exact it. I see that many of my fellow Canadians are aware of this pattern of human behaviour, while many others are not. For me, this somber perception explains aspects of many conflicts in the world: the civil and earlier independence wars in Algeria, the Israel-Palestine struggle, the War on Terror, even the Quiet Revolution in Quebec.

Arriving in Canada, I again saw injustice. Admittedly, it was substantially milder than what I had grown up with in Egypt. However, in a way it seemed worse: in Egypt, the troubles were within what had almost become one people; here, the injustice was by one ethnic group towards another. Since my "dees and dose" experience many years ago, whenever an anglophone complains about changes in Quebec, I tell the story of the English manager who wouldn't hire a francophone. Usually, eyes are averted and the subject is changed.

I continued with my new life and soon my mind turned to other things, but it was clear that this had not been an isolated incident. In the back of my mind, there was an intangible sense of foreboding and déjà vu.

Chapter 3: Growing Up in a Clash of Empires

If immigrants are vital, they will continue to be welcomed into Canada in large numbers. Native-born Canadians should be aware that New Canadians, though they may be well adapted, often retain some very different attitudes and perspectives on important aspects of human existence. This chapter looks at some such perspectives, as they relate to the historical conquests of the Europeans.

One perspective relates to once almost-forgotten but recently resurrected memories of wicked imperial European behaviour. These might result in a dog-eat-dog view of humanity and a new suspicion of current intentions and actions of the rich world towards the poor world.

Another is a perception I have, that many Canadians with ancestry from former imperial states apparently do not quite remember or recognize cruelty inflicted by their ancestral countries, and often actively resist being reminded. Such people flock to the writings of Western "scholars" who specialize in deflecting feelings of guilt or remorse. These latter specialize in spinning history in a way that absolves the West from ever having done anything immoral or ignoble.

I have also found that old feelings of inferiority inflicted by earlier subordination to foreign conquerors exert a sad influence on the mindset of some New Canadians.

A Dog-Eat-Dog World

The degree to which immigrants are affected by memories of pain inflicted on ancestral countries, varies according to factors such as personality, personal experiences and where in the world they come from. On an individual basis, some of these mental "burdens" may weigh heavily or not at all. Those who are affected most are from places where hurtful foreign intrusions are continuing today, thus bringing back old, half-forgotten memories.

In my case, I had believed the era of Western imperialism had ended; my concern had been centered about the threat of the Cold War becoming a nuclear war. Living happily in Canada, my memories of misdeeds by European empires had faded. But they were resurrected in the 1990s when so many Iraqi children were dying from malnutrition and a lack of the most basic of medicines. The Anglo-American aggression against Iraq in 2003 looked very much like the old imperialist ventures: my old memories came back and no longer seemed irrelevant.

My childhood and adolescent years occurred in the midst of rebellious nationalism and social upheaval, though the result of the latter left much to be desired. I was affected in a number of ways, among them my (usually subconscious) distaste for countries which, during the colonial era, amassed wealth on the backs of less advanced peoples through aggression and violence.

Starting in the mid-nineteenth century, the military technology of Europe became advanced enough for Europeans to go on a global rampage. Such expansionism was not in itself new: throughout history, whichever people gained a military advantage did much the same thing. There were the Macedonians, Romans, Arabs, Mongols, Turks—even Swedes—and many others. Nineteenth- and twentieth-century European aggression operated under the banner of something new, the sovereign nation-state.

When the British drove the Turks out of the Middle East, together with the French they carved up my old region into smaller colonies such as Syria, Iraq, Jordan, and Palestine so it would be more easily subjugated. Divide and rule. In the case of Egypt:

> "We ask, what happens in the 1820s, when the United States and Egypt both began their internal economic development programs in rather similar ways. Both were based on textiles, both had cotton, both had cultural producers. The United States had kicked out the British, so it was able to continue. The Egyptians had not kicked out the British, therefore the British intervened forcefully, and quite consciously and openly—you can read it in the public document—to block internal economic development in Egypt, because, as they said, 'We're not going to permit a competitor in this region, which we run.' And they did [run it], too, by force."[1]

The aim of the Europeans was to keep other peoples weak, backward, and divided. With the help of corrupt locals, they succeeded very well.

There is an embarrassingly large number of cruel imperial examples. Belgium, for example, lived in fear of Germany for a long

---

[1] Transcript of Evan Solomon interviewing Noam Chomsky, "Hot Type," 10 May, 2002, CBC (Canadian Broadcasting Corporation.) Online: <http://cbc.ca/programs/sites/hottype_chomsky911.html>.

time. A small country of about ten million people and two official languages, it did not pose a threat to any of its neighbours. All it wanted was to be left alone. Without any provocation, Germany attacked it during each of the two world wars. What are we to make of these brutal acts of aggression against a decent, helpless neighbour? The question itself entails an assumption that is not entirely true.

Yes, Belgium was helpless in relation to Germany. It could not commit aggression against its neighbours for fear of reprisal. However, it just had to look further afield to find a safe outlet for its completely unprincipled greed. It found weaker societies to victimize in the African Congo, where the people had no modern weapons and were not dangerous by European standards. There, Belgium wrote one of the many dark pages of European colonialism. At the beginning of the 20th century, during the "golden age" of the sovereign nation-state, rubber was an important commodity and natives of the Congo were pressed into forced labour to collect it. Men and women who did not meet their quota would be shot on the spot or have their ears, hands, or feet cut off.[2] It should be noted that the Congolese who lost their lives or parts of their anatomies had not rebelled against Belgium or committed acts of terrorism. They simply failed to meet their production quotas for rubber. Typical of the behaviour of nation-states, Belgium seems decent and helpless when confronted by a superior military power; towards the Congolese, it became a monster.[3]

Comfortably Tailored Memories

I am less than very pleased by so-called scholars in the West who deliberately avoid acknowledging the ruthlessness of former European colonial powers. Sometimes they actually defend the worst kind of behaviour. Some seek to absolve the West for its significant role in the wretched plight of the Arab and Muslim world today. They add insult to injury. Another more serious reason for my disdain is that such writers, by hiding the true extent of how others were hurt and wronged, contribute to the schism between civilizations. They make it more difficult for their own public to understand the rage against more recent Western aggression. I sense this indirectly helps fuel the growth and intensity of terrorism.

2 There are photographs of Congolese abused in this way in Taylor, *The 20th Century*, Vol. 3, p313; "The Congo under Leopold" by Roger Anstey.

3 More photographs and a much more elaborate account of this tragedy "of Holocaust dimensions" can be found in Hochschild, *King Leopold's Ghost*.

According to one view, Western military intrusions were not the cause of the Muslim and Arab World's decline from an advanced position of wealth and power. Rather, Western aggression is the result of such decline.

I beg to differ. Every powerful civilization eventually declines, and the same will inevitably happen to the West. When it was the turn of Muslim power to decline, it became about equal to Western power and an uneasy balance resulted. The big gap between them emerged when the West began to enter the Industrial Age and the scientific revolution gained momentum. The Europeans entered a new era while most of the rest of the world did not. Industrial Age technology led to the development of new weapons that could kill at a distance and on an unprecedented scale. Courage and valour alone were insufficient against such weapons.

I could choose any former empire—French, Portuguese, Turkish, Spanish, Italian or others—as examples for the following line of thinking. I have arbitrarily chosen Britain, because it happened to be occupying the country where I was born. To illustrate how I feel about what the old empires of Britain and France did in the Middle-East, let us engage in a thought experiment and ask whether the same thing could be done to Britain as was done to their victims. As the U.K. continues to decline from the peak of its former power over others, let us suppose a hostile power makes a technological breakthrough that gives it military superiority over the U.K. and its allies. It forces the surrender of Britain and occupies it. Could such a new colonial power do many of the same insidious things and, within some decades, bring Britain down to the miserable level of any developing country, formerly a colony of a European empire? I believe it could.

This new power would first make defeated Britain pay reparations for the war it had not started. Prior to the arrival of the British, Mysore had not been in a state of decline. It fought bravely but just did not have the advanced firepower the British had brought with them. It does not appear that either Britain or its East India Company were morally or socially superior to Mysore. It took four wars to finally kill the sultan and destroy Mysore on the way to subjugating all of India. The explanations given by British "scholars and historians" to morally support the "need" for the final British attack in 1799, were that the sultan was "intransigent"—that is, he tried to resist a malicious foreign power—and that the sultan was seeking assistance from the French, as if it were a crime to seek allies when attacked.

Next, the evil neo-colonial power would disunite the United Kingdom by force. Since such a malicious colonizer could do practically anything it wanted, it would destroy any social and political institutions that stood in the way of its complete control. It would establish its choice of unelected rulers in the dismembered parts of the former United Kingdom and allow them to enrich themselves by any means they saw fit. (Britain did just that in Egypt in 1922, finally placing the corrupt King Fouad I on the throne of Egypt, after unsuccessfully approaching other prominent families who preserved their honour and integrity by refusing to be lackeys.) It would support them by force and would help them crush any emerging leader or movement which strove for independence or tried to reunite the former country. It would try to create and exacerbate tensions amongst the Scots, English, Welsh, and Irish. One way to do this would be to draw the new borders to make sure that the fragments of the former U.K. were awkward and contained sizable dissatisfied minorities. Special attention would be paid to North Sea oil. In that area, a weak and vulnerable prince would be established and allowed to rule, while enriching himself and obeying his foreign protectors and masters. Such tactics could be relied on to bring troubles and debilitating divisions for years to come.

The occupier would tolerate corruption and discourage integrity in the splintered and subservient establishments. It would put down rebellion by any part of the former U.K. In exchange for protection, carefully-selected rulers would serve the interests of the occupying power, even against the interests of their own people. Such rulers would be designated "our moderate friends" until they failed to obey, at which time they would become "corrupt tyrants who must be removed for the good of their people." It would manipulate the educational system to suit its own needs. It would block economic development. It would destroy those sections of the economy that competed with its own industries.

Then, a century later, when the divided, occupied, and oppressed former Britain had sunk to abysmal lows, some "scholar" would write that the peoples of the British Isles had only themselves to blame. Meanwhile, the imperialists would perhaps claim to have brought even civilization itself to the "primitive" colonies by improving communication and transportation and building taller buildings than existed before. We can assume that these peoples would also be less than very pleased with the view presented by such scholars.

Interestingly, none of my disapproval is directed towards Canadians of European extraction. For some reason, I do not associate Canadians of English, French, Belgian, Portuguese, or any other extraction with the cruel excesses of former European empires, even though some may have perspective at odds with mine.[4] Curiously, I am not even anti-monarchy, being rather quite neutral about our Queen. If ever there were a referendum to abolish the monarchy in Canada, I would abstain and let those who feel strongly one way or the other about it decide. A reason may be that the social environment in Canada acts like a balm which heals old grievances as it soothes and consoles. Canada is a country like no other I know, with a benign and gentle nationalism and a remarkable lack of vindictiveness.

How Nationalism Came to My Country of Birth

It was not easy for an ancient society to do battle against the modern knowledge and techniques of the West. When Europeans developed their modern mindset and when their scientific methods and military technology enabled them to defeat older, traditional civilizations, fierce cultures which had hitherto been dangerous became easy prey. There is nothing like a Gatling gun to mow down brave men defending their turf with spears and ornate shields or beautifully-crafted swords.

At this point, Europeans' most dangerous adversaries were other Europeans, and the "Great Powers" competed and fought amongst themselves. It was principally in order to strike at British interests that Napoleon led an expeditionary force against Egypt in 1798. The land of the Nile, where I was born, would be changed forever.

"In the last decade of the eighteenth century, the French were looking on Egypt with increased interest largely because of their struggle with the British. Egypt could be France's granary, and its possession could control Middle-Eastern military and commercial traffic, providing a base from which to threaten the British in India."[5]

4 Canada's First Nations peoples might well disagree.
5 Anderson, *Politics and Change*, p58.

Though the French remained only a few years, they had brought with them savants—including scholars and members of their scientific community—and the shock of new intellectual and scientific ideas. The British responded quickly: shortly after the French fleet arrived, it was attacked and destroyed at the Battle of the Nile, in Abu Kir Bay, by a British fleet under Nelson. Cut off, the French forces' days in Egypt were numbered. The stranded French army capitulated a few years later and was allowed to return to France. The British evacuated the country in 1803. Though they had wanted to keep the French out, it appears a cost-benefit analysis convinced them it was not worth the trouble of occupying Egypt.

Native Egyptians, of course, had absolutely nothing to say about all this; they lacked the fleets, advanced weapons, and organizational skills necessary to participate in the violence in any meaningful way. They just watched the events unfold, prayed to God for an outcome favourable to them—or at least not very unfavourable—and hoped for the best. British disinterest changed as the acquisitive instincts of the Empire were aroused with the completion of the Suez Canal in 1869. The canal opened up a new, much-shorter route to their "milk-cow," India. Now the British wanted Egypt. They came back and took over the country in 1882. Through the power of Industrial Age weapons, the concept of nationalism, born in Europe, was spread around the world. The European idea of the sovereign nation-state was gradually adopted by peoples they conquered, then turned against European imperialism. Nationalism helped galvanize resistance to foreign occupation and spur wars of independence.

Egypt historically has been an attractive target for conquerors. I grew up in an environment created by the ambitions, interaction, and clashes of empires. The Ottoman Turks have been present to some degree or another since the 16th century. In the 19th century, the French and British empires hovered around the region competing for the prize. The British came to attach great importance to Egypt; they evicted the remnants of Ottoman influence and successfully blocked the French. Sixty years after they occupied the country, during World War II, they just barely managed to hold onto their prey by stopping the Third Reich, which made a brief and sensational appearance on the scene but failed to take Egypt when Erwin Rommel's Afrika Korps were finally defeated at El Alamein.

Initially, opposition to foreign intrusion was based on religion. Napoleon Bonaparte was made aware of this when he captured Cairo after his victory at the Battle of the Pyramids in 1798. Seeking to minimize resistance to the French presence, he declared to Egyptians that he and his soldiers had become Muslims. Alas, he was not widely believed—perhaps because, among other things, his men could not refrain from drinking alcoholic beverages and pursuing Egyptian women. Gradually nationalism emerged in Egypt in the late 19th century and became an almost-religious fervour. Resistance to European intrusion and colonization began to center around nationalist sentiment. In at least one case, nationalism and religious sentiment converged, as the Moslem Brotherhood emerged in the 1920s. Starting in the 1920s and 1930s, Egyptians rallied in earnest against British occupation.

My maternal grandmother was an activist for women's rights and against the British occupation of Egypt. She was a fierce nationalist. For much of her life, she carried a scar on her forehead where a British bullet had grazed her. She had been helping and caring for Egyptian nationalist demonstrators injured in the streets of Cairo by the British Army during an Egyptian intifada in the 1920s. She wore the scar proudly for the rest of her life.

The nationalism Europeans brought to Egypt fueled the resistance which eventually drove them out.

Are Conquerors Better Than the Conquered?

One of the sad legacies of European armies trampling on others is that some feelings of inferiority have developed among the downtrodden. Some New Canadians from former colonies bring memories of these troubled emotions with them. Others do not, or never had them.

My cousin Leila, who went to the same English school I did, wrote about the "curse of internalized colonialism."[6] After I decided not to go back to Egypt and to come to Canada, I suddenly found myself wondering whether my decision was related to an internalized colonial way of thinking. I was born in a country forcibly occupied by the British and dominated by Europeans. My extended family—or rather my entire social class—learned European languages and adopted European

6 Ahmed, *A Border Passage*.

clothing and other habits. We learned modern science thanks to the European presence. Did I admire the West so much and had I been so transformed that I no longer wanted to be Egyptian? Had my education in a French school, then a British one, had the insidious effect of turning me against my own kind?

This introspection was a difficult process, because using one's mind to examine one's own mind is intrinsically subjective and is quite the opposite of a detached intellectual process. I tried my best to be factual and concluded that the answer to one more question would go a long way to answering the first two: Did I feel that Western Europeans, including the British, were superior to me? I had no difficulty in answering with a resounding "no." I looked for evidence that I was not just in denial, to avoid embarrassment and to feel better. I found it easily. The best evidence of my pride in my Egyptian heritage is that I have passed on this pride to my children. They all have Egyptian names: Tarek, Karim, and Shereen. In their youthful exuberance, they sometimes go too far in boasting about their Egyptian background.

But I discovered that some immigrants from former colonies have indeed felt inferior to their "white masters," as happened on one of the occasions when we were invited to dinner by our good friends Andre and Raja Dirlik. Andre is a retired former educator at St. Jean Military College and Raja is a professional librarian. At one of these parties, we met a fine couple from Fiji, Mohan and Shayla, racially of East-Indian origin and for many years Canadian citizens. Mohan is an endocrinologist who obtained his degree in medicine in New Zealand. Shayla has a master's degree in nursing. I have always looked forward to dinners at the Dirliks' home. In addition to Raja's superior culinary skills, one can always anticipate an equally superior level of intellectual discussion. On this particular evening, the topic of conversation turned to European imperialism, and at one point Andre asked Mohan about his years growing up in Fiji.

"How did you feel about the British?"

"We felt inferior. We were made to feel inferior," Mohan answered. He told us how even though he had received exceptionally high grades at school, it had been extremely difficult for him to obtain a scholarship for university studies—such scholarships were for white British people living in Fiji. He eventually did get it. Once precedent had been broken, however, the scholarship was abolished. It is easy to imagine that many who grew up in British-occupied Fiji and elsewhere bear at least some emotional scars for the rest of their lives, and sometimes pass the resentment on to their children. Andre then turned to me and asked,

"And how did you feel about the British in Egypt?"

I took a moment to answer, since no one had asked me such a question before. There was silence as I pondered the question deeply. The suspense mounted. Finally I answered, "I felt equal or, I am embarrassed to say, a little superior."

"Ah," said Raja, exhaling as though she had been holding her breath, "that is the influence of Islam."

I think it was, at least partly. We have not been a deeply religious family. We do not pray regularly. We only sometimes fast during Ramadan. I do, however, enjoy reading the Koran occasionally. Sometimes one verse or another will give me goose bumps. I suppose that in Canada we would be called secular Muslims, though none of us would ever contemplate renouncing our religion. Islam builds up the dignity of every individual by insisting on the absolute equality of all, regardless of race, social status, or wealth. As part of our culture, we internalized these values.

The next question was: How is it that I don't feel European imperialists are superior? After all, they conquered many countries all over the world, including ours. In addition, I owe a great deal to ideas and discoveries from Europe. I greatly admire the modern scientific method they developed: measurement and observation, verifiability and repeatability. Europeans introduced electricity, the automobile, and modern banking to Egypt. To their eternal credit, the British gave the world parliamentary democracy, a marvel which fortunate countries have been able to adopt in some form or another. (It did not catch on in Egypt.)

The two most important explanations I came up with are universally human. The first reason why I do not feel the West is superior is that they learned a great deal from us when we were more advanced than they—for instance, they learned about experimentation, the basis of science, from the Arabs, who had built on the work of the Greeks. Without building on our algebra, I don't see how Newton (and the German Leibnitz) could have developed integral and differential calculus. Without calculus, the industrial revolution would have been unthinkable. Our advances in sciences, such as in chemistry and medicine, helped the British and all of Europe escape the Dark Ages. For us to learn from them now makes us even.

The second reason I do not feel Europeans are superior, is that European powers committed gross injustices in the countries they conquered. One cannot be unjust and superior at the same time—the two are mutually exclusive. The European powers that advanced into the Industrial Age before other societies have used this advantage on an unprecedented global scale and in some cases with a degree of ruthlessness and cruelty rarely surpassed in history. To use the knowledge of how to make a Lee Enfield rifle to capture other peoples and their lands, then siphon away their riches and resources, is dishonourable and immoral to say the least. People who behave in this manner are not superior to their victims; it may be argued that, at least with respect to that specific behaviour, they in fact are inferior.

In the same way, turning to Quebec's past as a colony of the British Empire, those anglophones who deliberately tried to make the francophones feel inferior simply because, for a certain time in a certain place, they had an advantage, are ignorant or wicked and thus by definition not themselves superior. Ironically, therefore, the behaviour of some of *les anglais* is a good reason for the Québécois not to feel inferior.

But lest the francophone citizens of Quebec be tempted to feel superior themselves, let me hasten to suggest that wherever they could, the French also behaved in this manner. Whenever it had the upper hand over people who could not match its military power, France behaved with destructive cruelty in order to benefit materially and boost the ego of its people under the banner of *la gloire de la France!* The French Empire was just as haughty as the British Empire, though it apparently tended to sneer more—or more overtly—at its victims. Even right here in Quebec, the ancestors of today's de souche population conquered the original First Nations and sometimes treated many as badly as or worse than they themselves were treated by the British after the Conquest of 1759. The "Red Indians" should not feel inferior to others who act like brigands, in this case the French Empire, just because the latter had muskets and better organization and knew how to march in columns.

But they should not feel superior, either. Before the Europeans came, there were wars between the various tribes and those who gained the advantage at a given time in a certain place, apparently enslaved, tortured, and killed members of other tribes. That is also inferior behaviour.

Finally, it would seem that no one is superior or inferior. As a species we have evolved certain characteristics that may today be judged as extremely unpleasant, though I suppose they were once important in helping us survive in difficult conditions tens or hundreds of thousands of years.

Chapter 4: Language Wars, Long Ago and Far Away

Language and My Identity

The language we speak is paramount in defining who we are—or who we think we are. What happens to a person like me, who acquires fluency in more than one language? The language I use most is English; however, I certainly have no interest in being English. I am fond of the French language, which I learned even before I understood English, though I am not and do not wish to be French. German enriched my life by opening a window to a wonderful cultural heritage, but I am far from being German. I was born into Arabic, though recently in Cairo I was told, in the usual friendly and polite Egyptian way, that I was not really quite Egyptian. So what am I? Where do I belong?

Do these questions bother me? Not in the least. I have no problem with the question of my identity. The diversity merely intensifies my feeling that I belong to the human race as a whole. I think Canadian society makes it easy to evolve such a multicultural and laid-back identity. I am Canadian.

Before coming to Canada, things were not that simple. I was raised in linguistic turmoil reflecting social troubles and nationalist wars. Arabic, powerful by virtue of tradition and being the language of an overwhelming majority, held its own in all classes. No matter how many foreign languages one knew, it was shameful for an Egyptian not to speak Arabic. In the first half of the 20th century, English and French competed against each other amongst the small upper classes, while Arabic competed against both. It is thus that, in Cairo, I grew up in a multicultural environment.

> "While foreign-sponsored schools taught European ideas in European languages, a native flowering of Arabic literature struggled to reconcile the vastly different worlds of the classical Arabic language and literary forms, the local Arabic vernacular and popular literary culture of Egyptians, and the foreign literary genres that expressed 'modern' individualistic conceptions of the self … In short, Egyptians faced a bewildering smorgasbord of different, and partly incompatible, cultural symbols and identities."[1]

---

1 Anderson, *Politics and Change*, p 148.

It may have been bewildering for some, but I found the cultural and linguistic environment where I grew up to be rich and diverse. I thoroughly enjoyed it. (That is probably why the presence of both English and French makes me more at home in Montreal than I would be in either a French-only or English-only city. Arabic is present here too: I regularly socialize with "good Quebecers of Egyptian origin."[2])

As was the fashion in Egypt, my father was educated in Arabic with an emphasis on English. He was an architect, and while knowledge of Arabic was a matter of pride and essential to any kind of career in Egypt, English was considered the language of pragmatism and engineering. Of course, he also learned French. My mother was educated in French, considered the language of culture and gracious living. Of course, she also learned English.

When a once-powerful culture declines, its language becomes less attractive to others. Arabic is a good example of this. From about the 9th to the 13th century, it was the foremost language of learning in the world. It was very attractive—if one wanted to be thoroughly educated and up-to-date, one had to learn Arabic, in the same way that English is essential for advanced learning today. With Arabic, one could pursue algebra (al-gabr), chemistry (al-chemia), medical science (the work of Ibn Sina and many others), philosophy (the writing of Ibn Rushd, Al-Razi, and many others), mathematics,[3] architecture, and even things like perspective drawing (Al Hassan Ibn Haitham.) Eventually there came a series of disasters, including bad rulers and the catastrophic destruction wrought by the Mongols. Over a period of about eighty years, Arabic ceased to be the universal language of learning.

As a child, I just caught the end of the demise of the Turkish language and culture in Egypt. When I was a child, my father went to work in a European suit and tie with a bright red Turkish-style fez on his head. Though the British had been the latest conquerors, the fez was a vestige of the once-mighty Ottoman Empire. But the former Turkish glory receded into the past: as the memory of Turkish power faded into history, so did the fez. In the 1950s, I remember suddenly noticing one day that my father did not have it on when he left for work. He never wore it again. As Ottoman power declined, people stopped copying its culture, outer trappings, and language. Even the Turks themselves began

---

2 As an open-minded minister of the separatist PQ once called me. (See chapter 17.)

3 The word "algorithm" is derived from the name of the Arab mathematician Al Khowarismi. Algorithms are necessary for the operation of modern computers.

mimicking Europeans. Egyptians who could afford to adopted the style and language, though not always the mentality, of the new European powers. My mother never wore any but European clothes.

My very first schooling—kindergarten and first grade—was in French. Afterwards, my parents decided that English would be the dominant language of the future and transferred me to an English school. (You were right Mom and Dad!) In addition to my French classes at school and private French lessons, my mother continued to speak and read to me in French. She told me stories about the Palace at Versailles, the French Revolution, Louis Pasteur and how Jean-François Champollion deciphered the Rosetta stone and unlocked the fascinating secrets of the hieroglyphics. This accounts for my knowledge and fondness of French language and culture. Everyday life, intensive private lessons at home, stern pressure from my father, and classes at school all contributed to my education in Arabic, a beautiful, flowery language. Educated Egyptians pursued fluency in English and French to gain access to the new knowledge of Europe. However, Arabic was the language of Egyptian nationalism, itself about a century newer than European nationalism. Not knowing Arabic was associated with not loving one's country.

As strange as this may sound, there was a language competition within my extended family and among friends and acquaintances, all Egyptian. Faced with a smorgasbord of cultural symbols, Egyptians were free to pick and choose. Over the unifying bedrock of Egyptian Arabic culture was a diverse layer, the result of many influences. While I continued in English through high school, some relatives and friends received a French education. Others went to Arabic schools, either because their parents could not afford foreign schools or because of a sense of patriotism. Many of those of us who went to English schools learned to feel superior to those who went to Arabic or French schools. Those who went to French schools tended to feel they were getting a better education than either Arabic or English schools could give. Many who went to Arabic schools learned that England and France were evil colonial powers that sought to keep Egypt weak and pillage its wealth and resources: families that put their children in foreign schools were dupes.

In visiting our relatives who went to French schools, we realized that they had "discovered" English schools were inferior to theirs. They believed the curricula were weak, homework was insufficient, and learning was not rigorous. Recently, when I questioned a friend (Egyptian Montrealer René Cressaty) who had been to excellent primary and secondary French schools in Egypt, he said that he could recall no attempt at school to make him believe that English schools were inferior. In the next breath, he added, "But it is well known that the French education we had is far stronger than the English." The message in French school was subtle and simple: *les anglais* were bad and so were their schools.

The British, too, were subtle. We were led to conclude "on our own" that our education was better than a French education. We "figured out" that while French teachers made their pupils mindlessly memorize vast quantities of information (thus the massive homework), the English taught pragmatic problem solving. We were told that education is more a frame of mind than the memorization of facts. Homework for French school kids entailed memorizing difficult words and their meanings. English homework required we look up and occasionally comment on difficult words and concepts in dictionaries and encyclopedias. The French required the learning of facts. We were taught to be careful with "facts": they are subject to change. I remember an example which our headmaster, Mr. Brandon Laight, used a couple of times to demonstrate how "timeless" facts can change. At least since Euclid in ancient Greece, it was a known "fact" that the shortest distance between two points on the face of the earth is a straight line. Then it was discovered that the earth was round and that the shortest distance between two points on the surface of the earth is actually a curve.

Furthermore, we thought that sports and physical education were practically non-existent in French schools. Sports build character. We had soccer, athletics, tennis, cross-country marathons, and more. We "concluded" that pupils in French schools would grow up chubby and unhealthy with no sporting spirit. No one ever said French schools were bad, but it was the "logical conclusion" that they were.

Linguistic conflicts were a visible reflection of social and political tensions. There were at least three components to the conflicting currents swirling around me as I was growing up. There was the rivalry between English and French. There were the conflicting perspectives of those Egyptians who entered foreign school systems and of those who could or would not (usually, but not always, the poor versus the rich.) Then there were the tensions between Egyptians as a whole and "foreign occupiers," reflected in conflicts regarding the Arabic and European languages, principally English and French. Eventually, for me, the chaos of these swirling conflicts was sublimated into a serene mental posture. I came to see languages as benign, a tool with which I could experience the best of what a variety of cultures had to offer.

Language as a Factor of Class Distinction

The arrival of Europeans brought a new mix of languages to Egypt. Growing up in Cairo, where a confluence of new empires was edging out the influence of an older one, the mixture of languages was an everyday fact of life. Arriving in Quebec, I took in stride the presence of both English and French. When it is necessary to switch from one to the other, I am not at all bothered.

On a wall in my home in Montreal, there hangs a testament to these layers of languages that have built up in Egypt over the centuries. Neatly framed is the passport of my father's maternal grandfather. It was issued on July 13th, 1898—sixteen years after the British landed in Alexandria ostensibly "to protect the thriving foreign community." The language of the people of Egypt was Arabic, but the passport is bilingual. It is in French and Turkish. That is French, Turkish, and no Arabic. The passport consists of one large sheet of heavy paper, about 36 cm wide by 28 cm high, with the headings "Gouvernement Egyptien" and "Passeport" at the top. Below are the details. French on the left and Turkish on the right. The passport is "Délivré à Son Excellence Ismail Pasha Sabry" and lists his profession as "Gouverneur de la ville d'Alexandrie." The Turkish, however, is in Arabic script written from left to right, not in Latin script as it is written today. (The passport predates Kemal Attaturk's reforms in Turkey.) I enjoy showing the passport to Arabic-speaking friends and watching their bewilderment when they read the Arabic lettering but cannot recognize the words or understand their meaning. Dr. Mohamed Ismail, formerly Consul General of Egypt in charge of the consulate in Montreal and responsible for issuing and renewing passports, was overwhelmed when he saw it. He spent a long,

long time scrutinizing every detail before shaking his head and heading for the buffet. The passport, over a century old, is signed by a Mr. Glenfield or Caulfield—the signature is difficult to read—an English official whose title is given as: "Le Chef de Service." There is also a smidgen of English on the passport. On the upper left side, outside the elaborate decorative frame printed on the robust paper, in tiny, unobtrusive print, it says, "Police Form No. 117." The rest of the passport is apparently unchanged from the pre-British days. Count on the English to leave well enough alone.

To summarize, my ancestor was issued a passport in French and Turkish, signed by an Englishman, in an Arabic-speaking country. No wonder educated Egyptians have a facility with languages! They also have no language hang-ups and will speak whatever language satisfies considerations of courtesy and the objective at hand. The document also shows that, though the British were in charge, French remained strong and appealing and continued to enjoy widespread use.

Appealing, that is, to the Egyptian upper and small middle classes. For until the 1950s, Egypt was largely an agrarian, feudal society. There was a clear distinction between the educated wealthy and the uneducated poor. The Arabic language helped define my identity as a proud Egyptian vis-à-vis the outside world. My knowledge of foreign languages, somewhat shamefully, helped establish me as a member of the upper classes.

Often throughout history, the elite of an occupied or dominated people imitate the ones who dominate them. In Roman times, throughout their empire those who could afford it usually learned Latin and tried to emulate the Roman lifestyle. In Egypt, everyone in a position to do so adopted European garb and speech. This differentiated the well-to-do from the less so. In our home, the family could speak French or English in front of the servants knowing they would not understand a word. It was a case of blatant and socially destructive arrogance that I did not recognize as such at the time. It was taken as yet more "evidence" of their inferiority. Phrases like "pas devant les domestiques" became an additional means of distinguishing us from the masses and reaffirming our lofty position in society and our divinely-ordained superiority. With the acceptance of European languages, many, consciously or not, became influenced by the attitudes and values of the

West, though they remained distinctly Egyptian. This cultural dichotomy exacerbated the schism between rich and poor.

Today it seems striking to me that we cared so little about the plight of the poor. The poor always constituted the overwhelming majority of Egypt's population, as they had everywhere else before the Industrial Revolution. I think we saw them as a fact of life, like the Nile and the palm trees along its banks. In retrospect, it appears we had a medieval view of society: we had internalized the perspective that society was like the human body, with each segment playing its role in conjunction with all the others. The poor were part of society just as limbs, say, were part of the body. I saw how my parents, uncles, and aunts were generous to the poor and regularly gave them money and food. But these were individual gestures of kindness. Though there were some calls to do something for the poor on a national scale, the idea did not catch on. Nor were we conscious of any injustice in the social structure. On the contrary, we felt we were fair and just towards the poor, as when we made sure to reward them adequately when they pleased us or when we arbitrated justly and impartially in disputes between them.

From what I can gather, until certainly the 17th and perhaps the 18th and in some places even the 19th centuries, the poor of Egypt were relatively better off than the poor in most of Europe. Egyptian society produced a surplus of many kinds of crops, while many in Europe went hungry. Egypt had a clement, generally comfortable climate while many Europeans had to scrounge for fuel and did not always manage to keep warm in winter. Though in both places most rulers were absolute monarchs, I don't believe that European aristocrats were less cruel or oppressive towards their poor than Egyptian ones. The class distinction between officers and ordinary soldiers in the British army which invaded Egypt appeared every bit as severe as class distinctions in Egyptian society. Language played a role in class distinction among the British, too. Different accents and manners of speech among the British clearly pinpointed social class. Nevertheless, in Europe, despite initial difficulties and social disruption, the Industrial Revolution gradually changed the plight of the poor there, who became less poor in relative terms. But in Egypt, agrarian society continued in its timeless way until the middle of the 20th century.

The stability was shattered by the 1952 coup, which ousted the corrupt monarchy and was widely supported by the people. When the plight of the poor showed no sign of improving by gradual evolution, a revolution occurred that removed the largely gentle but indifferent elite from power.

In my original homeland, where my identity was first shaped and nurtured, there had been severe class distinctions, injustice, and huge discrepancies in wealth distribution. Language played a key role in this. The wealthy learned European languages and could absorb new, advanced ideas with relative ease, thus increasing the gap between themselves and the poor and leaving the latter further behind.

Language and Nationalism

In my old country, until about World War I, there was no sense of patriotism or sense of belonging to a sovereign nation-state in the modern sense. As the British occupation dragged on, resentment and resistance grew. Emotions of nationalism introduced to Egyptians began to take hold. The British came to be resented as foreigners not "of our nation" (they did not speak Arabic and were infidels to boot) who should not have been there. Nationalist feelings escalated to a fever pitch in the 1940s and early 1950s. There was violence and blood was spilt. The occupation forces suffered increasingly from what today would be called terrorism. Things went from bad to worse, until the British had to leave.

Some developments following the British rule in Egypt may sound familiar to Canadians. Nationalistic language laws were instituted, one of the first actions of the new government. It was decreed that Arabic must predominate on all commercial signs, though other languages were allowed. Street and road signs in English had to be changed to Arabic. All correspondence with the government, hitherto primarily in English and occasionally French, had to contain Arabic text as well. Government tenders and other commercial transactions were also included. In this way, monolingual Egyptians obtained the right to work in Arabic only. (Interestingly, other languages were not prohibited and some tenders were trilingual.)

Though there was freedom of choice for schooling, non-Arabic schools were required to teach a minimum number of hours of Arabic.

Such was the contempt for Arabic among the powerful foreign elite that some foreign-language schools had taught none at all previously. Now, no one enrolled in a foreign-language school could graduate from high school without passing an equivalency exam in Arabic language and literature. It was a tough exam, and when my turn came, I barely scraped through. Zealous nationalists made an attempt to mandate Arabic as the language of education in all universities. The attempt was successful for most of the humanities but failed completely when it came to any department involved with technology, since modern science and engineering were imported from Europe. Finally, it was resolved that university education in science and engineering would be in English with "as much Arabic as possible." During my preparatory year in the Engineering Department of Cairo University (equivalent to first-year CEGEP), the only course given in Arabic, out of a total of nine, was chemistry. This was possible because the Arabs had done a great deal of original work in chemistry centuries ago and there was a foundation and vocabulary in Arabic. All the other courses—including mathematics, which I felt could also probably have been taught in Arabic—were taught in English. The pride of nationalism had come up against the reality of the power of English.

With the overthrow of King Farouk in 1952 came the first indigenous Egyptian government in almost 2500 years.[4] Through legislation, Arabic pushed aside English and French. The "ugly reminders of foreign domination," like horrible scars, disappeared from the streets of Cairo and other cities. Everyone felt good, including youngsters like me who had gone to foreign schools. We were still Egyptian first, and proud of our independence.

It may be interesting to note that by 2003, almost fifty years after the Egyptian language laws were enacted, signs everywhere in Cairo—on stores, businesses, billboard advertisements—are monolingual Arabic, monolingual English, and everything in between. Upscale shops in wealthy neighbourhoods tend to be English-only while in poorer areas Arabic predominates. French has practically disappeared. Over dinner, I asked a group of businessmen about what had happened to the language laws of our blessed revolution and was told they were still in place. No one cared to enforce them, however. Merchants and businessmen were free to choose whatever language was best suited for

---

4 Farouk was the last of a dynasty of rulers originally from Albania. They had come as mercenaries in the Ottoman Turkish army in the early nineteenth century.

their businesses and clientele. Language had gone from a nationalistic public issue to a private matter between buyer and seller.

Language and Violent Conflict

So fundamental is language to human existence, that there is an interdisciplinary debate as to whether or not the drive and ability to communicate in an orderly verbal manner (i.e. through formal spoken language, though not reading and writing) is instinctive, in the same sense, say, that geese instinctively fly south for the winter.

> "The evidence that grammar is innate is overwhelming and diverse. The evidence that a gene somewhere on chromosome 7 usually plays a part in building that instinct in the developing foetus' brain is good, though we have no idea how large a part that gene plays. Yet most social scientists remain fervently resistant to the idea of genes whose primary effect seems to be to achieve the development of grammar directly. As is clear in the case of the gene on chromosome 7, many social scientists prefer to argue, despite much evidence, that the gene's effects on language are mere side effects … ."[5]

But neither side disputes the enormous role of language. Not understanding another's language is a primordial alienating factor. It is easier to go to war against a people who speak a language we do not understand.

During my formative years, my environment included not just language wars, but also real wars. I was involved in one of them and felt that extreme manifestation of nationalism—also primordial—called "militant enthusiasm" by ethologist[6] Konrad Lorenz. As a teenager, I was armed with a Russian assault rifle, a bayonet, and some ammunition and waited for the enemy, the British and French. In 1956, they tried to occupy the Suez Canal, recently nationalized by Nasser, through an invasion that became known as the Suez War. Israel was asked to join so that the former masters of two dying empires could claim their blatant aggression was a police action. (That collusion with former imperialists helped cement in the minds of its neighbours the idea that Israel was merely an extension of European aggression in the region.) I never engaged in a battle. The only signs of the enemy I ever saw were hostile aircraft overhead. Other than the officers and commanders, our unit was

---

5 Ridley, *Genome*, p104-105.
6 Ethology is the study of the genetic basis of human and animal behavior.

made up almost exclusively of very young volunteers. Some of us had been to foreign schools and often conversed in English and French. However, under those circumstances, every one of us made absolutely sure never to utter a single word in English or French. We now saw it as the language of the evil enemy, one that our nationalism compelled us to resist by using our own Arabic language.

Teenage boys inexperienced in war are rarely afraid of it. Until their buddies are killed or maimed, it seems little more than an exciting game. My experience is nothing compared to those of the youth who fought in battles like the Somme and Kursk, or the conflicts in Vietnam and Chechnya. Though the enemy was stopped before they came anywhere near me and I never fired a shot in anger, one aspect affected me for the rest of my life. For a time I was armed and, though my determination was never tested, I felt willing and able to kill other human beings (of course, I could be killed first.) I experienced militant enthusiasm.

> "In reality, militant enthusiasm is a specialized form of communal aggression, clearly distinct from and yet functionally related to the more primitive forms of petty individual aggression ....A shiver runs down the back, and, as more exact observation shows, along the outside of both arms. One soars elated above all the ties of everyday life for the call of what, in the moment of this specific emotion, seems to be a sacred duty. All obstacles in its path become unimportant, the instinctive inhibitions against killing or hurting one's fellows lose, unfortunately, much of their power ....Men may enjoy the feelings of absolute righteousness even as they commit atrocities ....To the humble seeker of biological truth there cannot be the slightest doubt that human militant enthusiasm evolved out of a communal defense response of our pre-human ancestors."[7]

Language is an important distinguishing factor between "us" and "them." It helps define and channel the "specialized form of communal aggression" and direct it towards *les autres*. Such is the disposition of our species that it would not only have been legal for me to kill those non-Arabic-speaking invaders, it would have been commendable and brave, perhaps even heroic. I came to Canada keenly aware that over most of the world, throughout recorded history, violence has been and continues to be the principal arbiter in human affairs. I had reached the conclusion that the dominant socio-political structure on the planet, the sovereign nation-state, is one of the most vicious ever devised by man. One of its most powerful distinguishing features is language.

7 Lorenz, *On Aggression*, p231-232.

This is the background that had shaped my mindset when I arrived in Canada. True, I had for many years lived and studied in Switzerland, a refined, peaceful, and neutral democracy. But it is right smack in the middle of Europe, a continent with a violent and bloody history. Increasing my knowledge and understanding of Europe did nothing to reassure me. Furthermore, I discovered that the wonderful Switzerland of today, neutral and largely peaceful since the Congress of Vienna in 1814-1815, was only achieved after centuries of external and internal warfare. A small sample of Swiss wars over the centuries are: The war over the huge estates of the last of the Toggenburgs (Frederick VII), who died without an heir (1436); The Kappel wars (1529); the Villmerger wars (1653); the fighting in the streets of Geneva in 1738. Also, I could not help but be influenced by the fact that I found the modern Swiss to be somewhat xenophobic. They distrust foreign powers and are meticulously prepared for defensive war. They will go a very long way to avoid violent conflict; however, for decades after the end of World War II, during which they were neutral, they reportedly remained able to field an army of some 800,000 well-armed and trained men within forty-eight hours of perceiving a threat.[8] Their constitution allows the government to manufacture and deploy nuclear weapons quickly if judged necessary to counter a threat. Furthermore, every citizen of Switzerland is allocated space in a well-ventilated, reinforced concrete bunker built to help withstand the effects of nuclear weapons. Given the respect I had for the Swiss, all this only reinforced my perception that the first law of humanity is the law of the jungle.

My exposure to the turbulence of nationalism, counter-nationalism, and war alerted me to several factors which combine to inflame passions and stimulate aggressive nationalism. Having lived in many countries and studied the matter, I was able to formalize my thinking and put together a simple model for my own use. Language differences play a major role in this model. Because my professional career has included travel to and residence in a number of countries in volatile areas, I needed such a model to help me foresee where trouble and violence might erupt. It has been useful over the years, such as when I prevented a multinational corporation from putting its head office for the

---

8 The Swiss army is a militia composed mainly of "citizen-soldiers," similar to the Israeli army. In 2002, the reserves were downsized due to a greatly decreased probability of a direct military attack on Switzerland. The forces were modified to face "new kinds of threats."

Mediterranean and Middle Eastern region in Beirut a few years before civil war broke out. There were too many signs indicating the possibility of violence on a large scale. Over time, through direct observation and by studying works related to the subject, I identified four factors which I think reliably indicate a probable outbreak of violence. I consider two of the factors "instinctively" present in us as a species, and the other two fostered by man, usually by leaders and rulers.

The first characteristic is a straightforward and easily-observable part of our makeup as a species: group formation.

> "Man is a social being obliged by nature to live with others as a member of society."[9]

Man lives in groups and language is one of the most important factors distinguishing groups.

The second is our very low inhibition against killing our own kind. There are mechanisms that prevent most species of animals from killing or seriously injuring members of their own species. Species which have developed special killing techniques for dealing with their own prey seldom employ these when dealing with their own kind.[10]

Or, as Konrad Lorenz puts it:

> "I have shown that those inhibitions which prevent animals injuring or even killing fellow-members of the species have to be strongest and most reliable, in those species which being hunters of large prey possess weapons which could as easily kill a conspecific ...."[11]

In man, these inhibiting mechanisms are feeble: it is less difficult for us to kill each other. Especially since the advent of long-range weapons, killing is often unrestrained by pity or even unease at the shattering of flesh and bone. Lorenz's book contains a convincing presentation of this phenomenon. I have seen no evidence of inhibition against dropping "daisy cutters" on anonymous, unseen "targets" (humans) from a height of 30,000 feet or more. Nor did any kind of inhibition shake the resolve of those who killed thousands of fellow humans in the World Trade Center.

---

9 Lenski, *Power and Privilege*, p25.
10 Morris, *The Naked Ape*, p156.
11 Lorenz, *On Aggression*, p110.

Would it have been noble or despicable for me to use my assault rifle to kill "aliens" under "appropriate" circumstances? Noble, of course, says General Sir John Hackett.[12]

> "It is a distinguishing function of man, the political animal, to live in a society. The better able to do this, other things being equal, the better he is a man. But living in a group demands some subordination of the interest of the self to the interests of the group. The military contract stands out here as almost unique. It demands the total and almost unconditional subordination of the interests of the individual if the interests of the group should require it. This can lead to surrender of life itself. It not infrequently does. Thus in an important respect, the military would appear to be one of the more advanced forms of social institutions."[13]

To fulfill the military contract in conjunction with this more advanced form of social institution, a lack of inhibition against killing is required on a massive scale. The mass bombing of large cities in World War II is an example. During the Cold War, I was interested in what could happen to the world and read some books on the subject of nuclear war. How would the Soviets have acted in case of a so-called "limited war" in Europe? (Of course, it was only limited as far as non-Europeans were concerned; for the Europeans themselves it would have been Armageddon.) Nuclear weapons were an integral component of a European war and their use was built into Soviet tactics.

> 'The main mission of the [conventional] ground forces is not the destruction of opposing forces. Weapons of mass destruction, chemical and nuclear, with air support playing a major role, are used to destroy major troop groupings .... [Nuclear] weapons rather than forces should be used to destroy enemy forces whenever possible. The task of forces is to capture critical facilities, terrain, and other rear objectives."[14]

In other words, an assault by conventional Soviet armies would be slow and wasteful and should be avoided. The way must be cleared through use of weapons of mass destruction. There is no mention of pity for the millions of civilians who would be killed even before the troops began to advance. There is certainly no inhibition against killing "other" humans or *les autres*—in great numbers, whether they are civilians or

---

12 General Hackett was commander of the Northern Army Group in NATO and Commander-in-Chief of the British Army of the Rhine.

13 Hackett, *The Profession of Arms*, p140.

14 Douglass, *Soviet Military*.

soldiers. I believe a different language is a very useful and powerful attribute when identifying and categorizing the "other" as an enemy and thus lowering the inhibition against killing.

The first of the two "manufactured factors" that help to generate violence is the presence of domination or perceived aggression by those not of our nation.

The second manufactured factor promoting violence is the role of leadership elites in fanning the flames of nationalism and highlighting the present threat or past aggression, injustices, and humiliations "we" or our allies have suffered at the hands of "them." As destiny would have it, I was present in four countries that became involved in violent conflict, either directly or in support of a close ally.[15] Every time, without fail, the leadership of each country undertook the task of demonizing the enemy and fostering hatred and contempt. This was essential to lower the already-low inhibition against killing to an absolute minimum. It was achieved through various means, such as provocative speeches in fiery language by prominent figures and careful control of media coverage expressing salient points in simple direct language. A stark, unabashed expression of this manufactured factor is attributed to Reichsmarschall Hermann Göring:

> "It is the leaders of the country who determine the policy and it is always a simple matter to drag the people along, whether it is a democracy, or a fascist dictatorship, or a parliament, or a communist dictatorship. Voice or no voice, the people can always be brought to the bidding of the leaders. That is easy. All you have to do is tell them they are being attacked and denounce the peacemakers for lack of patriotism and exposing the country to danger. It works the same in any country."

When we are attacked, it is the responsibility of leaders to skillfully explain that the attack is an unprovoked and evil act. If we attack first, it is always a justified and astute pre-emptive strike. This must be done eloquently by articulate leaders who can move the people in their native tongue. It is always very useful when "our" people don't understand "their" language and opposing viewpoints. Woe to leaders who allow any hint of moral equivalency, for then their followers may hesitate or question.

---

15 I was in Egypt in 1956 when Britain, France and Israel invaded; in the U.S. in 1967, when its close ally, Israel, was at war with Egypt and Syria; in Greece in 1973, when war broke out with Turkey; and in Canada in 1991, when it fought Iraq as part of an international coalition during the Gulf War.

Putting the four factors together is not difficult. The risk of violence appears because humans form distinct groups (nations, countries) which compete and strive to harm or dominate each other, causing leaders to galvanize their people and promote religious fervour or nationalism (respectively, the ancient and modern forces for group cohesion, though religion seems to be making a comeback) to help them accept and mobilize for violent conflict, and a willingness to kill.

When I arrived in Montreal, my model was not yet clearly articulated, but I knew enough to be concerned. Though I was appalled by the "dees and dose" incident, a serious clash based on language, deep down it did not really surprise me. It fit comfortably into the framework of my understanding of group behaviour. Perhaps the francophone candidate applying for the position with my prestigious multinational employer never understood he was not hired to serve his own primarily French-speaking society because his English accent was "contaminated." But I realized this incident must have played out hundreds or thousands of times, and I felt that the Franco-Québécois collectively knew why they were not being hired or promoted. I had seen it all before; language wars long ago and far away had been a harbinger of worse things to come. I became demoralized by the predictions I could make.

The factors leading to violence were present. Language was a powerful element distinguishing between two groups. There was injustice against francophones. A perceived oppressor speaking a different language was clearly identifiable. There was a consciousness of a new group or nation forming. Many were no longer "French Canadian"; they wanted to be "Québécois." A new leadership, angry and humiliated, was emerging to define and foster a rancorous new nationalism. Lack of inhibition against killing our own kind began to appear.

It seemed reasonable to expect that militant enthusiasm would soon follow.

Chapter 5: Civilized and Reasonable beyond Comprehension

The decades-long stormy relationship between Canadian federalism and Quebec separatism is an eloquent demonstration to immigrants of the unusually civilized and tolerant nature of Canada and Canadians.

Shortly after my arrival in Montreal, it became obvious that many Franco-Québécois were very angry. Many saw themselves as having been betrayed and abandoned by France, conquered by the English, looked down upon, humiliated, and treated unjustly. Many had emotions ranging from dislike to hatred of "les maudits Anglais." In private conversations, even today, relaxed and friendly individuals can become uptight and defensive whenever the subject of Quebec history and Quebec-Canada relations comes up. Yet they have not gone berserk and have carefully controlled themselves in their struggle for self-fulfillment. To me and other immigrants with whom I discuss such things, this is unusual. Why? Because in the experience of individuals raised in many other parts of the world, troubles such as those in Quebec usually lead to violence.

Are Injustice and Violence Timeless and Predictable?

With a few notable exceptions, only a small proportion of the population of a country chooses to emigrate. People either voluntarily stay home to enjoy continuity, familiarity, family and childhood friends, or are unable to leave. Though not traumatized like refugees, who are forced out under threat of persecution and violence, many immigrants are at least a little troubled in spirit. It is discomfort with conditions back home that motivates them to move in the first place, to embark on an uncertain adventure in the hope of finding something better. That discomfort must be large enough to overcome the inertia of staying home.

Immigrants usually bring skills as well as new ideas and perspectives with them. Often, they also bring the mental and emotional baggage of the tensions or troubles they left behind. They tend perhaps to have a broader perspective on human affairs and a deeper sense of the dark side of human behaviour. They interpret events and make their predictions and decisions with a different mindset, one that is often uneasy, wary, and suspicious. In my view, this may be one of the reasons Quebec receives, per capita, a lower percentage of immigrants than the Canadian average. Some immigrants have legitimate reasons for not coming to Quebec, such as their desire to avoid educating their children in a language other than English. But others have avoided Quebec because they erroneously interpreted events here in the light of harsh and ruthless realities they have seen elsewhere.

It is apparent that war and violence are a constant throughout history. Plato said, "Only the dead have seen the end of war." An Arab proverb says, "Peace is the dream of the wise; war is the history of man." An article in the (Montreal) *Gazette* of November 7, 1999, showed that about 16% of the world's 192 countries were at war on that day.

Oppression is not only a matter between "alien" conquerors and their victims but is widespread within peoples. Except for relatively recent developments in a handful of modern democratic states, oppression of the ruled by rulers has been widespread. Current events, historical records, and my personal experiences confirm that those with the upper hand abuse those beneath them and routinely use violence to maintain the subjugation. Retaliation or rebellion necessitates violence and, if successful, results in those who were oppressed immediately exacting revenge and retribution through yet more violence. Rulers have most often attained power through ruthless violence; they and their descendants have kept or lost it through continued violence. In the region where I was born and raised there have been wonderful civilizations, but—except for Israel[1]—never a democracy. Many Canadians feel that politics is a dirty game. If they were familiar with what has been happening in the rest of the world, they would look kindly upon even the worst Canadian politicians.

In Canada, I have seen politicians forfeit their dignity and scramble to get or hold onto power. Nevertheless, this is usually done within the basic rules accepted by all. I would say that most politicians have the integrity (buttressed by a relatively high degree of transparency in the system) to do what is good for Canada and Canadians. In many countries, including a number I have lived in, politics consists of a ruling group of individuals holding on to power at whatever cost to their people, their countries, other countries, and anything else. Since such ruling groups make sure they leave no opportunity for others to attain power by peaceful means, the only way

---

1 Israel's democracy has been criticized as being primarily for Jews among themselves. Typical of the behavior of nation-states, it has had no inhibition against dispossessing and driving out people of other races and faiths.

to come to power is through intrigue, violence, and assassination. This means that many of the best people will give politics a wide berth. There are prominent families in Egypt which avoid politics.

One such lineage is that of the Taher family, with which I have strong links. My sister-in-law Malak is née Taher and today is a foremost florist in Egypt. My late aunt Nemat on my maternal side was married to one. Her late son, my cousin Adel Taher, was Egyptian Minister of Tourism for some years and was known to be a very apolitical minister, as far as that was possible. His father, my Uncle Saiid, was well educated at home by tutors. However, Uncle Saiid's own father, Taher senior, refused to allow young Saiid to learn a profession, saying that only little people who might one day have to seek employment needed to suffer such indignity. For centuries, or millennia, there has been a very distinct separation between small ruling classes, which came and went, and the large mass of the common folk. Mr. Taher senior was part of a ruling class that established itself in Egypt when the Turks conquered Egypt in the 16th century. He himself was a descendant of an Albanian family that came to Egypt in the early 19th century. He was born near the end of that century and inherited a large feudal estate, the core of which was passed down from the original Taher Pasha himself. In 1803, the great Mohamed Taher Pasha had ruled Egypt for less than a month.

Today, the Taher family is gentle and civilized. The traumatic memory of the original Mohamed Taher Pasha is probably one of the strongest reasons why his descendants tend to shy away from politics. In 1801, he was sent from Turkey to Egypt at the head of an Ottoman army. He was of Albanian origin but was raised as an aristocrat in the Sultan's palace in Istanbul and was trusted by the Turks. His task was to assist the Ottoman governor of Egypt, Khusrau Pasha,[2] in bringing the Mamelukes under control. The Mamelukes were a caste of warrior lords who had controlled Egypt until the arrival of the Turkish conquerors some centuries earlier. Though they had been defeated by the Ottoman Turks in the 16th century and no longer ruled Egypt directly, for centuries they remained a powerful class with whom to be reckoned. These fierce warriors were acting too independently and often disobeyed the Ottoman sultan in Istanbul.

---

2 At the time, the title "pasha" was similar to "viceroy." There was only one pasha appointed by the Ottoman Empire in each of its dominions; the position was equivalent to that of American administrator Paul Bremer in Iraq. When Taher arrived, only the ruler of Egypt, Khusrau, was a Pasha. Subsequently, Taher was the Pasha of Egypt for a short time. Later, the ruler of Egypt bestowed the title of "pasha" on others and it came to mean something like "duke."

Historical records and family lore differ on some of the details on how things developed.[3]

As commander of the Ottoman army, Taher Pasha is said to have amassed great wealth in a short time by confiscating for himself lands and properties he fancied. He had to be careful not to transgress when it came to property belonging to the ruling Turkish and Albanian class and also the still-powerful Mamelukes. But when it came to native Egyptians, it is said he did not hesitate to threaten those who crossed his path. Apparently, he regularly engaged in mystical night-time rites featuring chants, little bells, whirling dervishes, and the like. According to some historians, Taher was "odd." Within a couple of years, he deposed the Ottoman governor, Khusrau Pasha, and became the new ruler of Egypt. As his second-in-command of the Ottoman military force, Taher (soon to become Pasha) selected his brother-in-law, Mohamed Ali. Mohamed Ali's sister had borne Taher a son, Ahmed. Taher felt more secure having a family member whom he could trust close by. As soon as the new pasha assumed power, however, Mohamed Ali hatched a plot to get rid of his brother-in-law.

The army that had come from Turkey under Taher Pasha included a contingent of Janissaries, a special Turkish elite guard similar to the Roman Praetorian Guard. There was a contingent of Janissaries already present in Egypt when reinforcements arrived with Taher Pasha's army. There had been delays in the payment of wages to the Janissaries previously stationed in Egypt and Mohamed Ali used this to stir up trouble. He told them that Taher Pasha had gold but refused to release it. One day in 1803, about 250 Janissaries, armed and angry, proceeded to Taher Pasha's palace and demanded their money. They found Taher Pasha practically unguarded. It has been rumoured, though there is no evidence, that his own son Ahmed had conspired with Uncle Mohamed Ali to draw away most of his father's guards. Taher Pasha imperiously told the Janissaries he would pay their wages starting from the date of his arrival but had no money for them for previously unpaid wages. He said that if his second-in-command Mohamed Ali felt they were owed something, they should go to him for payment. An altercation followed. The Pasha's head was cut off and thrown from a terrace onto the street below. To add to the horror, a couple of days later his body had to be buried without its head because it couldn't be found. Later

---

3 For the story of Taher Pasha, I relied on private manuscripts in Arabic, interviews with Taher Pasha's descendants, Arabic publications, and King's *Historical Dictionary of Egypt*.

it was located and, after a skirmish, retrieved by his relatives and buried with the body. Taher Pasha had ruled Egypt for twenty-six days.

Now Mohamed Ali became ruler of Egypt and Pasha. He ruled cautiously and ruthlessly and developed a reputation for being able to kill his perceived enemies before they killed him.[4] Rumours of conspiracy were fueled when Mohamed Ali rewarded his nephew Ahmed Taher by making him "Prince of Upper Egypt" and appointing him to the post of Director of the Customs and Tax Department. That position was known for bestowing on whoever held it the ability to amass great personal wealth in a short time. A few years later, Ahmed developed a mysterious sickness and died. There was never any proof but one rumour had it that uncle Mohamed Ali Pasha had had him surreptitiously poisoned because the young Taher seemed to be developing certain unhealthy ambitions.

Growing up, I heard such stories of intrigue and murder. Later I learned that the histories of rulers in practically all other countries were very similar. In England, France, Italy, Japan, Germany—practically everywhere—the histories of monarchs and competing dynasties are replete with intrigue, treachery, torture, assassination, execution, and horrendous, selfish wars. Only in a handful of Western countries did democracies develop, and these are simply amazing to me given the entire recorded history of humankind. Unfortunately, in most of the rest of the world, the struggle for power continues in the same old disgusting ways. There is no shortage of examples. Until the 1990s, hundreds of millions of people in Eastern Europe lived under rulers whose mentalities were not much different from those of Taher Pasha and Mohamed Ali.

My father often said, "Don't break the law. If you really don't like the laws of the society where you live, you have the option of moving away." In retrospect, it is interesting that he did not say, "Don't break the law. If you really don't like the laws, work to change them." Perhaps he did not want my impetuous youth to get me into trouble. An earnest attempt to change the laws in a dictatorship by anyone other than the dictator and his friends can lead to imprisonment, torture, and death.

My mother always anxiously implored us: "Stay away from politics."

---

4 Mohamed Ali continued to have problems with the powerful Mamelukes. In 1811, he finally patched up his differences with them and reached an accord. He invited them all to a gala dinner at the Cairo Citadel to celebrate their newfound harmony and the end of tensions. Over 200 of these feared warlords came, including the most powerful and wealthy. Inside the Citadel, he trapped and slaughtered them all, though legend has it that one escaped. The power of the Mamelukes was destroyed forever.

Democracy Is Amazing

Having lived in Canada for many years and in Switzerland before that, I have come to take fair and free elections for granted. I routinely follow the shenanigans of our politicians and am often amused or revolted, like everyone else. But on pensive days I feel wonder, even awe, at how it was possible for such a democracy to come about, where the power of the powerful is extremely limited by ordinary people, where rulers are selected by the people and removed if they fail to perform, and where they are unable to torture or kill the people who would remove or replace them.

When I came to Canada, I could not conceive of a revolution without violence. The term "Quiet Revolution" was an oxymoron. I knew that in traditional societies the rulers often abused the people and could only be removed through violence. But I also knew from stories like Taher Pasha's that when the rulers are of a different race or ethnic background, the contempt and abuse can be much worse. He and other rulers were not Egyptian and, even though within the ruling class of Turks and Albanians there was competition for power and property and tales of intrigue and murder, there was also an important element of respect and cohesion. This class considered itself far above native Egyptians and collectively treated them like dirt. Even before the Ottoman Turks came to Egypt, the then-ruling Mamelukes behaved in the same way. They were non-Egyptian and came mostly from the Caucasus. A conflict between two strong Mamelukes was a serious matter. But the antagonism would be temporarily frozen and they would immediately join forces to crush, torture, and sometimes kill any Egyptians who tried to use the conflict between them to benefit themselves in any serious way.

When I had lived in Quebec for a couple of years, I began to perceive a loose similarity between the old troubles in Egypt and the situation of the Québécois. Taher Pasha, Mohamed Ali Pasha, and thousands of others engaged in soldiering, administration, and trade, had come from Albania and Turkey. They were not Egyptian and couldn't speak Arabic. Their descendants remained the dominant class in Egypt for a century and a half. Though that class became Egyptianized and came to live and work in Arabic, it was still considered a "foreign ruling elite" by many. In 1952, its power and much of its wealth was stripped away by "regular" Egyptians. In Quebec, I saw that the dominant class was of English (and Scottish) origin. It remained distinct, hardly spoke French, and ruled over a large majority of francophones. The English elite tended to look down upon the Québécois, as the Turkish-Albanians had looked down upon native Egyptians. Would there be a revolution here too?

Seeing the stratification of Quebec society along linguistic lines and the anger of francophones, I naturally envisioned awful scenarios. I saw a people prodded and inflamed by ambitious leaders with personal agendas—after all, I "knew" that all political leaders are motivated by personal agendas. I felt there was a probability that some French Canadians in Quebec would sooner or later arm themselves and demand immediate, unconditional independence. As always everywhere, the federal government would declare martial law and in send troops because the selfish and self-serving English elite would not stand to lose any territory their ancestors had conquered fairly and squarely.

Possibly, civil war would erupt. There could be chaos and blood on the streets of Montreal. I had no difficulty envisaging this. When I was a child in Cairo, my father was driving my brothers and me to our cousin Ninette's birthday party when we suddenly found ourselves in an area where buildings and shops were burning. The streets were almost deserted. I remember there were no other cars, only a few panic-stricken people running in different directions. We drove past a man sitting on the sidewalk holding his head, his face covered in blood. Nobody was helping him. My father remained very calm and smiled a little to reassure us, made a slow and deliberate U-turn—at least it seemed very slow—and we returned home, safe but shaken. My youngest brother, Aziz, cried because there would be no party, colourful balloons, or delicious birthday cake that day. Many years later, on bad days, I could see buildings burning in Montreal in my mind's eye.

Though all this may seem exaggerated and perhaps even paranoid to some Canadians born here, my view of the world included the possibility that the awful events that I saw and heard about as a child might occur elsewhere. Prior to my arrival in Canada, I had heard about incidents involving bombs exploding in mailboxes in Montreal. Even though there had been some casualties, I did not attach much significance to these, since they were minor by global standards. When I learned more about the *Front de Libération du Québec* (FLQ) and its terrorists (or freedom fighters, depending on one's perspective) and gained a better understanding of the situation, in my mind these incidents became an omen of things to come.

I saw visions of Quebec nationalist fighters engaging the Canadian Armed Forces with hit-and-run attacks. They would attack federal assets and English businesses. Separatist guerrilla and terrorist groups would blow up targets in Quebec and probably in Ontario. The heavy-handed army would go around destroying things with its heavy weapons. The anglos of Quebec would retaliate by forming secret death squads to assassinate prominent separatists. Underground federalist terrorist groups would blow up enemy targets and perhaps carry the war into parts of the countryside. Well-armed English militias would be formed to defend their neighbourhoods and anglo volunteer fighters would come from the rest of Canada to help their compatriots. Even some Americans would arrive with their guns, if only for the excitement.

Eventually, when the casualties and damage were great enough and everyone grew tired, there would be a ceasefire. It was more difficult to speculate as to what could happen next. Perhaps, following tense negotiations, federalist and separatist areas would be delineated. The separatist area would become an independent and strictly French-only Quebec. The rest of Quebec's territory would stay in Canada. It could be expected that ownership of some territory would remain disputed and would be used by leaders on both sides to inflame passions and provoke violence for years or decades to come, as is still the case in Kashmir decades after gaining independence from the British. There would be a population exchange between the territories as there was between India and Pakistan, not necessarily peaceful or voluntary. Newly-independent Quebec would have an area two or three times the size of France, where non-francophones would not be welcome. English would be prohibited across the entire territory. (At the time, having recently arrived, I was not aware of the Aboriginal dimension.) There would be pressure on francophones all over Canada, no matter how federalist and loyal they were, to "go to your new country" and "go tell René Lévesque to take care of you." Especially in areas of the former province of Quebec, this message would be persistent and harsh. Because of the hatred generated by the bloodletting and the loss of life, francophones would be afraid to speak French outside independent Quebec.

Perhaps the events following the civil war would not unfold this way exactly, but it would not be a happy time. On good days, I chided myself for these thoughts, believing they were too pessimistic—nothing like this would happen here. I went about my life and work normally, but I was saddened. We had just arrived and did not want to contemplate leaving Montreal. We were happy here.

Then in 1970 came the October Crisis. My predictions appeared to be coming true. On October 5th, the British trade commissioner was kidnapped and the government was forced to allow radio broadcasts of the kidnappers' manifesto, standard activities related to guerrilla warfare. The FLQ demanded freedom for what they called political prisoners—those who had earlier committed the acts of violence that I had once thought inconsequential. On October 10th, Quebec's labour minister was kidnapped. Here we go, I thought. As I easily foresaw, the army moved into Quebec and hundreds of suspects were rounded up, in my mind a typical response from the government. Trucks carrying soldiers drove by. Armoured vehicles prowled the streets of Montreal. Infantry patrols seemed to be everywhere.

Today, I can hardly believe that I immediately went to Pascal's, the now-defunct hardware store, and purchased a rifle and some ammunition. I had no idea what I would do with them. In retrospect, it seems like some kind of Pavlovian reflex. There was fear, tension, and a feeling of crisis in the air. After seeing the soldiers and the weapons in the streets, something in my mind clicked. Even though I went about life normally in every respect on the surface, at a deeper level, powerful old memories took hold. As a teenager, I had seen soldiers and guns in the streets of Cairo, but then I had also held a weapon. Now, I was driven by some subconscious, primordial urge to defend myself; my fingers needed to grip a weapon. I was agitated and insecure and would have fought fiercely, though I did not know whom I would be fighting. There was no reasoning involved. Whom was I supposed to fight? No idea. The separatists? As far as I could see, there was no separatist army. Terrorists? Whose side were they on and where would I find them? The Canadian army? Unlikely. Perhaps gangs of rampaging vigilantes or criminals? That seemed a little out of place in Montreal, but one never knew. I was mindlessly driven to obtain a weapon to defend my lovely wife and myself (there were no children yet.) Though my everyday behaviour was normal, I was in some kind of trance. I told the salesman at Pascal's that I wanted to hunt deer.

Even today, I believe my early predictions were reasonable and astute. This is the way things are done all over the world. It is normal and predictable human behaviour. But civil war did not break out in Canada.

I don't know a word to describe how I felt as I gradually realized there would be no violence. I know what such a word would mean, if it did exist. It would mean something like "slowly startled over a number of years."

Based on how I saw the world, there was no way to anticipate or easily explain the developments in Canada and Quebec. That Canada was a democratic society was not the only factor that determined the outcome of the crisis, but it was a critical one. My early predictions, reasonable and believable as they were, proved to be wrong because Canadians, including Quebecers, were civilized and reasonable beyond my comprehension.

Thanks, Canada. Thanks, Quebec.

That things did not happen the usual way in Quebec shook my framework of perceptions regarding some basic rules of human existence. But I eventually recovered my composure and realized that my perspective was valid, and that what we have here is one of a few wonderful exceptions. I was enveloped by a warm, glowing feeling about Canada. Over the years it became clear that in addition to avoiding domestic war, my new country strenuously avoided involvement in foreign wars, except in peacekeeping. After September 11th, like most Canadians, I was severely jolted. However, even as many Canadians were afraid of terrorist attacks here, I was almost certain they would not happen. I was certain that Canada was not perceived abroad as a threat to potential terrorists from among the oppressed and downtrodden of the world. I hope that perception does not change.

Democracy, Respect, and Integrity

When musing over how such a rare exception could exist on our brutal planet, or how it could have come about in the first place, I found myself focusing on the differences between what I saw in Canada and what I had previously come to view as the norm. The essential differences I could identify were: first, a genuine internalization of democratic values; second, a greater respect for the self-interest of the individual than I had seen anywhere except the United States; and third, widespread integrity.

To most Canadians, "understanding democracy" is generally taken for granted. It is simple: we have rules that lead to a government being elected according to how the population votes in periodic elections. There are occasional dirty tricks and some cheating. Dirty tricks can backfire and cheats risk being found out, resulting in a costly political price. Many don't bother to vote. "No big deal." Well, to me it is a huge deal. It is a startling new development in human affairs that so far only a minority of humanity enjoys.

Practically all Western democracies respect individual rights but, in my view, often not to the same degree as in North America. In Europe, the mindset of citizens gives the self-interest of individuals much weight but still relatively less weight than transcendental concepts such as the "state," the "nation," or the "collectivity." I have encountered numerous examples of how Europeans give transcendental importance to "the authorities" and their rules. To many North Americans, they are little more than meddling bureaucrats who thrive on over-regulation. An incident that illustrates how Europeans expect their choices to be limited, and in fact seek out and try to clarify artificial limitations before they do anything, occurred when I was staying with my friends Ruth and Ted Grunau in their beautiful mansion near Toronto. Also staying with them at the time were a couple of very polite and clean-cut German students whom the Grunaus had invited for a visit to Canada. We interacted for a couple of days; they asked many questions and took many photographs. As we were parting, I asked them what they thought of Canada. They said many nice things, but then one of them added, "One thing we don't like is that there are many situations where there is no indication of what one should do."

The other explained, "Back home in Germany, everything is regulated (he used the word *vorgeschrieben*) and all instructions are clear. One knows exactly what to do in any situation. Here it is loose and chaotic. It is not organized and in many cases we don't know what to do."

"Don't you realize that when there are no rules and regulations to channel your actions, it means you are free to do whatever you like, as long as you behave in a reasonable manner and don't hurt anyone?" I asked. No, they did not realize this, and went back home without understanding an important virtue of Canada, one they could not photograph.

In Canada there are fewer obstacles in the way of citizens pursuing their self-interest, more leeway to be themselves, and less pressure to conform to narrow national and social standards determined by the authorities, tradition, or the race, religion, and language of a local majority.

In Europe, people are less tolerant of those outside their respective countries of origin. It is the easiest thing in the world for many Europeans, in ordinary conversations and completely without embarrassment, to insert any nationality other than their own to complete the phrase: "I don't like..." Having lived in Europe for many years before coming to Canada, I had also become like that. I remember in the early days making off-the-cuff remarks about not liking these or those peoples. I was quickly cured by the negative reaction to my biases and to the way I bad-mouthed other cultures. Once, years after becoming a tolerant Canadian, I was at a dinner party in Cairo. Another Egyptian-Canadian and I had a rambling conversation with a Spaniard who lived in Germany and worked for the European Monetary Fund. After half an hour or so, in a friendly, conversational manner, we drew his attention to the fact that he had managed to say he did not like the Swiss, the British, and the Italians at different times, all within a twenty-minute chat. We said that in Canada we had learned not to speak like that of others. I must have been feeling a little cruel because, with a little smile, I told him that my wife was Swiss. Speaking to what appeared to be simply two Egyptians in Cairo, he could not have suspected anything like that. He became very uncomfortable. Of course I forgave him. I had once been like that myself.

So entrenched is the I-don't-like-such-and-such-a-people mindset in Europe that even corporate settings are not entirely spared. When I held an executive position in Europe in a multinational corporation, I often participated in meetings with other executives to discuss procedures or policies or to tackle problems. Many nationalities were represented at these gatherings. These were well-educated, professional people. Everyone acted politely and professionally when face to face, but behind each other's backs, on rare occasions, there was quite appalling behaviour.

Once in a meeting when an opinion was expressed, I said "G. V. (an executive from France not present at that meeting) is responsible for this product line. I spoke to him earlier and he feels differently. He says..." and on I went, describing G. V.'s professional opinion.

The first time, I was astounded by the reply: "G. is a Frenchman and their mentality is petulant and strange, so naturally he would say something like that." I had never come across anything like this in a corporate environment in the U.S. or Canada.

Another time I suggested we follow D. H.'s recommendations, since he was an expert on the matter at hand.

"Oh come on! For heaven's sake! You know the Germans..."

Neither D. nor any other colleague of German nationality was present. I came to wonder what might sometimes be said about me in my absence. A person originally from Africa—quelle horreur!

Coming to Canada from such an environment, I was not expecting the basic respect I found among separatists and federalists, anglophones and francophones. There is tolerance at a fundamental human level in spite of very major differences in opinion, passions, and concerns. At first, the civilized and reasonable behaviour of federalists and separatists had a somewhat surrealistic aura, at odds with my previous experience. Here I found people who wanted to break up a country and others who wanted to stop them. Yet, on the whole, they went around being polite to each other and sometimes showing respect for each other's point of view. Unthinkable. Fantastic! In spite of my fear of separatism—emotions shared by most immigrants—I learned to take my cue from civilized Canadian behaviour. I was cordial and polite with the indépendentistes. I came to like some as individuals. Some became good friends.

In addition to democratic values and a broad acceptance of differences among people, the most important feature of a civilized society is a commitment to decency among its citizens and the self-discipline to abide by the rules even when they appear to go against one's self-interest. That is an important part of integrity and is most important among those with wealth, power and privilege. It is such an important ingredient in the success of Canada that I would like to focus on it. Compared to what I have seen elsewhere, among anglophones, francophones, federalists, separatists, undecideds, and whoever, the overall level of integrity in today's Canada is high. Sure, there are dirty tricks, wrongdoings, dishonesty, outright fraud, and criminality here. But overall there is more integrity than lack of it. There are many places in the world where an understanding of democracy might exist but where there is insufficient integrity to sustain it, especially among the elites, who care only about maintaining and benefiting from their privileged status.

It is not my purpose to pick on any one country. However, I remember an example which I feel reflects the situation in most of the world. On the CBC program "counterSpin", a panel discussed the aftermath of the military coup that brought General Pervez Musharaff to power in Pakistan. Avi Lewis was the moderator, and a couple of the participants were of

Pakistani origin. Two opposing viewpoints emerged during the discussion. One held that the Pakistani government had been elected democratically and that therefore the military coup should be condemned. The other viewed the democratic process as corrupt; the elite had no integrity and manipulated the elections to rotate power among its members under the guise of different parties, while taking turns at enriching themselves. Therefore, someone said, the coup could be justified. Then one of the participants of Pakistani origin said that, in his opinion, it was not just the members of elite who had unfairly controlled the government that were corrupt, but that a lack of integrity was widespread among all classes of Pakistani society. Though I had been aware of this in a general sense, I don't know why I had not clearly articulated the phenomenon to myself in so many words. In a flash of revelation, or rather of recognition of what I already knew, I realized that my own country of origin, Egypt, at this time in its long and often illustrious history, suffers from the same disease. I personally know many Egyptians, in all walks of life, who are solid in their integrity. Still, in all segments of society, from electricians and other trades people to professionals to shopkeepers to government officials, including even (gasp!) some ministers, the proportion of those who lack integrity is too high (though definitely excluding the president of the republic and the minister of the interior or homeland security.) In Cairo, when I once made the mistake of complaining about insufficient integrity, I got a defensive answer:

"Well, there is plenty of garbage going on in Canada, too!"

"For sure," I said, "and there are plenty of people here in Egypt who have the highest integrity." To keep it simple while still making my point, I added, "In Canada, there is 75% integrity and 25% lack of integrity. With us here it is the other way round, there is 25% integrity and 75% lack of it."

In my view, in societies that do well there is a "critical mass" of integrity among its people. I cannot define this critical mass of integrity or of how it comes about, but I can recognize a number of factors that create the right environment. In this environment, there is a genuine, widespread sense of personal honesty and integrity among most individuals.

The "Avalanche Effect" of Corruption

I have been concerned about the question of integrity among rulers for a long time. In my early twenties during my studies in Zurich, I wrote an article in Arabic for a student magazine published by the Arabischer

Studentenverein, the Arab Students' Association. The article was about corruption among the powerful. I was concerned about the corruption in Nasser's regime but did not specifically mention Nasser and wrote in general terms. Everyone, including the Egyptian Embassy in the capital, Bern, knew who the subject of my piece was. As a teenager, like many other Egyptians, I had considered Nasser a hero who had stood up to the imperialists. But by my twenties, my perspective had changed, and I became very troubled by the corruption and deceitful practices of the regime. In my article, I suggested the existence of an "avalanche effect" of corruption among a people or society. I wrote that corruption gathers strength when those engaged in it do not fear punishment or prosecution. One who benefits from corruption and is not punished by a superior or some other authority persists in this manner for material gain or some other advantage. In a hierarchical society, such as socialist Egypt at the time, if no superior steps in to put a stop to the corruption, it continues and quickly grows as others join in. If the superiors themselves are corrupt, they will tend to ignore the corruption of subordinates or will often share in the booty. The only people with no superiors, I wrote, are the ones at the very top.[5] Therefore, corruption must start at the top. When it does, it begins to cascade down the ranks in what I called an avalanche of corruption, gathering momentum until all society is infected.

It appears to me that even in societies which are not strictly hierarchical, lack of a critical mass of integrity makes it unlikely that corrupt actions will be punished. In Canada today, due to the presence of a critical mass of integrity, there is a significant probability that a lack of integrity will be detected and formally or informally punished to some degree. Further, there is often protection for individuals who, due to their integrity, refuse to participate in corruption, or who blow the whistle when they see wrongdoing. In dictatorships, those who would alert society to the wrongdoings or plain foolishness of those in power are silenced by any means necessary. In a country such as Egypt, those in the minority who maintain their integrity—including ministers—are to be highly praised and warmly congratulated. They must learn to function in a difficult and hazardous environment in which, when it comes to personal gain, the majority is flexible with regards to matters of commitment, straight talk, conflict of interest, duty-consciousness, sense of fair play, and so on.

---

5 In proper democracies, the voters are supposed to be at the very top. Nasser's Egypt was very far from being a democracy.

In Canada and Quebec, it is clear to me that those who lack integrity are in the minority. Fanatic Quebec separatists who, after losing two referendums, went home peacefully each time to carry on with their lives and wait for another chance, have integrity. Unconditional Canadian federalists who accept that separatists, who want the destruction of their country, may sit in the Canadian Parliament and become Her Majesty's Loyal Opposition, have integrity.

It seems to me that there is a relationship between democracy and integrity, though I do not understand it fully. A lack of democracy can destroy integrity, as those who speak out against abuse are silenced, through physical force if necessary, and others become afraid to contradict the powerful. A lack of integrity can undermine democracy, as particularly those with wealth, power, and influence can pass unjust laws and corrupt the system to gain an immoral advantage. (A "spin culture" fostered in a media industry controlled by a few wealthy groups is a form of corruption.) In any case, democracy and high levels of integrity, together with a high degree of tolerance, competence, and well-entrenched respect for each and every citizen, make it easy to put up with even the absurdly cold Canadian winters.

It does not take much to trigger violent conflict among humans. I expected the outcome of the troubles in Canada to be a francophone-anglophone war. According to a Ukrainian proverb: "When the banners are unfurled, all reason is in the trumpet." I saw angry rallies with hundreds of flags and banners. All my thinking about how francophones would transgress and anglophones would retaliate, or vice versa, all my thoughts about majorities crushing minorities, gradually diminished and my understanding, admiration, and respect for Canada grew.

Part II

Relationships, Likes and Dislikes

Chapter 6: Anti-immigrant Currents

Canada is well-known internationally as a country that needs and welcomes newcomers. Most Canadians have positive feelings towards immigrants, as quickly became evident to me upon arrival. There are also a number of secondary, unfriendly currents; this chapter looks at some of these.

One example of particularly damaging hostility towards immigrants attempts to make an economic case for drastically reducing immigration to Canada.

Another is a new and targeted anti-immigrant sentiment originating in the U.S., directed specifically at immigrants from another civilization…the one in which I was born and raised. A direct result of 9-11, it has inevitably found an echo here: the recent surge in fear and suspicion of Muslims and immigrants from the Middle-East.

Economic Arguments

It has been alleged that the current level of immigration is too high and hurts the economy of Canada. I have not seen a convincing argument to support this. Prominent author and journalist Diane Francis is among those who support this opinion. In my view, the best and most useful aspect of her book[1] on the subject is its exposure of the weaknesses relating to the screening of refugees and to government inefficiencies in dealing with illegal immigration. She relates a number of horror stories of which Canadians should be aware. The worst and least useful aspect of her book is the way legal immigration is confused with false refugees and illegal immigrants. Unless readers are very alert, they may come to associate problems related to undesirable and illegal entrants into Canada with mainstream, legal immigration. This can create the illusion that all immigration is detrimental to Canada. Tediously meticulous reading is required to avoid falling into the trap.[2]

---

1 Francis, *Immigration*.

2 As just one example, the last paragraph on page 62 defames legal immigrants by mixing in damning statistics on illegal immigrants and refugees, then sandwiching the results between a reference to immigrants in part of a sentence at the beginning and one sentence at the end. I had to read it more than once to untangle refugees from immigrants. A clear distinction between immigrants and refugees would have been more lucid and more useful.

One thesis presented by Ms. Francis is that immigration policies were more-or-less sound until 1986 and that changes introduced that year were dangerous and damaging to Canada. Yet, in 2002, Canada's economy led those of the world's industrialized nations. Surely, if the immigration policies adopted in 1986 really were as harmful as Ms. Francis maintains, the damage would have caught up with us by the time her book was published sixteen years later. There is obviously some benefit to the "total of 3,035,615 persons" which Canada admitted between 1986 and 2000. The fact that over three million newcomers did not adversely affect Canada's economy is a rebuttal of Ms. Francis' thesis. The opposite may be argued: immigrants constitute most of the annual growth of the Canadian work force, and thus are at least partly responsible for our excellent economic performance.

Happy Immigrants Make Good Citizens

The book denigrates family-sponsored immigrants and complains that after 1986, too many arrived under the "family reunification" category rather than as "economic" immigrants. According to the figures[3] presented by Ms. Francis, between 1986 and 2000, for every skilled immigrant selected on the basis of economic value, about one other immigrant was a sponsored relative. Is that really excessive? Does an immigrant selected for his or her desirable skills really have to come here all by him or herself? On average, should he or she not be allowed to bring in just one more person, even if that person is completely dependent? Are immigrants not human beings, and can we feel comfortable denying them the ability to bring in, on average, just one person they love?

Ms. Francis makes a coldly calculating suggestion: focus on accepting immigrants of economic value to Canada. She suggests that inhibiting the "family reunification" category would be economically beneficial. The problem I see with her argument is that if we treat immigrants as purely economic assets, then they will tend to reciprocate. They will see Canada in terms of dollars and cents, a purely economic opportunity. They will calculate how much they are benefiting and, when it makes sense, leave and move on to a better opportunity elsewhere. After gaining Canadian experience and becoming solid

---

3 Ibid., p 42. About 44% of all entrants were sponsored immigrants and 40% were economic immigrants. (The remainder were mainly refugees.) That is a ratio of close to one to one, or 100:110.

contributors to the strength of the workforce, they also might decide to take their money and other benefits and go back to what they would perceive as their one and only true home.

In an extreme example of how people coldly calculate the economic benefits of living abroad, many workers, at all kinds of skill levels and from every continent, live and work in Middle-Eastern countries rich in oil and poor in talent. It is understood by both parties that the mutual interest is purely economic. Foreign workers are never made to feel at home. They are there just for the money. Once they take their money and go, few if any have any interest in the well-being or future of Kuwait or Saudi Arabia. That is far from the kind of immigrant I would like Canada to attract. It needs newcomers who will enhance our population and become an integral part of it. I want them to be loyal, to feel completely at home, to develop a lasting affection for their new country and to stay on for good. Cold immigration policies which disregard human considerations will deter the best and brightest, the strongest human assets available. There is an economic cost attached to harsh immigration policies.

In the case of my own family, my two brothers and I came completely independently from one another, each being accepted by Canada on merit. Later, when we were settled, our father and mother, now deceased, came over under the family reunification category. As their age advanced, they did require increased medical attention. However, the economic contribution to Canada expected from their three sons (we all arrived with university degrees), their three daughters-in-law, and their seven Canadian grandchildren (all with university degrees and now able to participate in the work force) far exceed the medical costs of my parents' final years. To be coldly calculating, each of my two brothers and I brought in a mere 0.667 of a person under the family reunification category. Is that too much?

Globalization and Unskilled Workers

Ms. Francis' book mentions a valid concern for the most vulnerable Canadians. These are "the young and uneducated native-borns."[4] Unskilled and uneducated immigrants compete with them for jobs. As I say elsewhere, the problem today is that if low-income, unskilled workers do not come to Canada for certain types of jobs, then many of

---

4 Ibid., p 62.

these jobs will migrate abroad to find such workers. Globalization is responsible. Some decades ago, during the Industrial Era, even workers without a high-school diploma could make a good living in factories protected by powerful unions. Nowadays, foreigners—whether abroad or in Canada—can compete with uneducated native-born Canadians. Either these low-income foreign workers can come here for low-income jobs, or, if they stay abroad, many jobs can leave Canada and go to them. Ms. Francis does not demonstrate that the latter brings greater economic benefits to Canada than the former.

Immigrant Children and Language

> "One out of five entrants was a child under fourteen years of age who arrived in Canada without either official language, thus adding a huge burden to Canadian public schools."[5]

This statement could stir up anti-immigrant emotions in Canadian parents concerned about the well-being of our schools. It deserves closer scrutiny.

For one thing, it refers to "entrants," which includes those other than legal immigrants; this yet again muddies the water. For another, language is an important criterion in the selection of legal immigrant families, while for refugees humanitarian considerations are paramount. The statement conceals the important corollary that 80% of entrant children under fourteen spoke at least one official language. What excellent value added to our population! Some of these children have been to expensive schools overseas and have a greater mastery of English or French, or both, than does the average Canadian-born child.

The 20% who speak neither official language do require the allocation of some resources, initially, to integrate them into their new schools. According to my old friend Steven Lawrence, an experienced professional educator, saying that immigrant children add a "huge burden" to Canadian public schools is an exaggeration. The overwhelming majority of these children quickly absorb the language of their school environment, even though they may speak another language at home. Their arrival is a wonderful gift to Canadian society and native-born Canadians, whose birth rate is too low even to maintain existing population numbers. They can grow up to do very well.

5 Ibid., p 67.

Erin Anderssen reports that

> "One in five Canadians in their 20s are the children of immigrants. Driven to make good on their parents' sacrifices, they tend to excel beyond their peers."[6]

Whatever languages they speak, those who come at a very young age will develop official language skills indistinguishable from native-born Canadians. They will enhance the population, work force, and consumer market and help prevent a decline of Canada's demographic weight in the world. These advantages overshadow the increases in expense Canada incurs to help the mere 20% of children who don't know either official language for the brief period after their arrival.

"War on Terror"

With regards to the War on Terror, again, legal immigrants can be carefully screened. No immigrant I know wants to see terrorists and criminals enter their new country. However, no immigration system can completely block the threat, as Ms. Francis writes, and there can be no doubt that terrorism is bad for the economy. In addition to tightened security, the most effective way for Canada to combat terrorism on its own soil is not to engage in death and destruction overseas in support of injustice and oppression.

"What criminal or terrorist problems do immigrants and refugees visit upon Canada?"[7] asks Ms. Francis. Again, she lumps legal and illegal immigrants and refugees together, though they are different in many ways. Apparently, she seeks to persuade Canadians that immigrants must be especially feared as a source of terrorism in their country. Yet, because the core of Canada's foreign policies are benign, I cannot imagine that any terrorist entrant would be willing to give his or her life in order to attack Canadians. No one hates Canada. On the contrary, there is much respect abroad for Canada's moral stands, as in when it refused to participate in the second U.S.-led attack on Iraq. It is the United States that must fear terrorist attacks. Our responsibility is to prevent terrorists from using Canada as a base or transit point to attack our ally, the U.S.

---

6 Anderssen, "The New Canada."

7 Francis, *Immigration*, p125.

It is my view that our American friends are in far greater danger from terrorism by native-born Americans than from immigrants. Why? Immigrants from Muslim countries can be identified easily and subjected to scrutiny. As the War on Terror painfully drags on, efficient systems are in place to identify, racially profile, and spy on such people. They are easy to target based on their names, countries of origin, appearance, religious affiliations, and so on. Their actions will be watched, and the tiny minority that may seek to commit terrorist acts will be less difficult to detect and apprehend than native-born criminals and terrorists in the wider population.

The greater danger will come from non-Muslim Americans who themselves feel oppressed by the system and who wish to strike back. They may or may not sympathize with Muslims. Some maintain that there is no aggrieved underclass in America...or if there is, that their standing is their own fault. Others can see an ominous, growing gap between rich and poor. It has been said that, among Americans, there are resentful pockets living in Third World conditions.[8] Inevitably, some turn to violence as a means to achieve what they perceive as justice. They will find a way, rightly or wrongly, to blame others for their plight and justify their actions as self-defense.

A growing number of native-born Americans are converting to Islam, changing their names, and living according to Islamic tradition. The overwhelming majority are frank and honest people who love America and appreciate and enjoy its many freedoms, including freedom of worship. However, the perception might grow that Muslims are being singled out. Subterfuge could then be expected. As in the time when early converts to Christianity were persecuted by the ancient Roman Empire, some conversions to Islam will be done secretly. To avoid detection by the national security apparatus, some will not change their names or their modes of behaviour. They will keep their original names, such as Williams, Walker, and Padilla (not to mention McVeigh, who apparently had no interest in Islam and just wanted to strike at a government he called "out of control".) They will be very difficult to detect as they live apparently normal, low-profile lives. A tiny minority of these will turn to violence. Some will be detected and stopped. But because they can be of any ethnic origin, defense against them will necessitate a huge, expensive security machine, one that is suspicious of

---

8 More on these "discarded citizens" in Chapter 15.

everyone. That will be a drain on the economy. Nonetheless, it will sometimes fail. Some undetected native-born terrorists will get through. These are far more dangerous than immigrant would-be terrorists, who stick out like a sore thumb. Because they can be easily identified and "marked," immigrants are unlikely to pose as much danger as aggrieved, violently-inclined native-born terrorists.

The Added Value That Immigrants Bring

An important omission in Ms. Francis' book relates to the valuable economic impact of immigrants. For example, there is no calculation or estimate of the total dollar value of the skills immigrants bring with them. According to her figures, just under one half of legal immigrants are skilled workers. (The other half consists mainly of family-sponsored immigrants.) There is substantial economic value for Canada in receiving chemists, machinists, nurses, and others who have been trained and educated at no cost to the Canadian economy. In my case, private British primary and secondary schools and a post-graduate engineering degree from a world-class European university cost Canada nothing. In a book about the economic impact of immigrants, it would perhaps be useful to include estimates on the many millions of dollars worth of education immigrants bring with them.

Furthermore, immigrants come with commercial contacts and an understanding of the economies, needs, markets, languages, habits, and methods of other cultures. These are of high economic value to Canada. I know a number of immigrants who have contributed handsomely to the exportation of Canadian goods and services. One good friend has been directly involved with exports of about $200 million worth of Canadian industrial products, working with a team consisting of foreign business people living overseas and native-born Canadians. He also helped export tens of millions of dollars worth of American industrial products. There are many immigrants from all over the world who regularly contribute in the same way.

In addition to those engaged in fraud and "scams," there are immigrants who arrive with literally millions of dollars that they intend to invest and spend in Canada. There are rich and very rich people who are genuinely looking for a new home, just as there are less rich and poor ones.

There are others who also believe that immigration is a boost to the Canadian economy.

"There is no question that immigrants are needed to make Canada prosperous. The facts are there to prove it. According to a 1994 study, the economy typically grows during periods of high immigration, primarily because many immigrants start companies and invest money in our economy. Immigration is expected to account for all labour force growth in Canada between 2011 and 2016...From 1999 to 2001, the economic immigrant class was the largest of all classes... "[9]

The Canadian economy benefits very well indeed from the money that wealthy immigrants bring, from the dollar value of the education of skilled workers and professionals, and from the economic impact of the increase in exports resulting from the special knowledge of immigrants. I looked in the index of Ms. Francis' book for "benefits" or "economic benefits of immigrants" and found no entry.

Racism or Business Decision?

Some anti-immigrant feelings in Canada appear to be based on racism. It is noteworthy, however, that some of what is called racism may better be described as "inter-ethnic antipathy." In addition, problems ascribed to racism may rather be due purely to business decisions and the profit motive. For example, a newspaper headline screams: "Racism Holding Immigrants Back, Study Says."[10] I looked at that study[11] and did not reach the same conclusion.

The research "focuses on levels of employment, earnings, family incomes, and poverty rates of recent immigrants compared to those of the rest of the Canadian population." The study finds that

"Recent immigrants...particularly visible-minority immigrants...have experienced high rates of unemployment and high levels of underemployment in low-wage jobs which often do not match their skills and formal credentials....foreign-born visible minorities and recent immigrants were much more likely than other Canadians to experience persistent low income...Some authors have attributed discrepancies in income and employment among racial groups to racism."[12]

---

9 McGinn, "Immigration."
10 Eric Beauchesne in *The (Montreal) Gazette*, Monday, 25 February 2002.
11 Smith, "Rising Tide."
12 Ibid.

Though racism might sometimes be a factor, I do not believe it is the primary reason for the problems facing foreign-born Canadians, especially recently-arrived immigrants. Sometimes when I am traveling overseas, the question of racism in the Canadian workplace arises. I proceed to pose the following riddle to those wishing to know more about discrimination in Canada, some of them potential immigrants: "Suppose a Polish-Canadian businessman is looking to hire a sales engineer for his computer and software business. He puts an advertisement in the papers and from the responses he identifies five candidates that appear qualified and interesting. He invites each to an interview. The five are of English, French, Chinese, Egyptian, and Polish origin. Which one would he hire?"

Not always but most often the answer would come quickly: "The Polish candidate." Some would add "of course." Then I would say, "Not necessarily. I believe that any astute Polish-Canadian businessman would hire the candidate that, taking everything into consideration, he believed would help maximize the profits of the business."

I can think of an important reason why recently-arrived immigrants might be at a disadvantage when applying for certain types of jobs, one unrelated to racial considerations. Recently arrived from a perhaps very different culture, an immigrant might have difficulties interfacing with a Canadian customer base. One's level of formal education is important but not in itself sufficient to satisfy the specific requirements of various high-paying jobs. It takes time and effort to move oneself mentally from one country to another. Some immigrants manage better than others.

The study seems to support my contention that racism in Canada has little bearing on the findings that immigrants from visible minorities have lower average incomes than native-born Canadians:

> "Very large gaps in earnings and annual incomes were found between foreign-born visible minorities and other Canadians...Fortunately, the gaps in annual incomes and earnings between visible minority persons who were born in Canada and those of other Canadians were much smaller, or non-existent."[13]

If racism played a large role, incomes of Canadian-born and immigrant members of visible minorities would be much closer to each other, and those visible minorities who were native-born would

---

13 Ibid.

encounter the same problems as those born abroad. Rather, it is the unfamiliarity with the mentalities and attitudes in the workplace that handicap recent immigrants applying for certain jobs.

Hey! Who Is Picking on My Part of the Canadian Mosaic?

Eventually, I learned not to care in the least whether or not other ethnic groups in Canada were biased against my background. However, I realized afterward that the Canadian mosaic can be hurt by the collective biases of its ethnic groups. Black people in Canada have been targets of prejudice by non-Blacks from many other ethnicities and may suffer discrimination, which could lead them to do less well economically and otherwise.

In the past, there has been overt bias against Jews in Canada. Near our home is a prestigious golf club which, decades ago, refused membership to people of the Jewish faith. Their response was to establish an equally nice Jewish golf club nearby. Not every group, however, can be smart and diligent enough to counter bias against it. Today, such discrimination manifests itself only among intolerant and narrow-minded individuals. Officially, Canada's governments and institutions protect groups from harassment and hate crimes.

The attacks of September 11th drew my attention to the special type of inter-ethnic conflict that can occur when one specific ethnic, religious, or racial group is singled out as a result of conflicts abroad. Since its inception in 1867, Canada has been linked very closely first to Britain, then to the United States. Until about World War II, enemies of Britain were automatically also enemies of Canada. As a result, during World War I, Ukrainians in Canada were interned because their original homeland was on the wrong side of the conflict. During World War II, the same happened to those with Japanese ancestry. When the strong links of affinity and dependency transferred from Britain to the U.S., there came pressure for Canada to be hostile towards enemies of the latter. I wonder, as a Muslim Canadian from Egypt, could the "War on Terrorism" affect me? Could Canadian society as a whole—or substantial components of its mosaic—turn on me?

Erin Anderssen reports that

"Canada has confirmed its standing as one of the most diverse nations in the world...a kaleidoscope, according to the national census, of culture, languages, and nationalities that amounts to more than 200 different ethnic groups..."14

She writes that Canada is becoming ever less homogeneous and that we will be faced with more "intergroup challenges" which, it is hoped, we will meet successfully.

Muslims and Middle-Easterners are now an established component of the Canadian mosaic. If bad came to worse, to which ethnic group would those who watched (spied on) me and others making up the Muslim mosaic belong?

Canada's special character is threatened by the new global situation. With the disappearance of the U.S.S.R., the U.S. is far less inhibited in using military force abroad. If Canada supports the U.S. in every war against a foreign county, will the corresponding component of the Canadian mosaic routinely come under suspicion and pressure? Are all components of the kaleidoscope expected to turn on one of its parts every time the U.S. threatens another country? I am relieved to be able to answer "no." There would be grave consequences for Canada as we know it, if ever the answer became "yes."

This is a matter that concerns the very core of who we are, of our Canadian values and culture. Our population has become so diverse that we simply cannot afford to continuously engage in wars overseas every time the U.S. scolds us. No group in Canada, no matter how influential, could be sure it would not be the next target of suspicion.

After the attacks of September 11th, there were threats and some attacks against some individuals perceived to be Muslims or Arabs in the U.S. (Due to deep and penetrating ignorance in the American milieu perpetrating this kind of violence, Sikhs, Hindus, and...as in the time of the Crusades...even Christian Arabs were targeted.) There seem to have been some cases in Canada, too. However, I am very proud that the overwhelming majority of Canadians proved to be broad-minded, tolerant, and more difficult to manipulate than most other peoples.

---

14 Erin Anderssen, "Immigration Shifts Population Kaleidoscope," *The Globe and Mail*, 22 January 2003.

Our Canadian "knack" for coping with "intergroup challenges" must help us find a way to live with the U.S. while resolutely protecting the integrity of our mosaic. That will sometimes be difficult in the light of the U.S.'s either-you're-with-us-or-against-us attitude. It will become ever more difficult the longer the U.S. maintains its current foreign policy, whereby it seeks predominance in the world through violence whenever it unilaterally deems it necessary. At this point, the "War on Terrorism" is expected to continue for a long time. In my view, if it ever becomes a de facto war against Islam, it could become a new Hundred Years' War. Although the U.S. is very powerful, the faith of Islam has superior staying power, strong growth potential, and a great appeal, particularly for the downtrodden everywhere. I don't even want to think about the possibility that a war with North Korea could erupt. I refuse to even contemplate the nightmare of having to join the U.S. in a war against one-quarter of humankind.

Could I Ever Become a Separatist?

A long war in Iraq would entrench antagonism in the U.S. towards Muslims and Arabs. By osmosis, attitudes in Canada could follow suit. However, hostile attitudes will not spread uniformly among Canadians. According to one study,[15] 60% of English-speaking Canadians supported the U.S. in its zeal for war against Iraq, as opposed to only 44% of Québécois. That makes me thankful that the government of Canada is so strongly influenced by francophone Canadians. It also briefly made separatist former premier Landry of Quebec thankful for being able to seize on yet another difference between Quebec and Canada, this one affecting the life or death of perhaps tens or hundreds of thousands of people: Is Quebec less keen than English Canada to kill defenseless people?

A hypothetical and as yet far-fetched question arises. Could I ever become more interested in living in an independent Quebec than in my Canada? Such a change is still unthinkable, but it has now become conceivable in theory. There are many hypothetical "ifs": if the war lasts a very long time; if Canada gets sucked into ever more unjust wars overseas because of attachment to U.S. policies; if a Canadian penchant for killing people in faraway lands materializes, then increases the

15 By Jack Jedwab, released on Monday, February 17, 2003, based on a January 2003 poll by the three firms of Taylor Nelson Sofres, Gallup International and Léger Marketing.

chances of terrorist revenge; if this results in my piece of the Canadian mosaic becoming the target of severe discrimination and racial profiling, harassment and abuse; if Quebec washes its hands of all this and refuses to participate in the bloodletting overseas and racial profiling at home; if Quebec recoils at the cruelty of *les anglais* (and their "typical behaviour" in the view of some hard-line separatists) and wishes to pull out of Canada. Would I then possibly think of voting "yes" in the next referendum on separation? I suppose, possibly, yes. In that hypothetical situation, in theory, I might decide that I could feel more at home in a separate Quebec where all non-Québécois-de-souche are equally "less equal than others," than in a Canada that, as a whole, will specifically target me, my section of the Canadian mosaic and, potentially, my descendants. We can speculate that in the case of another close referendum, if thousands in Quebec think that way and vote "yes" instead of "no," the separatist option could win.

It's all speculation, of course. Still, I never thought such ideas would ever cross my mind. Out of respect for Canada's integrity and cohesion, the individual components of the Canadian kaleidoscope must be especially careful not to target each other for special abuse because of conflicts overseas.

In my case, the "rival group" with the most potential for mutual hostility, tensions, and conflict is, at least in theory, the pro-Israel lobby. Fortunately, the troubles at Concordia University in Montreal seem isolated and limited. On the whole, the relationship between the two communities has, with some exceptions, been placid and largely respectful. Yet each side is naturally expected to root for and try to assist their side "over there," within limits. How far can each ethnic or racial group allow itself to go in pursuing its rivalry with its Canadian "opponents?"

Chapter 7: Interethnic Dissonance? Muslims and Jews?

In February 2003, former Prime Minister Brian Mulroney said that anti-Semitism was growing.[1] About two months earlier, the *Jerusalem Post* had reported a rise in anti-Semitism in Canada. In between, a national poll showed that over 40% of Canadians supported a limit on Muslim immigration.[2] Could it be that Canada is saying, "A pox on both your houses! Don't bring your hatreds here! Don't use Canada as a platform for your conflicts!"

A little more than a year after 9-11, a number of reports appeared in the Canadian media about a rise in anti-Semitism, against both branches of Semites: Arabs and Jews. In both cases, discrimination against Semites has old roots. I have not looked into the reasons for traditional anti-Jewish discrimination and persecution in Europe over the last centuries. According to Mr. Mulroney, it is "born in ignorance and nurtured in envy." As for anti-Arab, anti-Muslim sentiment in the West, it is well over a thousand years old.

Almost any factor that distinguishes between human groupings can serve as a basis for conflict. Religion is certainly such a factor. In the view of most Muslims I know, some "Christian church organizations" have deliberately and consistently fostered such enmity over the centuries. According to this view, many Christian religious leaders have feared the central Muslim idea (also present in Judaism?) that no intermediary is needed between man and God: each and every individual can communicate with Him directly through prayer. As I understand it, in Catholic doctrine, there is an "original sin" which taints all humanity and salvation is only possible through the church. Over the centuries, brilliant theologians such as Thomas Aquinas have developed sophisticated philosophies and a reliable conceptual structure to link man to God in this way. In the view of Muslims, the church felt threatened by a new faith

---

1 Michael Friscolanti, "Anti-Semitism Growing: Mulroney," *The (Montreal) Gazette*, 10 February 2003.

2 Mike Blanchfield, "Canadian Attitudes on Immigration Hardening against Muslims: Poll," *Ottawa Citizen*, 21 December 2002.

that came along and said that, essentially, the service it offered was not really required. Thus, there has been a centuries-long campaign of defamation against Islam, Muslims, and the Prophet Mohamed.[3]

The large numbers of people converting to Islam did nothing to ease the tension and hostility. I will not get into a theological debate but will give an example. Among the popular slanders propagated against Islam is that it was spread by the sword. Actually, war in Islam is not allowed except under very strict and narrow conditions. For example so-called "pre-emptive" war is not allowed. An example of allowable war would be to protect the freedom of speech of those who would explain the Muslim faith, if rulers of non-Muslim lands attempt to forcibly suppress their message. This specific reason for Muslims to wage war is not applicable to Canada and the United States, since both countries allow complete freedom of expression in this regard. The most populous Muslim country in the world is Indonesia. No Muslim army was ever involved in bringing Islam to Indonesia. Muslim ideas were expressed freely and those who wished to convert did so without compulsion. According to the 2001 census, Islam is the fastest growing faith in Canada. Part of the growth comes through conversions: I never heard of anyone being converted by force.

Some Muslims express anger and outrage when, now and then, some firebrand preacher in the U.S.—perhaps a TV celebrity—insults Islam or the Prophet Mohamed. In my case, such tirades usually elicit a chuckle. Obviously Islam is competing too successfully and over the centuries has attracted away a great deal of potential business. Perhaps I should take the matter more seriously, however, since prominent extremist religious figures have impressionable "flocks." Constantly reminded to be faithful enemies of Islam, they might widen the rift and increase tensions in their own society and internationally. Some of them might hold prominent positions and use their authority or public voices to plot wicked mischief. Fortunately, the great majority of the Christian clergy today are secure, tolerant, respectful of other faiths, and not prone to hurling insults at the competition. The pope in Rome is generally considered by Muslims to be the most important among the many Christian religious leaders in the world. He has consistently repeated a message of peace and mutual respect.

---

3 Islam does not respond in kind. Christians are considered "People of the Book"—who have their own different and respected way—while Christ is a prophet of equal stature to Mohamed, as is Moses.

Muslims and Jews: A Benign History

The historical relationship between Muslims and Jews has been much more benign. While Europeans Jews were suffering and dying under severe persecution and pogroms, culminating with Nazi genocide, in Muslim countries they could amass wealth, own property and businesses, and enjoy religious freedoms like everyone else. In Spain, under Muslim rule, there had been a centuries-long "Golden Age" for Jews. Christians too were respected, well off and free to worship as they pleased. This state of affairs lasted for about seven centuries. Over hundreds of years of Muslim dominance, under no ruler was there a policy to massacre Christians or Jews. There was no systematic campaign of forcible conversion to Islam. When Muslim rule finally succumbed to Christian supremacy, the result for Jews and Muslims was the Inquisition, ethnic cleansing, and genocide.

Al Maimun (b. 1135, d. 1204), known as Maimonides[4] in the West, was an Arab Jew of Spanish origin. A genius to many, he wrote some of his greatest Arabic works in Egypt, where he is honoured to this day. In modern times, Emmanuel Mizrahi Pasha was a prominent, wealthy, and respected Jewish Egyptian during the reign of King Farouk I. As my parents recounted, so wise, honest, and trusted was Emmanuel Pasha that sometimes, when serious tensions and conflicts arose between the Egyptian monarchy and the British occupation authorities, he was called upon to mediate and calm everyone down. We were proud of our Egyptian Jews.

> "Because of the spirit of tolerance inherent in Islam, Muslims, Jews, and Christians coexisted in harmony from the beginning of the Islamic Empire, through the Ummayid and Abbasid eras, until the end of the Ottoman Empire. It is also interesting to note that when French Jews began to flee the Nazi occupation of France the only country to offer them refuge was Morocco under the late King Mohamed V."[5]

For the first time in history, Jews have power over Muslims. In Palestine, they are not repaying their former friends and protectors in kind. In 1948, Arabs and Muslims everywhere saw their Palestinian brothers dispossessed, driven out of their homes, off their lands, and away from their towns, hills, and valleys to make way for Jews from everywhere and anywhere else. Jews are not treating Muslims as they themselves were treated in Spain, Egypt, and elsewhere in the Arab and Muslim world. This will not be forgotten for many centuries.

---

4 According to the *Encyclopaedia Britannica*, his full name was Abu Imran Musa Ibn Maymun Ibn Ubaid Allah.

5 Article by Ossama El-Baz, chief political adviser to President Mubarak of Egypt. *Al Ahram Weekly Online*, 2—8 January 2003, no. 619, <http://weekly.ahram.org.eg/2003/619/focus.htm>.

I pray that Jews never again suffer persecution as in the past. In the unlikely event of such a renewed horror, I hope enough time will have elapsed—preferably with apologies and restitution—for the Muslim world to forgive, and to again take Jews in, shelter, and protect them, according to our time-honoured tradition.

> "Did the spirit of brotherhood between the Arabs and Muslims, on the one hand, and Jews on the other, continue after the creation of the state of Israel? Sadly, one must answer that this spirit was impaired for a number of reasons. Firstly, the methods used by the founders of Israel against the Arabs of Palestine were brutal. Secondly, Israel, and the Zionist movement abroad frequently used Jewish and Israeli interchangeably. This confusion caused Arabs to wonder whether the conflict that had erupted in Palestine and later spread to other Arab countries was between the Arabs and Israel or between the Arabs and the Jews."[6]

I was not confused; I came to Canada with a negative perception of Israel but not of Judaism. That is because of what my parents taught me regarding Jews and Israel many years before. When I was an adolescent, some years after Israel's creation, my parents sat me down for an important talk. I knew immediately that something serious was afoot, because they took me into their bedroom and closed the door, so that the servants would not hear. In retrospect, it seems that they were concerned about the racist behaviour of Israel. They worried that it might reflect on all Jews, including Egyptian Jews. What they said to me was that though Israel was behaving in a wicked and brutal manner towards non-Jews in Palestine, that did not mean that Jews as a whole were bad. Essentially, they said, "Jews OK; Israel not OK." In the beginning, it wasn't exactly clear what all this was about. Still, I remember the message well, because my parents repeated and reinforced it several times.

It seems that initially, at least in Egypt in our social circle, the creation of a Jewish state in Palestine was not immediately viewed as necessarily a bad thing. I heard stories about how, in 1948, some Egyptian Jews were congratulated by their non-Jewish friends. It was the brutality and injustice against non-Jews in Palestine which changed that benign view.

My First Palestinian

What I learned from my parents about the tragedy in Palestine was "received knowledge." I had never met a Palestinian. Only later, in my early

6 Ibid.

twenties, did I meet Joseph C., a Palestinian from a prominent and wealthy Christian family. While other Palestinians lost everything and most ended up in refugee camps, he had the good fortune of being able to study in Switzerland because his family had considerable assets outside Palestine. His father had owned various assets, including a large estate in Palestine that included fruit orchards. One of his lucrative businesses had been exporting citrus and other fruits to Europe. Joseph and I became good friends. I remember once my wife-to-be, Heidi, and I drove with him in his blue Volkswagen Beetle across the border to Stuttgart, Germany, where we spent a long weekend seeing the sights.

On rare occasions, Joseph talked about his family's misfortune. When he did, his primary emotion was not hate, rancour, or vindictiveness. He just seemed bewildered. He told me that he remembers that, as a child, "a band of armed Jews," mostly in uniform with some in civilian clothes, banging on the door of the family home. He caught a glimpse of them— they mostly looked like foreigners, Europeans—before he was pulled inside the house and away from the front door. Apparently the household was told to "be east of such and such a place within twenty-four hours, or the same will happen to you as did in Deir Yassin." By then, everyone in the Arab world knew that the village of Deir Yassin was the site of a "demonstration massacre" where the entire Arab population—about 250 men, women, and children—were killed by Jewish terrorists. Law and order had broken down and there was no protection for Joseph's family. It was decided they would leave "for a while, a few days" to a safer area until things settled down and peace and security were restored. They could not go back in a few days and still cannot go back today.

Joseph said that they learned that the same thing had happened to all other Christian and Muslim families in what had been a prosperous mixed neighbourhood. Only Jewish Palestinians were allowed to stay in their homes and keep their properties. His family's home and other properties were simply taken by Jews. I suppose the beneficiaries were mainly European survivors of the Holocaust, though some poor Palestinian Jewish families may also have benefited. Joseph C. told me the deeds of his family's estate were in his possession.

"Then it is your land," I said very naively. "Why not claim it?"

"They passed a law saying, essentially, that it is no longer my family's land," he said indignantly.

There is no reason to believe that Joseph's orchards do not continue to produce juicy, sun-drenched citrus fruits, only now someone else pockets the profits. Of all the money these and other orchards have earned since then, of the countless billions more Israel has received from Western governments, from regular and substantial private donations, from the billions in German reparation payments, and so on, Joseph C. has received not a cent. I have never knowingly purchased a citrus fruit—or anything else—grown in Israel. For all I know, it may have come from Joseph's estate. Though I understand the reasons for the creation of a Jewish state somewhere, I find what was done to Joseph, his family and many others difficult to forgive and forget.

Leave the Hatreds Behind

I brought my parents' wisdom and Joseph's story with me when I immigrated to Canada. I still felt that "Jews were OK, Israel was not" in spite of continued injustice and oppression and the perception that such behaviour had the support of a majority of Jews. Within a year of starting life in Montreal, I learned something of great importance about inter-ethnic relations through my interaction with the Jewish community of the city. All immigrants should internalize this important rule of conduct in their new country. I believe everybody coming to Canada, or already here, should adhere strictly to the following rule: Don't bring to Canada the old malice and rancour of your old country, ancestors, religion, or culture. In other words, bring as much of your identity as you like, but don't let your view of troubles overseas induce you to act in a way that is detrimental to Canada or any other Canadians. Treat all Canadians as Canadian first.

For me, this principle was strongly reinforced by a specific event. Shortly after being given responsibility in Quebec for a large U.S. corporation's line of medical electronics products, I had an experience where members of a "rival group" behaved towards me in this fair and just way. As sales engineer, it was my job to keep abreast of demand for our products, and one day I discovered that the Jewish General Hospital was issuing tenders to purchase medical equipment for intensive care units and other applications. Israel and Egypt had been in a state of war since 1948. At that specific time, they were engaged in an intermittent shooting war with deployment of both air-forces and heavy artillery; there were casualties on both sides. Being emphatically Egyptian, it was "logical" for me to assume that the Jewish decision-makers at the hospital would feel antagonism towards me. It was unlikely I would be able to do any business there.

Still, it was my job to do my best; I owed it to my professionalism and to my employer, for whom I had great respect. I went through the motions as best I could, preparing the ground and talking to those I had discovered would be on the purchasing committee making the final decision. These consisted of a number of doctors, the head nurse, and others, such as the hospital engineer, Mr. Alec Sebe (the only name I remember, since we subsequently became friends), and high-ranking administrators of the hospital. There were other excellent companies bidding, including, if I remember correctly, General Electric and Marcel Dassault of France. I was familiar with the French company—they also supplied warplanes to the Israeli air force. I often felt I was wasting my time, since many of the names were clearly Jewish and some others may or may not have been Jewish. But I put these thoughts aside and persisted to the best of my ability.

Finally, the day of my big, decisive presentation came, the meeting that would make or break the sale. The committee asked tough questions, but I was well-prepared. After the presentation, on the way back to the office I mulled over in my mind what reasons I could give in my report as to why we had lost the order. A few days later, the decision was made. The Jewish General had given the order to me, the "enemy"! It was because, as I learned later, I had convinced the committee that our equipment was the best suited and that I would make sure they would be well taken care of in matters of after-sales support, preventive maintenance, and repair. It did not matter that I was Egyptian, even at a time when Egypt was a sworn enemy of Israel.

That experience reinforced my basic principle on this matter: I have always treated any person of Jewish origin with whom I have had any dealings—whether a chartered accountant, dentist, or job applicant—as simply Canadian. I don't ask about their degree of support for Israel. I work with whoever gives me the best product or service at the best price.

Another thing I learned, which made life easier, was not to worry too much about inter-ethnic rivalry. Though I was very proud and gratified at having won the purchase order despite strong competition, and felt enlightened by the impartial behaviour of my new customers, it actually would not have mattered had I not received this order. There were many other, non-Jewish, customers, and I could have made a good living anyway.

This is the way it is in multiethnic Canada. In most cases, it matters little if a member of one ethnic group is narrow minded enough to be biased against members of another ethnic group.

Not long after my arrival, I recognized that the Jewish community of Canada helped me and served my interests in two fundamental ways. The first was a result of the discrimination Canadian Jews had suffered in many walks of life.[7] Their fight against discrimination helped end bias against all minorities, including mine (at the very least, at the official level.) They were instrumental in the struggle to change Canada for the better. By the time I arrived, the battle had been largely won for pluralism and respect for all, including French-speaking Canadians, throughout Canada. I benefited directly from their struggle and sacrifice. Thank you, Jewish community.

The second issue that placed Jews and me (and most immigrants) on the same Canadian team was the dread of Quebec separatism. They knew, as did other minorities such as the Greeks and Italians, that an independent Quebec, with an 80% majority of one race and culture, would be a setback for all who did not belong to that 80%. It was ironic and strange: when I arrived, Jews and I were on the same side in Canada, while Israel and my original homeland were mortal enemies back in the Middle East.

Equality and full integration in Canadian society does not preclude dislikes between groups of different races or ethnicity. Perhaps some Turkish Canadians don't really accept Armenian Canadians, and vice versa. So what? If Serb and Albanian Quebecers dislike or even intensely hate each other, as long as there is no violence, there is little impact on the lives of either group or on Quebec as a whole. Different groups in Canada may naturally sympathize with the causes of their native countries and try to assist in some way. However, I believe strict constraints must be respected: absolutely no violence and no selling out of Canada's laws or interests for the sake of some conflict abroad.

At a practical, everyday level, it is a betrayal of our wonderful Canada for Serbs and Albanians, Israelis and Palestinians, or Russians and Chechens to bring their biases to these shores and act upon them to hurt Canadians of other ethnicities. It is fine to have pride in one's background, but I have no respect for Canadian individuals or groups who put the priorities and interests of a foreign country or cause above those of Canada.

---

7 Just one example: for a long time, McGill University did not accept Jews at all; it maintained a quota system through the 1940s.

Much worse, it would be a crime and a sin to replicate violent conflicts going on elsewhere in this peaceful and civilized country. For those interested in violence, there is plenty of opportunity in bloody conflicts going on all over the world—if you want to engage in violence for some foreign cause, go and fight over there. Some Canadians do.

I do consider it normal and legitimate, however, for components of the Canadian mosaic to try to sell their own view of foreign affairs. Jewish groups have had a head start in establishing themselves and gaining influence in Canada, and are thus able to influence the media or the government in a way favourable to Israel. Arab groups, many of whose members are much more recent arrivals, are still establishing themselves and have not been anywhere near as effective. Only recently have their voices and votes begun to have an impact. There is a great mismatch between the resources, know-how, and influence of the pro-Israel lobby and of pro-Palestinian voices. The owners of CanWest Global and the Southam newspaper chain in Canada are fervent supporters of Israel and discourage criticism of its actions. I am sure they would be appalled if a Mr. Mohamed Something gained control of an equivalent media empire and told his people, "Whatever Palestinians and Arabs do, don't make them look bad."

Troubles at Montreal's Concordia University aside, the violent overseas conflict between Israelis and Palestinians has so far had only a low-key echo in Canada. There have been outbursts of rhetoric here and there, sometimes followed by an apology. The real rivalry is in the mainstream media and in political influence, where there has been a huge mismatch in favour of the pro-Israel lobby. For decades, the media propagated Israel's viewpoints and spin on events in the Middle East. The Jewish community became so accustomed to seeing one-sided reporting in Israel's favour that they internalized this unbalanced reporting as truth. Israel could oppress and torment Palestinians with impunity, never having to worry about damage to its reputation and image in Canada and most Western countries. Recently, the media has begun to shift towards more balanced reporting. I feel that many in the pro-Israel lobby sincerely and genuinely believe that the media is turning against them, rather than just moving towards middle ground. I suppose that, in relative terms, it must look to some like an "anti-Semitic conspiracy."

Though the Zionist lobby in Canada is expected to actively promote Israel's interests (by trying to interpret and spin all its actions as good, moral, and so on), it needs to worry far less about the promotional and political activities of the Canadian Arab community than vice versa. The first reason for this is that the Jewish population of Canada established itself much earlier and has had more time to gain understanding and influence; it is thus far more effective. There are two additional reasons why apologists for Israel need to be only minimally concerned about their rivals in Canada.

The first is that Muslims and Arabs have not been overtly and relentlessly discriminated against in North America. On the contrary, by the time they began to arrive in substantial numbers, the ground had been prepared for a genuine welcome. Jews routinely suffered discrimination, sometimes severe. That prompted them to establish organizations to defend themselves, such as the B'nai Brith and others. Today, in addition to defending Jews against anti-Semitism, these organizations also use their resources to assist Israel. Most North American Muslims have not felt compelled to develop such organizations for themselves, at least not so far. If, after 9-11, the defamation of and discrimination against Muslims and Arabs grows, they will naturally begin to pay attention and divert much more of their time, energy, and resources to defending themselves in social and political terms. Muslims, too, can learn about the need for acquiring media outlets and developing "extraordinarily good friendships" with politicians. As far as I can tell, at the time of this writing, there appears to be no urgent need for this in Canada. I hope the need for drastic self-defensive political and legal action will never be forced upon Muslims in Canada.

The second reason pro-Israel support may not be matched any time soon[8] is that most Muslims and Arabs who have immigrated to Canada have done so because of alienation from their old countries. It does not go without saying that an Iraqi from an Iraq ruled by Saddam Hussein, would enthusiastically go looking for ways to help "the old country," when all that means is supporting a ruler who has terrorized him or her and perhaps killed family members and friends. Arab immigrants may sympathize with the cruel plight of the Palestinians, and "do what they can." But how much

---

8 In my view, the pro-Israel lobby should be very concerned that continued cruel and unjust oppression of Palestinians will make it impossible to stem the growing hostility towards Israel in Western countries. In Europe, Israel's image has been badly damaged and sympathy is being lost.

effort and dedication will anyone, from anywhere in the world, apply to support any regime "back home" which they see as corrupt, undemocratic, exclusionary, cruel, and ruthlessly willing to sacrifice the interests of the country for the sake of remaining in power?

In stark contrast, Jews in Canada can love Israel as an embracing second home. They have a choice of political parties to support, all of which—at least in theory—respect all Jews everywhere. They can travel there and express their opinions freely. To me, that is a clear example of why the free muddle of democracy is more powerful than the coerced order and uniformity of dictatorship. (I must add, though, that a more advanced political system such as the Israeli one does not give one the moral right to abuse those with a less advanced political system.) It seems to me that the progress made by the Canadian public in understanding the plight of Palestine is only in small measure due to the efforts of the Arab-Canadian community. It is due much more to the fair-mindedness of Canadians and the perception of how badly Israel treats a weak and vulnerable people. In addition, there is growing discomfort among an increasing number of moderate Jews at the treatment of the Palestinians, whom Israel turned into "occupied refugees" decades ago and who even now "naively and unrealistically" persist in demanding justice. Such compassionate Jews are often unpopular with Zionist Jews, not to mention Israelis.

The Importance of "Self-Hating" Jews

Jews who speak out against injustice and oppression in Palestine are called "self-hating Jews" by extremists and religious fanatics, who will stop at nothing and seem unable to gauge when enough is enough. Palestinians have been pushed to such desperation that some have violated the rules of their religion, which prohibit attacks on civilians. It appears to me, in layman terms and without a full understanding of what really happened so long ago, that some Palestinians have followed the example of mighty Samson (Shimshon) of old. Betrayed, blinded, imprisoned, humiliated, mocked, and with nothing to live for, Samson helped his people by committing a suicide attack, bringing down the temple indifferently on himself, civilians, soldiers, the elderly, women and children. We all belong to the same species: similar circumstances induce similar behaviour.

Times are changing, and now benign Jewish voices can more often be heard criticizing Israel, sometimes severely, in the mainstream media.

Sometimes, my "Jews OK/Israel not OK" perception is reinforced. In an article in *The Globe and Mail* entitled "Zionism Doesn't Define Jews—It Divides Us," Gabor Maté writes:

"The modern identification of Jews and Israel emerged largely as a reaction to the Nazi genocide. Although it may represent the majority view today, it should not be taken for granted. Historically it never has been. It is unlikely to persist...The Palestinians continue to be disenfranchised, disposed and humiliated....[In] the words of an Israeli officer who chose this week to join dozens of his comrades in jail rather than serve in an army of brutal occupation: "I will do my time in a visible prison for a few months for refusing to enlist in Israel's academy for prison guards: the IDF, Israel's 'Defence Forces,' which have been imprisoning an entire people for thirty-five years."

This is some of what a "self-hating" rabbi had to say:

"We have no doubt that would Jewish refugees, have come to Palestine not with the intention of dominating, not with the intention of making a Jewish state, not with the intention of dispossessing, not with the intention of depriving the Palestinians of their basic rights, that they would have been welcomed by the Palestinians, with the same hospitality that Islamic peoples have shown Jews throughout history. And we would have lived together as Jews and Muslims lived before in Palestine in peace and harmony."[9]

I have learned that such deep divisions freely expressed are no sign of weakness. Rather, they are an indicator of the great strength of a people. It is not my place to involve myself in debates within Canada's Jewish community, but I do have two points to make. First, I admire the freedom and tolerance both in Canada and amongst Jews everywhere. A diversity of opinions and opposing viewpoints are openly expressed and graciously allowed, even for the most basic and gut-wrenching issues, no matter how grating or unacceptable to a few, to many, or to the majority. I wish this noble attitude prevailed in the region where I was raised. Had that been the case, perhaps I never would have left to become an immigrant to Canada. Over there, it is rather the opposite: usually, whoever has the upper hand suppresses all opposing viewpoints.

Secondly, in my humble opinion, so-called self-hating Jews are of great value to Judaism and thus to all Jews. By expressing their views, they make it impossible—or at least unfair and unreasonable, even racist—for those

---

9 Weberman, Rabbi Mordechi. "Because We Are Jews," June 2003;
<http://www.marchforjustice.com/Becausewearejews.php>.

who have suffered at the hands of Israel to hate all Jews. The virtues of free expression and mutual respect will prove to be of incalculable value as the decades unfold. For I fear that Israel will probably, though not inevitably, continue to be at war for decades, or perhaps generations, longer. I believe this will occur because, at the time of this writing, Israel's persistent wars, rather than winding down, appear to be expanding into a war against all of Islam. It could take another few decades for the Muslim world to mobilize effectively.[10] In the tragic eventuality of war lasting one or two centuries, it makes a difference whether it will be one between Judaism and Islam, or the sovereign nation-state of Israel and Islam. Many of its enemies believe Israel could "win" and have some decades of peace and quiet, or it could lose and change into something else. In contrast, Judaism, Christianity and Islam will be here "until Doomsday".

I know that I will always see Israel in a negative light until there is justice for Joseph C. I cannot let down my fine old friend as long as the conflict continues and he and his people have not forgiven or forgotten. I am helpless to help him and the other refugees, many of whom have suffered much more than Joe's family. So does my opinion really matter? It does, because it is shared by tens or hundreds of millions who matter very much, even though they are currently weak, divided, and—in the view of some Israelis—contemptible. I do not doubt that Israel has an arsenal of nuclear, chemical, and biological weapons. But for the security and permanence of Israel, it is not enough for Israelis to say that this is their land and enforce their claim through violence and the threat of greater violence. True and secure ownership of anything depends on the freely-given, formal, legal, and moral recognition of others. Unelected Middle-Eastern governments who recognize the Israeli state for their own purposes and without the true consent of the people, or Palestinian leaders who give in under duress, do nothing to validate the state of Israel in the long term.

Islam Is Here to Stay

It would save much trouble if everyone understood the following basic fact: the Muslim world stretches from Morocco on the Atlantic through the

---

10 Being a populist faith based on the conscience of each individual rather than on a centralized, hierarchical organization, Islam took about forty years to mobilize against the Crusaders who captured Jerusalem in 1099 (and immediately massacred the inhabitants, Muslims and Jews alike.) It took almost 200 years to completely eradicate the military power of the Latin states in the Arab world.

Middle-East, far and wide in Asia and south into Africa. It is irrevocably Muslim. It is inhabited by about one and one-quarter billion people; a number that is growing steadily. Like other civilizations, they have had their ups and downs. Non-Muslims who live in peace and harmony with Islam have been welcome. Forces such as crusaders, imperialists, and communists managed to gain a foothold on Muslim areas for varying lengths of time, but all of them eventually disappeared like dust in the wind. Israel has maintained a hostile presence in the Muslim world for over half a century. Cultivating a peace that does not rely on belligerent militarism and threats might serve its future well.

A Lost Hope for Peace

Only once was I truly hopeful that peace would come to the region. That was when Israeli Prime Minister Menachem Begin and Egyptian President Anwar Sadat reached a peace agreement with the help of President Jimmy Carter in 1978.[11] For a while, it looked as if Palestinian rights would be looked after and peace might spread throughout the entire area. "At last," I thought. "Perhaps all will end well and I will finally be able to go over there and hear the fabled Israel Symphony Orchestra." I am fond of Gustav Mahler's music and thought that a great orchestra mostly comprised of Jewish performers would do a sublime job of interpreting it. I even went so far as to inquire as to when Mahler's Second or Third symphony would be on the program.

Alas, having made peace with Egypt on the Western Front, Israel opened up the Eastern Front by invading Lebanon and ignoring the United Nations' resolutions to cease and desist. When Israeli heavy artillery bombarded densely-populated Beirut, I was reminded of World War II footage of German artillery shelling Warsaw, at that time overcrowded with refugees. I suddenly realized there would be no peace soon, because Israel—a typical sovereign nation-state—appeared to attach no value to the lives of the people of the region where it wanted to establish itself, and because it was too powerful to overcome anytime soon. The Israel Symphony Orchestra and Mahler's symphonies would have to wait.

---

11 *The Camp David Accords*, signed 17 September, 1978
(see <http://www.jimmycarterlibrary.org/documents/campdavid/index.phtml>) led to the award of the 1978 Nobel Peace Prize to Sadat and Begin.

Can Israel's Neighbours Ever Accept It?

At the time of this writing, more than half a century after its creation, Israel still says it is fighting for its very existence. Israeli casualties are proportionately higher than they have ever been. The sympathy for Israel and Jews that followed World War II is eroding. This is called a "resurgence of anti-Semitism" by pro-Israel spin doctors, who perhaps actually believe it. I see much of it as hostility that would be directed at any people of any race who dehumanized and tormented others in the way Israel is doing. Germany is getting over its guilt about the atrocities of World War II. In Europe in mid-2002, on a German TV channel I heard talk of "the infamy of having made it a taboo to criticize Israel for all these years." Such talk on public German television would have been unthinkable just a couple of years earlier. From what I can see, attitudes against Israel are hardening over much of Europe. Accusations of anti-Semitism are not silencing people as they used to.

In August 2001, I became very angry at a spate of articles promoting all-out war against the Palestinians. I sent an e-mail to some of my friends. They liked it and sent it to more of their friends and acquaintances. I was encouraged and also sent it as a letter to the Montreal *Gazette*. I knew it would not be published, even though that newspaper was still owned by Mr. Conrad Black, who was more open to opposing viewpoints than the current owners. Sure enough, it was not published. Among other things, I think it was too long. In any case, it didn't matter, because many had seen it on the Internet while my primary aim was to let off steam.

```
August 24, 2001
To: A bunch of friends and acquaintances and The
Montreal Gazette

From: C. Rifaat


Where is the wisdom of the Jews?

    In my perception, the Jews are an ancient people with
many centuries of wisdom and experience in the ways of
man, punctuated by suffering which has sometimes been
among the most extreme. The vicious excesses against them
in Europe in the last couple of centuries have justifiably
```

led them to accumulate the influence and power needed to defend themselves. Having accumulated a comfortable reserve of power, it is a small step from defending against injustice to applying such power to oppress others.

I am having difficulty detecting wisdom in Israel's current actions. George Jonas (The Gazette, Sunday August 19) alludes to "illusions" about the prospects for a non-violent resolution to the conflict in Palestine: perhaps, he writes, war is the only reality. Such a war would presumably be between a powerful Israel confident of victory and destitute Palestinians, and would possibly involve Arab states weaker than Israel. In Levon Sevunts' article (Thursday, August 23) we read that Palestinians are not really victims and deserve what is and has been happening to them.

Being myself from an ancient country with a long historical perspective (Egypt), I see that most peoples have at one time or another had a turn at being a superior military power. Rarely, however, does a nation at the height of its power realize that it is only a turn and that it will sooner or later be over, inevitably.

In some cases, for any of a number of reasons, the once-powerful oppressor declines and weakens without ever suffering the wrath of the formerly oppressed. In my judgment this is unlikely to be so in the Middle East.

In principle, former Prime Minister Ehud Barak was on the right track: it is wise for Israel to pursue peace from a position of seemingly overwhelming power. The trouble is that Israel still does not appear to understand the region in which it lives. Islam strongly discourages compromising with injustice. Those who are perceived to commit injustice are despicable and contemptible, no matter how powerful. On the other hand, biding one's time until the right circumstances emerge is acceptable, as long as the spirit is steadfast. Thus, Sadat and King Hussein of Jordan—both unelected—did not lead their people "into accepting the State of Israel," as Sevunts' article reports. The great majority of Egyptians I know have not accepted the state of Israel, but rather have accepted the need to bide their time. I suppose it is the same with the majority of the 250 million Arabs as a whole, not to mention the billion plus Muslims in the world.

Mr. Barak's government was far-sighted in its quest for peace.[12] It not unreasonably felt that the Palestinians would be "realistic" in the modern Western sense and bow to the agony imposed by a "superior power": they would accept a somewhat reduced level of injustice, in exchange for some much needed and overdue relief. The result of Mr. Barak's effort is surprising and revealing. After more than half a century of destitution and wretched living conditions, the Palestinians refuse to compromise on the question of justice. They will not accept any injustice, period. It is as if the perceived injustices of 1948—when Palestinians were driven from their lands and homes—occurred only last week. The passage of time does not soften their desire for justice. If Israel genuinely inclines towards peace with the Arabs and would like bygones to be bygones, then it is the duty of Muslims, who comprise the overwhelming majority of Middle-Easterners, to also incline towards peace. But first injustices must be reversed. Palestinians must be allowed to return home to what today is Israel proper or be compensated fairly. Otherwise they may well continue their struggle for another fifty years, or however long it takes. Some Israelis mock what they call Palestinians' lack of realism and their "missed opportunities." The situation is viewed differently by the other side. The Koran says: "O believers endure, and surpass all others in endurance."

It appears to me that pro-Israel articles such as the two mentioned above may be aiming to "prepare the public" for more war in the Middle East. However, using Israel's power to extend the violence now will simply entrench the contempt, hatred, and desire for revenge among its enemies for many, many generations to come. I don't know when the Jews' turn at being more powerful will be over. All I can see is that Israel currently behaves as though it believes its reign will last forever.

Where is the wisdom of the Jews?

C. R.

I can see now that I was angry. For one thing I used "Jews" and "Israel" almost interchangeably, against the principle my parents taught me. More

---

12 Some, such as "self-hating Jew" Noam Chomsky, say Barak's peace plan was a sham and did not give Palestinians a viable state. Chomsky points out that no map of the proposed solution has been made available in North America, lest the general public see the unfairness. Perhaps late Israeli Prime Minister Rabin could have done better.

importantly, I did not mention a hope for peace. I suppose that means I am not optimistic: Israel is very powerful and the other side will not give up for primordial and timeless reasons. The Koran says, "Expel them whence they expelled you"[13] (though complete financial or other fair and full compensation might be acceptable.) There is also a saying that "Jerusalem is either Muslim or at war" (but it could be divided, with each side claiming it has the real Jerusalem.)

Since then, things have become worse for the Palestinians. The all-out war George Jonas favoured in his article has been unleashed and Israel has sent heavy weapons into some of the most densely-populated civilian areas in the world. The shame of finding it necessary to send tanks into refugee camps has bothered some Jews, but not others. The second war on Iraq appears to have improved Israel's position and improved its substantial advantage in negotiations with the Palestinians. But even if new representatives of the Palestinian people give up the "right of return" to their lands and homes of 1948, it will have been done under duress. The door will remain open for a resumption of the struggle in a decade or two, or whenever the situation changes sufficiently. It appears to me that Israel does not understand that.

Palestinians have had almost no support from the rest of the Muslim world. Yet they have been able to deny Israelis peace and security. With or without American help, through the conquest and occupation of part of the region, I believe that "bashing" Arabs to keep them quiet for a decade or two can work only for a short while. As long as Israel cannot become a prosperous and peaceful little country like Holland or Belgium, the Palestinians will not have lost the struggle.

For the proponents of a "might makes right" doctrine in Israel and elsewhere, I have two suggestions. First, in today's fast-changing world, "might" can more quickly abandon those it favours for a while and migrate to others. Second, globalization endangers the mighty even at the peak of their power, as ideas and passions spread rapidly and as weaker opponents are allowed a wide-ranging ability to work their mischief and inflict damage.

Is there a way out? Only one, I believe. Israel must change and stop treating Palestinians as subhuman, whether they be Muslim or Christian. My fine friend Joseph C., his offspring, and all the others must be dealt with fairly. Palestinians must obtain full justice and equality in human, social, and religious terms. Then I will finally be able to say: "Jews OK; Israel OK."

---

13 This is not perceived to be someone's frivolous opinion, subject to deal-making and bargaining. It is the word of God. Religious intractability is not a characteristic of Jewish settlers alone.

Chapter 8: The U.S. and I.
Fluctuating Admiration

The Famous Balancing Act

As a Canadian, like most Canadians, I am keenly aware that the United States plays a major role in my life and in the life of my country. Early on, even before I became Canadian, I learned we must balance two aspects of our very good relationship. On the one hand, we want to remain good friends, allies, and trading partners. On the other, we have worked hard to keep sufficient distance so as to maintain our own identity and culture. Since 9-11, this balancing act has been more difficult. The pull in two opposite directions is being exacerbated by the War on Terror.

I strongly support helping the U.S. prevent further terrorist attacks. But I am uncomfortable with Canada being drawn into the bombing and killing of pre-industrial peoples in remote lands. Coming from a former colony myself, I am sensitive to that kind of cruel mischief, inflicted by Western countries over the last century and a half. It is immoral to add to the misfortunes of those already much less fortunate than we are. In Iraq, little twelve-year-old Ali and other children had been worse off than Canadian children even before he was orphaned and his arms ripped off by a cluster bomb. I do not want Canada's reputation as a peacekeeper and honest broker to be jeopardized, and furthermore, I don't want to do anything to attract terrorism here.

Jean Chrétien's Liberal government did its best to maintain balance in these difficult times: it developed a strategy of support, which we owe the U.S., while avoiding distasteful aggression, which we owe to ourselves and our moral standards.

Our reliance on the U.S. is not just a matter of economics: we also rely on it for our security. Due to my perception of the behaviour of the sovereign nation-state as amoral, ruthless, and guided by greed and fear, I believe that, had it not been for the might of the U.S., many big powers—such as Germany, Japan, and Russia—would have been tempted to seize at least part of this huge territory and its resources.

Notwithstanding my appreciation of the importance of the U.S., I am very happy to be Canadian and very proud and gratified by the differences between us. There are two differences I especially value. One is our compassion: we are much less belligerent and oppose hurting and killing the weak and vulnerable abroad. The other is the fact that it is much more difficult for the established powers here to manipulate public opinion.

Intermittent Approval

Before ever setting foot in North America—and ever since—my perception of the U.S. has been characterized by alternating waves of approval and disapproval. Often, I have felt affection for the U.S., believing it to be a special and praiseworthy phenomenon in human history. Other times, I have felt betrayed by what had seemed an admirable friend to humanity but had turned out to be just an ordinary "real country."

When I was growing up in Cairo, like countless millions of youngsters all over the world, I was seduced by the fun and excitement which was America without ever having been there. I loved American comic books. There had been a brisk trade in comics at school. I knew all about Batman, Little Lulu and Tubby, Nyoka the Jungle Girl (whatever happened to that early and tentative feminist prototype?), Captain Marvel, Tom Mix, and all the others. So popular was this "purest form of American art" that our headmaster once banned it. Perhaps he felt that the comics were beneath the dignity of a fine British school; perhaps they competed too successfully with the English stories and novels for young people's attention. A short time later, the ban was lifted and the vibrant comic book exchange was re-opened during break ("recess" in North America.) We did not know why the ban came or why it went. As a teenager, I received a gift subscription to *Newsweek* and read it avidly. In childhood, the biggest treat my parents could give us was an American movie or a matinee featuring Tom & Jerry.

There was much goodwill towards America and its culture reached far and wide. Such was my infatuation with all things American that, as a young adolescent, I once carved "The Kid From Texas" with a screwdriver on a prominent wall at the entrance of our apartment building. The superintendent spotted me just as I had finished and was showing off my handiwork to my brothers. He threw a fit. Obviously, I thought, the problem was that he could not read English. I sympathized. Since he did not comprehend the words, I understood his anger and tried to placate him.

"This is a movie about cowboys," I explained helpfully. "It is from America and showing at the Rivoli cinema." The superintendent became hysterical. I wavered, but stood my ground and said, "It is starring Audie Murphy and is in Technicolor." He went berserk and I had to flee. It was hard to believe, but apparently the unfortunate man had never heard of Audie Murphy. My father paid to repair the damage and included a generous tip for the superintendent.

When I was in my teens in 1956, the British and French invaded Egypt—with a young Israel in tow—and it was explained to me that America had been instrumental in helping us. The U.S. put enormous pressure on the invaders and refused to give loan guarantees to the British, who needed them to pursue their aggression. What is known as the "Suez War" ended: the enemy withdrew. In Egypt, there was euphoria about the U.S. that rubbed off on me. Unlike Europe and its imperialists, America had no colonial history in the Middle East. At that time, it was respected and admired as a big, strong, fair-minded, and friendly giant. I did not understand politics but America's role in helping underdog Egypt was not surprising to me. The U.S. had acted true to form. Like John Wayne, it had gone against the big bullies (Britain and France, like the railroad or cattle barons) and helped the little guy (Egypt, like the simple and vulnerable homesteaders.) America was great.

Later still, when I was studying in Switzerland, my feelings about the U.S. started to turn sour. America seemed not so great; in fact, it seemed pretty mean. The reason for this change in perspective was the Vietnam War. Even though I had grown up in an anti-Communist family, I strongly disliked the spectacle of a big power bombing weak and vulnerable people, destroying what little they had and killing or maiming them. What the U.S. did in Vietnam—dropping napalm and Agent Orange on a largely agrarian society—did not seem like things Audie Murphy would do. That influenced my choice of destination: when I decided to emigrate, I avoided the U.S.

Why Did I Not Choose America?

Immigrants go through an emotional buffeting of a kind not experienced by native-born Canadians and are changed by the experience. Few just decide one day to pack up their bags and move to another country. It is usually a difficult and intimidating matter requiring a period of thinking, hesitating, and weighing options. It requires dissatisfaction with the existing situation. It requires the clear-headedness to ask the right questions—why do I want to leave, what am I looking for, and where can I find it—and a healthy dose of emotional fortitude. Then, after determining the answers, it is essential to muster the courage to sever old ties and leave familiar surroundings for an uncertain future in a strange country. Some just cannot take that last step. I was fortunate to have a choice of two familiar places in which I could live and work: Switzerland or Egypt. The problem was that I did not want either.

After obtaining my degree and while pursuing another in Zurich, I began to realize that I did not want to go back to Egypt, my original homeland. These were troubled times for me. I had been a happy youth growing up in Cairo—young, idealistic, and nationalistic. I had always felt that after my studies, I would go back home and pick up where I had left off. My education would be valuable to me and to the country. But the military dictatorship that had replaced the corrupt monarchy had deteriorated to a point where I felt I could not function in that environment. Meanwhile, my exposure in Switzerland to one of the purest forms of democracy had changed my way of thinking.

Gamal Abdel Nasser, the revolutionary leader and president (dictator), had been a hero to me as a teenager. Back home, he was credited for the final push to drive out the British and for bringing independence and dignity to Egyptians. Egyptians felt Westerners were against him because, outrageously, he would not bow to their will. With their more advanced technology and better organizational skills, Europeans had become accustomed to having their way with defenseless peoples. For a century or so they had dominated and oppressed the Middle East and, though they had been driven out, still instinctively resented insubordination from their "underlings."

When newly arrived in Switzerland, such was my infatuation with "Nasser, the Saviour of Egypt" that I sometimes stuck a picture of him on the inside cover of the binder where I kept my lecture notes. One day, when I returned from a break between lectures, the picture was missing. After the lecture was over and the professor had left, I asked loudly who had taken the photograph. For the next couple of days during breaks, I went around asking the students whether anyone knew who had taken my picture. It was an international student body, and on the third day a student from Germany, Peter Kuhle, pointed out the guilty party. I confronted the "thief." He admitted taking the photograph but refused to return it, saying something to the effect that Nasser was threatening Europe. I issued a threat of my own, that I would take the matter up with the university administration. He still refused to return my property. After several failed attempts to retrieve the photograph, I went to the Rektoratskanzlei and reported the matter, saying I wanted it back. The administrator looked at me gravely and said that this was more than just theft; it was a political matter and an insult to me and my nation. He suggested we resolve the problem without involving the administration, since the student who took the picture could even be expelled from the university. When I explained this to the student, he said he would give me back my picture if I promised not to bring it to class. I refused but got it back anyway. I kept it in the binder for the rest of the semester as a gesture of defiance. No one touched it again. Remembering my emotions at the time helps me understand the seductive passions of nationalism and patriotism.

Unfortunately, after ending foreign domination, Nasser soon established an oppressive regime modeled after the Soviet Union and Eastern Europe. Though it was certainly less harsh, stories reached me of people being arrested for derogatory remarks, or even mere honest criticism of the leadership. I heard of members of the same family spying on each other for the regime. Over a few years, my adulation turned to intense dislike for Nasser. He had created an environment completely unacceptable to me and I would not go back to Egypt.

I was fortunate to have an alternative. I could stay in Switzerland. I spoke two of the official languages and had a fine degree many Swiss could only envy. As a student, Switzerland had been a paradise for me. My life revolved mainly around what I called s^3 (or s-cubed): studies, sex, and skiing (not always in that order.) I gave little or no thought to democracy, politics, the future, or anything else.

But after graduating, my thoughts began to turn to my long-term future. Though I still enjoyed Switzerland, had lived there many years, and was well-adapted, I was nowhere near integrated into Swiss society. If I had stayed on, it would have taken a long time to obtain Swiss citizenship; in the meantime, my rights would have been restricted. Also, the authorities and the *Fremdenpolizei*[1] could decide not to renew my annual residency permit for any reason or no reason. I had the impression, rightly or wrongly, that even if I obtained Swiss citizenship, I still would never be considered a "real Swiss."

Professor M. J. O. Strutt, who headed the Institut für Höhere Electrotechnik (Institute for Advanced Electronics Engineering) where I was continuing my studies, was a Swiss citizen of Dutch origin. He used to joke about "a hierarchy of Swissness." The real Swiss, those with the proper genetic credentials, he would say, are the descendants of the Germanic tribes, the Allemanen, who came from the north to settle in the third century A.D. onwards. The next-most-real Swiss are the descendants of those from the few cantons which in 1281 formed the "Everlasting League," the nucleus of modern Switzerland. Next in line, and almost as good, are the Swiss who heroically stood their ground at the Battle of Sempach on July 9, 1386, to defeat the shining knights of the mighty Hapsburg Empire and thus achieve independence. Lower down the hierarchy of "real Swiss" are the citizens of Geneva, since that former city-state only joined the Helvetic Confederacy much later, in 1814. At the very bottom of the hierarchy, my professor would say, we find the "sort-of-Swiss-but-not-really": foreigners who had obtained Swiss citizenship, like himself. I was not interested in staying on in Switzerland.

Neither Switzerland nor Egypt, the two countries I knew well, suited me. Where, then? It would have been disastrous to make a mistake with something so serious. Imagine cutting ties, selling my roadster (I still miss that convertible), all my furniture, and my piano, saying goodbye, and moving somewhere which then turned out to be wrong for me.

Since I became Canadian, whenever I am asked about Canada as a destination by people who are thinking of emigrating, I always say the same thing: "If you leave your country of origin to settle permanently elsewhere, choose a country to which you can genuinely belong and in which you can be really at home. Canada is one such country." It was an

---

[1] A special police department set up exclusively for foreigners, who are officially referred to as "strangers."

important criterion for me once I had decided to move on from Switzerland but not to return to Egypt. That meant going to Australia, the United States, or Canada.

Australia seemed very far away. Also it appeared at the time, rightly or wrongly, that the country was dominated by a large majority originally from England. It therefore seemed too much like going to England. Just as today I am not attracted to the idea of a Quebec nation dominated by the French, at the time I was not attracted by an Australia dominated by the English.

When I decided to look for a new home, my perception of the U.S. was not as favourable as it had been in my childhood. Still, America was wonderful. It welcomed all humanity. It was fun and a great place to build a future. However, two thoughts made me hesitate.

First, I had been born and raised in a patriarchy. Though by no means the most male-dominated society in the world, Egypt is a country where men are in charge, although women can be very strong—even dominant—inside the home. All evidence I had seen led me to believe the United States was an extreme matriarchy. I was a young, single, macho male from the Middle East and quite exuberant about my masculinity. At that impetuous time, there was no way I was going to put myself in a position where women, or even a woman, would try to walk all over me! Rightly or wrongly, I was discouraged from going somewhere where I thought I would have to act like a wimp, pleading and obedient, to avoid trouble with the opposite sex. In retrospect, I think that my youth and inexperience led me to confuse the institution of marriage with this aspect of American culture. Nevertheless, many years later, I still believe I was at least partially right.

The other problem related to the tensions between the U.S. and Egypt at the time. Nasser was dubbed "Hitler of the Nile" by the U.S. media. I assumed this was because he had been cozy with the Soviet Union and would not accept the "injustices in Palestine," that is, the creation of Israel. Nasser was the principal reason I would not be returning to Egypt and I felt that the label was not completely outrageous[2] (though "Stalin Lite of the Nile" would have been somewhat more accurate.) What bothered me was that the media were nurturing a dislike for Egypt and Egyptians in the American general public. I felt an armed conflict or all-out war involving Egypt and the United States was

---

2 It was a complete fantasy to think that Egyptians under Nasser could generate anywhere near the military power or wreak even a fraction of the havoc as the Germans under Hitler, but the smear suited the aims of the "Establishment" in the U.S. so it was used often in the media.

likely and was affected by memories of when, as a teenaged volunteer militiaman clutching a Russian-made assault rifle, I had waited in a Cairo suburb for British paratroopers.[3] I was looking for a new home. What would my situation be if my new home went to war with my old home? Could I belong fully in America if the U.S. leadership whipped up militant enthusiasm against Egyptians in its public? I thought it better not to take a chance.

From what I could tell, Canada was more balanced between extreme matriarchy and extreme patriarchy. Also, it did not have awesome fleets scouring the oceans of the world, enraging peoples and drawing hatred and hostility. I had been corresponding with my good friends, the Alailys, in Toronto, and they seemed to like their new country very much. They convinced me that I could be at home in Canada. My wife-to-be, Heidi, and I were madly in love. We had what was probably the most serious talk of our lives. She said she would be happy to come with me to Canada, and so here we are.

I applied for landed-immigrant status in Canada and was accepted. As chance would have it, I almost immediately left to spend about eight months in the U.S., much of it in the Boston area. Now I was experiencing America first hand and things were falling into place. The Vietnam War wound down and my perception of America quickly improved. Soon, it soared.

Should I Have Chosen America?

I've always admired how Americans are determined to try to make everyone feel respected and at home, regardless of race, religion, or ethnic origin. I saw examples of this in everyday life, as in the episode involving the policeman and my driving test (described in Chapter 2.) Another, more significant example occurred at work.

Once on the way to the cafeteria with some colleagues, we passed a small chapel. The curtain was open and I could see a plain Protestant cross, a Catholic crucifix, and a six-pointed Star of David. I stopped and looked into the small enclosure. My co-workers stopped too.

"Hey, what about me?" I asked.

"You are not represented by one of these symbols?" someone asked.

"No," I replied. "I am not particularly religious and I am pretty sure that I will not be praying here, but that is beside the point. It is a matter

---

3 The invasion force never made it that far into Egypt.

of symbolism. If we are all here together, I should also have my symbol, the crescent."

We walked on to the cafeteria and I soon forgot about the chapel.

My job was to provide technical support to the sales force. Sales engineers called me frequently with technical questions about our product lines. If I could not find an answer from the technical literature, I made direct contact with the engineers at the facility who designed the products. About a week after the chapel incident, my phone rang. When I picked it up, I froze: the voice at the other end identified himself as the number-two man in the division, ranking up in the stratosphere above me. I had never had anything to do with him, just occasionally caught sight of him here and there in the facility.

"Hey, how are you doing, Cherif?"

"I'm fine, thank you," I heard myself say. I suppose I should have said, "...and how are you?" but I did not; I was too tongue-tied.

"Do you have a few minutes for me to see you?"

"Sure," I said. "I'm at my desk."

"OK, I'll be over in five or ten minutes."

We hung up.

"Stupid! Stupid!" I thought to myself. "Of course I am at my desk; he had called my extension, hadn't he? Now he will think I am a moron."

I had a few minutes to compose myself and collect my thoughts.

"At least I know he is not coming to fire me," I thought. "If I were being let go, that task would be performed by a much lower-ranking manager. But usually people he wanted to talk to went to see him in his corner office. Why was he coming to my lowly desk? Help!"

When he arrived, my co-workers sitting in desks around me, including my supervisor, Jack Cunningham, were taken by surprise and fell into an alert silence. When we started to talk, my co-workers moved discreetly out of earshot. My experience with European bosses is that many act aloof and godlike. In America, I discovered that, in most cases, the higher the rank, the more personable and relaxed the attitude. Experienced bosses and young trainees spoke to each other almost as equals. When the VP came to my desk, he very quickly put me at ease with questions regarding the comfort of my apartment and told me he had been told I was doing a good job. Then he said:

"I understand that you had a comment about our chapel the other day."

So that was it. This was no time to back down. "Well, there are other religious symbols, but not mine."

"And your symbol would be a crescent? You feel there should be a crescent in the chapel?" Someone had briefed him in detail.

"Well, yes. Don't you agree that if we are all equal, we should all be represented equally?"

"Of course I agree," he said. There followed some small talk and he wished me luck and went back to his office. My mystified and slightly-awed supervisor, Jack, came over to my desk with a couple of others.

"What was that all about?"

"Oh, something about the chapel," I answered vaguely.

A couple of weeks passed and the chapel was removed completely. Years later, when I had moved up in the company, someone who had been involved reminisced and said to me that I had created quite a stir. After much debate, it had been decided at the "highest level" that while all faiths should be equally represented, many new additions would make this impractical. The best way to achieve equality was not to display any symbols at all! (One day, I must remember to ask a European, perhaps from France, what would have happened to a young, new, and foreign trainee who encountered a cross of Lorraine and asked why his crescent was not right up there beside it.)

In Egypt, I had been treated with dignity and respect, because I belonged to a privileged class. In Switzerland, I was treated fairly but was a rather irrelevant outsider, a foreign student. In the United States (and later Canada), I was treated with dignity and respect, because it went without saying and because most Americans feel that this is how everybody should be treated. I cannot forget that.

I found the U.S. gave me, and everyone else around me, more respect as individuals than any other country I have visited. I also found the same tolerance and respect in Canada when I returned after my extended stay in the U.S. I found ordinary Americans, like Canadians, to be decent and honest, with a strong sense of fair play. This will be met by disbelief, or at least surprise, by many in countries that have been bombed by America.

In discussions with non-Americans, I would sometimes acknowledge some wrongdoing by the U.S. here or there, but I would always add something like: "Every country I know that became more powerful than others attempted to conquer or subjugate others and expand its territory. Between 1945—the end of World War II—and about 1948, the U.S. was the only country with nuclear weapons. It could have used these to conquer the world. It never even tried. Which other big country do you know would have acted in the same way? (Following the 2003 attack on Iraq, I believe that fewer non-Americans than ever will accept this argument. In fact, I have stopped using it.) During the Cold War, I was whole-heartedly for the U.S. Once, in Europe, someone said that I was more pro-American than Americans.

When the Cold War ended, the United States and its allies had won a victory perhaps greater than any in history. I was happy that Communism, which I considered a scourge, had been defeated with very little violence (considering the arsenals at hand.) Thank you very much, America—we owe you a great debt of gratitude.

Canada Suits Me Better After All

Soon after the end of the Cold War, in the early 1990s, my perception of the U.S. took a sharp dip again. Why this time? Because I felt that the U.S. had begun to adopt certain traits of the despised, defunct European colonial powers. I had considered the U.S. an exception, a happy special case. But now it was beginning to act according to my model of typical nation-states, basing its policies on greed and fear. The fear of destruction by the awesome Soviet nuclear arsenal was gone and was not replaced by any other fear. The United States could define and pursue its "national interests" with much less inhibition, since no one could match its power.

It was not until 2002 that I saw author Samantha Power interviewed by Evan Solomon on the CBC program "Hot Type." She enabled me to articulate to myself that my perception of the United States fluctuated over the years according to whether or not its actions abroad, as I perceived them, were living up to its values, as I understood them to be. She proposed a "gap between American values and American foreign policy."[4] Over the years, without realizing it, I had judged America according to how large or how small I perceived that gap to be. As an adolescent and teenager, I had learned about American values, the fundamental virtues of justice and fairness, in American comic books, movies and from its lack of a colonial history. My first, formative

---

4 Samantha Power, *A Problem from Hell.*

impression of the U.S. was very positive. The influence of U.S. fiction was so strong that I eventually internalized the values it promoted. In my teens, that benign impression was confirmed by real events in the real world: America helped a victimized Egypt against a coalition of malevolent states.

Thereafter, every time the U.S. used its great power to pursue an unjust foreign policy—especially when killing the weak and vulnerable to impose its will—I felt as if betrayed by a friend. Initially, it seemed to me that American imperialist behaviour, such as in Vietnam, was a careless or accidental deviation from what I "knew" the "real America" to be like. Later, living and working in the U.S. confirmed to me that most Americans really want to live up to the ideals of their country—to be moral and just and special among peoples. With time, however, I realized that the U.S.'s fairness and respect for the human rights of its own citizens did not extend to "alien" peoples outside America's borders. I "discovered" that, in many respects, America is really much more like ordinary countries than I had thought.

Though my opinion of the U.S. has been low since the first Gulf War, I experienced a surge of sympathy right after September 11, 2001. I was hit especially hard by the sight of people having to choose between being burned alive or jumping to their deaths. Years ago, my own cousin Leila had to make that choice: she jumped from an eighth-floor window. Unbelievably, miraculously, she survived when she landed on a large protruding air-conditioning unit on the seventh floor directly below her. There, in her nightgown, she clung on for dear life, until rescued by firemen. Later, I visited her while she was recovering in hospital from her burns and asked, "Did you aim for the air-conditioner?"

"I did not even realize it was there."

"How could you bring yourself to just jump like that?"

"I was standing by the window, frantically waving and in a panic about what to do. Cherif, I tell you, as soon as I felt the flames licking my back, nothing mattered except getting away. I just instantly jumped. No thinking of any kind was involved. Perhaps unconsciously I felt that the few seconds longer I had to live before I hit the pavement would be a merciful choice compared to the flames."

I still do my best not to think of the people who jumped out of the twin towers.

However, notwithstanding our great sympathy for those who lost their lives in New York and Washington and those they left behind, I and many other Canadians cannot help feeling that U.S. foreign policy contributed in no small measure to the 9-11 attacks. Like all "real countries," the U.S. has engaged in imperialist policies and in valuing its own interests above the self-determination and even the lives of citizens of other countries. At the same time it has talked about spreading democracy, its actions have too often been in support of evil and corrupt dictators (Somoza, Noriega, and others in Central/South America, and also the Shah of Iran and even Saddam Hussein.)[5] As much as it has prided itself on courage in the defense of its citizens' civil liberties, it has been accused of exploiting the 9-11 attacks to justify the repeal of those same liberties for all Americans.[6]

After the 2003 attack on Iraq, my goodwill towards the U.S. went into sharp decline. I am horrified to see that some aspects of America are beginning to resemble the revolting environment of Third World dictatorships in the region where I was born: a criticism in official circles of those who show "too much" concern for human rights, immunity for those allegedly engaged in war crimes, a formal foreign policy that allows blatant aggression against others for gain, and "manufactured news"[7] to manipulate the public. These examples of corruption can only be generated within the highest ranks of society.

---

5 For a list of U.N. resolutions vetoed by the U.S., including a resolution that

"affirms the right of every state to choose its economic and social system in accord with the will of its people, without outside interference in whatever form it takes" (1981)

and

"measures to prevent international terrorism, study the underlying political and economic causes of terrorism, convene a conference to define terrorism and to differentiate it from the struggle of people from national liberation" (1987), and "to set up the International Criminal Court" (2001),

see <http://www.krysstal.com/democracy_whyusa03.html>.

6 Evelyn Nieves reported in the *Washington Post* (20 April 2003) <http://www.washingtonpost.com/ac2/wp-dyn/A64173-2003Apr20?language=printer> that

"A number of cities across the country are passing resolutions that urge local law enforcement and others to refuse government officials who make demands under the U.S. Patriot Act when these demands appear to 'violate an individual's civil rights under the Constitution'."

and that

"Across the country, citizens have been forming Bill of Rights defense committees to fight what they consider the most egregious curbs on liberties contained in the Patriot Act."

7 Arundhati Roy, "Instant-Mix Imperial Democracy: Buy One, Get One Free," speech presented in New York City at The Riverside Church, 13 May 2003, sponsored by the Center for Economic and Social Rights. Ms. Roy suggests that there has been movement from "manufacturing consent" to "manufacturing news," as was evident with regards to the 2003 attack on Iraq.

I am truly concerned that unless corrected, the U.S. will fall victim to the same "avalanche effect of corruption" I wrote about in my student days.[8] I still maintain firmly that integrity and fairness is widespread among ordinary Americans. However, if this kind of corruption grows and begins to cascade down through the American social hierarchy, Canada will not be spared.

I do have residual respect for the United States because I owe that to Canada,[9] its good neighbour and my home, and because I still believe it has some excellent aspects and values. But I would like to maintain a distance between us. The gap between its stated values and its actions has become too wide.

---

8 See chapter 5.

9 See, for example, the Canadian Department of Foreign Affairs and International Trade's report on the International Commission on Intervention and State Sovereignty <http://www.dfait-maeci.gc.ca/iciss-ciise/> for a quite different approach to international relations, and "Canada Cares Too Much About Personal Liberties: U.S.," *The Ottawa Citizen* (1 May 2003.)

Chapter 9: The Burden of Contradictions

As an immigrant from a former colony unfairly subjugated by a foreign power, I must live with a number of intellectual dilemmas. Three of these are covered briefly in this chapter. They are examples of the mental discomfort that might be caused by crossing cultures and the need to see certain issues from both sides.

The "Gap" Revisited

The gap between the expressed values of the United States and its actions, touched upon in the previous chapter, is one of the mental burdens weighing down on me. On the one hand, the U.S. is a country with many excellent values and attributes. I very much like America's fundamental respect for every individual, regardless of racial, ethnic, or religious background, even though this value may be violated by some individuals or groups. I like the professional working environment and the pursuit of excellence. I respect the great achievements in science and technology and am grateful for their contributions to human knowledge. I admire and have benefited from the marvelous freedom to pursue economic opportunity. (I like Jay Leno and Frasier, too.)

On the other hand, I intensely dislike the natural propensity of the strong to kill, abuse, and rob the weak. Intellectually, I know that to be the way of humans but am unable to sit back and think, "Oh well, humans will be humans." It is especially difficult when this behaviour involves a country I have liked and respected. I disliked the U.S. during the Vietnam War: the struggle to defeat communism did not excuse the killing of so many poor and vulnerable villagers. I disliked the support for Saddam Hussein as he gassed Kurds and Iranians.[1] I dislike America's duplicity in preaching democracy while conspiring to overthrow democratically-elected governments, such as in Iran and Chile. For decades, America has been an accessory to the vicious plight of the Palestinians.[2] I hated the cruel shortages of food and medicines for Iraqi children and the many deaths.

---

1 See, for example, "Saddam Was Not Always Washington's 'Demon'."
<http://truthout.org/docs_03/040603G.shtml>.

2 See <http://www.krysstal.com/democracy_whyusa03.html> for the many U.N. resolutions—on everything from basic humanitarian questions to censure of Israel for illegal acts—which were vetoed by the U.S. Richard Perle, one of the architects of the "Project for a New American Century" and the war on Iraq, worked to undermine the *Camp David Accords* in the summer of 2000: see
<http://www.guardian.co.uk/israel/Story/0,2763,342857,00.html>.

However, in my case, the most important decision of my life was forced upon me not by the U.S. but by a local tyranny in Egypt under Gamal Abdel Nasser, a mentor of Saddam Hussein and enemy of the U.S. I was driven away from my old country by my refusal to subject myself to a dictatorship. When I arrived in the U.S., I was welcomed warmly and given the freedom to be myself. I had never experienced such liberty before. (My previous stay in Switzerland had been temporary, as a foreign student.)

I agree with those who felt that the U.S.-led attack against Iraq in March 2003 too closely resembled the imperialist actions of colonial times. Britain certainly would appear to be the right partner for such retrograde ventures. It is an experienced consultant in matters of imperial wrongdoing. It can assist the U.S. to divide and rule. It can help understand and apply time-proven techniques for undermining and weakening societies and draining their wealth, while creating a façade of improvement. At the time of this writing, despite the joining of forces of old imperial experience and modern overwhelming firepower, to the surprise and dismay of the "Coalition", things are going badly in Iraq. What happened? Is the U.S. not following Britain's advice? Has Britain lost its imperialist touch? Perhaps the time for violent empire building is past. Perhaps the 2003 attack by Western powers against Muslims was one too many.

How much will the gap between American values and behaviour grow? The United States has unwisely—some would say amateurishly—trapped many of its men and resources in a guerrilla war, which could last a long time.

"The guerrilla has the initiative; it is he who begins the war, and he who decides when and where to strike. His military opponent must wait, and while waiting, he must be on guard everywhere.... The guerrilla fights the war of the flea, and his military enemy suffers the dog's disadvantage: too much to defend; too small, ubiquitous and agile an enemy to come to grips with. ... Time works for the guerrilla both in the field—where it costs the enemy a daily fortune to pursue him—and in the politico-economic arena."[3]

Terrorism appears to be expanding: I trust that our fearless leaders of the Free World are astute and careful enough to make sure that the "global war on terror" does not evolve into a "global guerrilla war."

---

3 Taber, *War of the Flea*, p22, p29.

I tentatively deduced at least two things from setbacks to the U.S. First, following decades of abuse from the West, victimized peoples are apparently sensitized and primed to immediately and violently resist colonial-style aggression. Second, the "foreign fighters" going into Iraq to help resist a neo-colonial occupation, may be a foretaste of how globalization can enable an ever more unified "resistance" by the weak. (I rather suspect that many of these fighters do not see themselves as "foreign", meaning from outside the borders of Iraq. Western powers deliberately drew those artificial borders to weaken the region. They probably see themselves as simply coming to the aid of their Muslim brothers. However, American soldiers certainly are foreign fighters in Iraq.)

If the resistance in Iraq continues and the Americans continue to try and subjugate it, they would have to resort to ever more cruel force. The gap between what America has become and what it imagines itself to be will continue to grow. It will become ever more uncomfortable and awkward to straddle the gap.

A Hope Reversed

My second dilemma has the potential for the most dire of consequences. It concerns a hope I had developed living in Canada and enjoying a free, democratic society. Since I became Canadian, whenever I visited any Middle-Eastern country I was reminded of stark differences. As most Canadians know, civil liberties over there are severely restricted. National security is paramount, as "the state" must protect itself from outbursts of dissent from the people or any threat to the power of the unelected regime. Quality of life is sacrificed for security. Remaining in power is the highest priority of dictators. Intelligence services are given highest priority and are concerned primarily with spying on their own peoples. Arbitrary arrest and detention without charges is common. In times of trouble, these secretive organizations assume even greater importance, as do police and other law-enforcement agencies; their power and influence peaks as the rights and security of individual citizens declines even more.

For many years, I have been hoping to see the authoritarian, quasi-police-state environment in the region of my birth move towards the freedoms of North America. Instead, I have seen the freedoms in the U.S. degenerate in the direction of the levels of those in Egypt and other developing countries. Canada is somewhat affected too. The consequences of prioritizing security measures in North America since 9-11 are still far from what they are in primitive dictatorships. For the most part, it is specifically-targeted groups that feel uncomfortable: mainly Muslims, some non-white, native-born Americans, and miscellaneous political activists. The longer the aggrieved in distant lands are motivated to strike at the U.S., the longer the "War on Terrorism" will continue, the higher the probability will be of terrorist attacks, the more urgent the need will be for an increased focus on security, the more freedoms and liberties will be compromised, the more Canada will be affected, and the more American and perhaps Canadian societies will come to resemble those in undemocratic countries. My hope that things will improve over there has ebbed; now I merely hope that our society here does not come to resemble what I left behind. This is a tragedy, the magnitude of which at the time of this writing is being slowly recognized in North America.

How I Benefit from Injustice

The third dilemma arises from my being born and raised in a developing country, which, like many others, suffered invasion and occupation by a predatory Western country. The contradiction arose when I moved to the Western world which, as a whole, reaped material benefits from its unjust and immoral imperial aggression against the weak and vulnerable. I believe I understand both sides of this unequal relationship and have a deeper perception than most of those who know only one or the other. I left behind a plague of political corruption which, though it exists everywhere to some extent, is out of control in much of the Middle East. Incompetence compounds the problem. The West is not solely to blame; however, Western imperial powers deliberately contributed to these deficiencies, aggravating and prolonging them to weaken their victims so that they might better control them—a sad example of hurtful corruption.

Part of the wealth and prosperity of today's West is the well-deserved result of astute planning and hard work. But another part results from what I would call "ill-gotten seed-capital for industrial expansion, acquired through violence against militarily weaker societies." Having moved to the West, I find myself in the situation of benefiting from an environment achieved partly by injustices inflicted on peoples in other parts of the world, including where I was born and raised. This is the main reason I would not be comfortable living in countries that are former colonial powers, while I could see myself living in a country like Switzerland, even though it is rather unfriendly towards newcomers. Today's Canada, of course, is just right.

Neither Canada nor Switzerland enriched itself by killing people overseas. However, they and some others did benefit in a secondary and indirect way, by interaction and trade with countries that did commit crimes against the weak and vulnerable. Given the nature of our species, it would be too harsh to blame them for not choosing poverty instead.

Neither Canada nor Switzerland participated in the Anglo-American invasion of Iraq in 2003, which many call illegal, immoral, and unjustifiable. Morally, Switzerland is slightly ahead of Canada in this respect: it is completely neutral and would not consider participating in an invasion of Iraq or any other country. The government of Switzerland could not itself decide to participate even if it wanted to: involvement in any war would require approval by the people through a referendum. I am certain the answer would have been no, had the Swiss been asked to participate. In Canada, there were some pro-war demonstrations and some of the population advocated joining in this unequal conflict, believing Canada's prosperity to be dependent on at least some servility towards the greatest economic power in the world.

Immigrants like me who come from parts of the world at one time or another subjected to Western violence can empathize much more than other Canadians with the additional fear and misery piled upon existing fear and misery. I wonder if the matter can be quantified. Why not try to carefully weigh moral considerations against material benefits? What is the minimum acceptable threshold of monetary return to Canada before it agrees to participate in aggression against the Third World? Put another way, how many dollars of increased GNP should Canada expect to gain, or avoid losing, for every man, woman or child killed or maimed, to make participating in such wars worthwhile?

It would appear that Canada puts too high a price on human life to participate in the killing of yet more Iraqis. While some hundreds spoke in favour of joining the "Coalition of the Willing," some 250,000 people demonstrated against the invasion of Iraq in my Montreal alone, and similar demonstrations took place in cities across the country. If Canada had held a referendum, there is little doubt what the answer would have been, even though some business lobbies and politicians warned that retribution from the U.S. might hurt Canada's economy if we did not go along. The Liberal government chose a middle way, holding back from participation in the invasion of Iraq while providing support for security in the Persian Gulf. Canada would not be killing defenseless people for material gain. My burden is somewhat alleviated. My thanks go out to Canada for that.

Chapter 10: Tormenting the Weak and Vulnerable

I believe the Bush administration is being truthful when it expresses a fear of weapons of mass destruction in the hands of "rogue states," otherwise mostly known as former victims of Western imperialism. With such weapons, the day may come when formerly-oppressed countries will demand compensation for the injuries they suffered in the colonial era, and in subsequent neo-colonial activities of the U.S.

"Pay up to make us prosperous, too, or else we both go down. But you rich folk would lose more than we would, since we have nothing much to start with. As a first step, you will eliminate your unfair farm subsidies so that our own farmers can export and improve their lives a little. And we mean now!"

Such a threat would be called "justice" and "retribution" by the Third World and "blackmail" by the West. Despite official condemnation of the 9-11 terrorists by many unelected governments, emotions in the Third World ranged mainly from ambivalence to jubilation. That is because in regions traditionally tormented by the West, it seemed about time that someone struck back. Do the many millions in the poor world feel that the vicious attack might improve or exacerbate their sad plight? The question is moot. There are many who feel that revenge usually requires sacrifice. There is much hatred.

In my view, the United States has garnered somewhat more hate than it deserves. In addition to the results of its own policies, it has inherited the bitterness and resentment first engendered by the old colonial powers. As the old "savagely unjust" European empires expired, America stepped in to play a seemingly similar role. The old bitterness was redirected and added to the hate newly generated by the U.S. Its modified version of the old colonial style remained just that, until 9-11, when it was renamed a "clash of civilizations."

How to Attract Hostility and Hatred

My interest in seeing an end to old abusive imperial practices is twofold. First, though I have been away a long time, I still empathize with the downtrodden, having been exposed to their gloomy perspective in my youth. Second, I do not wish to attract their hostility and hatred to my new country, because in our increasingly shrinking world, there is a risk of very undesirable consequences here.

Polls taken a year after 9-11 showed that a majority of Canadians believed U.S. intrusions overseas were at least partly to blame for the attacks. (Such intrusions also generate public support for extremists.) On this issue, I agree with the majority of Canadians. The Gulf War of 1991 is but one of several motivators for the attacks on the core symbols of U.S. power, the Pentagon and World Trade Center. For the minority of Canadians who don't think blame must be shared at least a little by the U.S., here is my opinion on how a substantial portion of the population in my old country and region have internalized the saga of the 1991 Gulf War:

There was a widespread perception in the Arab and Muslim world that Saddam Hussein was a ruthless dictator who routinely and cruelly eliminated his enemies. Those who would have chosen to live under his rule were the destitute whom he did not fear and those—destitute or not—who could garner some benefits from his regime. In the 1980s, the U.S. supported this brutal unelected ruler when he attacked Iran, at the time still a new, shaky, and confused Islamic Republic, brimming with fanaticism and resentment against the U.S. in particular. Iraq was given carte blanche to procure weapons and military technology. Western companies flocked to supply billions of dollars' worth, including the know-how and materials to produce missiles and weapons of mass destruction.

Iran was helped too: the immoral policy of the West was to help keep the war going as long as possible. Never mind the death toll among Iraqis and Iranians. When Saddam used chemical weapons against Kurdish villagers in 1989, the U.S. looked the other way. At that time, the mainstream media showed scenes of dead women and children once or twice, then the subject was dropped. The flow of military assets to Iraq continued. A couple of years later the war ended, unfortunately from the U.S.'s perspective, when Iran could not continue and sued for peace.

Suddenly, Saddam Hussein was no longer useful and became a menace, heavily armed and continuing with programs to build rockets and weapons of mass destruction. Iraq became a threat to U.S. interests, especially in oil. It could eventually neutralize Israel's nuclear weapons advantage through a mini-balance of terror. This was unthinkable: the Arabs must be kept weak and divided. It was time to provoke Iraq by pushing Kuwait into arrogantly demanding the repayment of the billions it had paid in support of the war. (These payments, incidentally, had helped protect the Emir of Kuwait and his family from Iran and from some of his own people, many of them Shiites, like the great majority of Iranians.)

There was no warning given to Iraq not to attack Kuwait; in fact, the U.S. appeared to have no objections. When Saddam attacked, they threatened to evict him through war. President George Bush (Senior) said this would be done "for the sake of peace and security in the region." That sounded good and noble, until people realized he had said nothing about human rights, democracy, social justice, and an end to oppression. To the people of the area, "peace and security" became a code for: "a divided Arab nation governed by corrupt and easily-controlled rulers." No equivalent to Bismarck or Garibaldi or even George Washington must be allowed in that region.

Suddenly, the old, horrendous footage of dead Kurdish families—helpless victims of Saddam's barbaric chemical attacks two years earlier—were dug out of the archives and played over and over again to Western audiences. The purpose was to horrify them as part of a general media blitz to "prepare the public." Next, they proceeded to easily defeat Iraq, but they didn't change the regime. They did not assist the Kurds to the north or the Shiites to the south, despite encouraging them to rise up against Saddam. Saddam Hussein's regime was allowed to remain in power for two reasons: to serve as a counterbalance to Iran and to frighten local kings, emirs, and sultans into allowing U.S. forces to remain in the area for their own protection. The continued presence of U.S. forces in Saudi Arabia is one of the reasons for the fury of Osama Bin Laden and literally millions of others. (But who cared, since they were far away and weak and could not strike at us?)

To make sure Saddam remained somewhat powerful but not an unmanageable threat, the U.S. had U.N. inspectors sent to destroy dangerous weapons which could threaten to destabilize the "peace and security" of Iraq's neighbours, but they left him with sufficient conventional weaponry—tanks, helicopters, short-range rockets that could not reach Israel—to control Iraq. In addition, they imposed debilitating economic sanctions, ignoring the deprivation civilians would suffer.

Madeleine Albright, while she was secretary of state, was once asked by a reporter about the plight of Iraq's children. Though I know very well that humans have a low inhibition against killing and tormenting humans, I was still very surprised to see and hear her chilling answer on U.S. national television: "We are willing to pay that price."

I don't know how anyone in her position could compound the perception of ruthless arrogance by saying something like that. I am so glad she did not add: "We would most certainly not be willing to pay the price of our children dying from malnutrition and lack of medicines." The question of human rights—or even of human life—did not interfere with the U.S.'s pursuit of its interests. In the face of malicious intrusions by outsiders, the tyranny and terrible crimes of Saddam become a related but separate issue in the perception of those living in that tragic region. I cannot help but feel that among those who rejoiced at his downfall and humiliating capture, were the growing numbers of fundamentalists committed to a struggle to change the behaviour of the United States in the Muslim world.

With such a view-of-the-world widespread in the Middle-East—where it is "the truth"—Canadians can judge for themselves whether they are justified in their rage against the United States. The fact that Americans have their own different "truth" matters not at all.

To me, the professed desire to bring democracy and freedom to Iraq was merely an excuse for a new aggression. (The U.S. proposed a series of excuses, in an apparent search for the most persuasive.) If the U.S. really wanted to bring democracy to the region, it had had a wonderful opportunity after driving out Saddam's forces from Kuwait. The unelected Emir and his family had fled. The U.S. could have brought in a democratic system. It could have kept him away, told him to go live in London or Paris and just enjoy his billions. Or it could have brought him back to Kuwait, while insisting that he reign as a titular head of state, while a freely elected leadership ruled. When oil was discovered in Kuwait after the expulsion of the Ottomans from the region, the British declared Kuwait a country, and their protectorate. The Emir and his family were supported by Britain in a prime example of casique, or puppet government: "O glorious Emir, our moderate Arab friend, you will at all times obey us and take care of our interests. In exchange, we will protect you and allow you to enrich yourself and your family beyond measure." By bringing back the Emir, everyone in the region could clearly see that the U.S. was following the example of the defunct British Empire.

At the time of this writing, Iraq has not fared better. Just after President Bush's speech to the United Nations General Assembly in September 2003, Paul Knox wrote:

> "The most revealing truth-twisting in Mr. Bush's address concerned the Iraqi governing Council, the body hand-picked by the U.S. authorities to help it run occupied Iraq. The country isn't even close to holding a postwar election. Nevertheless Mr. Bush called the council 'the first truly representative institution' there, and referred to Iraq as a 'young democracy.' ... Mr. Bush's words show how dangerously debased the word 'democracy' has become."[1]

It is little wonder that the capital of positive feelings I had held for the U.S. has declined noticeably since "Operation Desert Storm" (also known as "Operation Desert Slaughter"), except briefly after the 9-11 attacks, when, in a state of shock and anger, my sympathies were with the victims.

Class Struggles: From National to International

Following the media closely and talking to friends from many backgrounds, it seemed to me that practically all of us from all backgrounds shared the same severe shock on September 11, 2001.

I realized, however, that I felt something more than most Canadians and Americans. Essentially, I had immigrated to Canada to flee the wrath of the poor. Suddenly, I felt that the wrath of the poor and weak, which I had fled long ago from a place far away, had caught up with me in North America.

In my old country, the oppressed majority had been ruled by a small, wealthy, and indifferent elite. Their masters treated the peasants like dirt. My thinking has been permanently affected by the outcome of that situation. I have learned that when the oppressed poor overthrow their oppressors, sometimes the result might be no better than what existed

---

1 Paul Knox, "Bush at the UN: he seems faintly embarrassed." *Globe and Mail* (24 September 2003.)

before. What I had really fled, therefore, was the unfortunate result of the malicious interaction of the many poor and the few insensitive rich.

Until the end of the Industrial Revolution, it appears the struggle between the powerful rich and the weak poor had generally been between different social classes of the same countries. Now the scale has become global, and the struggle is growing to include the hatred of those in poor regions towards those in rich parts of the world. In the old, insular world of self-centered sovereign nation-states, those who perceived themselves as victims of injustice feared and loathed their local tyrants. The oppressed struck back within national borders or within distinct geographic limits. In the new environment, the weak have struck at their perceived tormentors halfway across the world.

Do the Jews "Control America"?

I regularly travel to Egypt, usually about once a year. In heated discussions, I insist that the American people are fundamentally more moral, just, and fair-minded than most other peoples I know. I have been told innumerable times, and often shouted at, that "the Jews control America." No, I say, the Jews just have an influence in America, one which is sometimes strong. It is very strong when it comes to Middle-Eastern issues and the interests of Israel. I talk about my own experiences there, such as the incident involving the chapel in my workplace. I tell my relatives and friends that I have seen how each religious, ethnic, and racial group favours its own but how there is nevertheless a nationalistic cement that holds most people together despite inter-ethnic rivalry. That cement is based on an ideal of fairness, the freedom to prosper, and respect for the law and human rights.

Yes, I say, the ideal is sometimes compromised and there are religious and racist fanatics, too. At the risk of oversimplifying to people who have not lived in the U.S., I say that various ethnic, business, trade union, religious, and other groups try to push their own agendas with politicians, the various levels of government and public opinion, in a political and media free-for-all. Some American groups are much more influential than others. These can achieve gains for themselves, sometimes at the expense of other groups. I say that the United States has been described as "special-interest driven."

Everywhere throughout history, wealth and power concentrate. "Amreeka," as it is pronounced in Egypt, is no exception. Simply put, in the democratic and free U.S.A, the power to rule is not concentrated in the hands of one man, clique, royal family, or the leaders of a political party. Nor is the power to rule absolute or unopposed. Nevertheless,

> "We are obliged to define as the goals of a given society those ends towards which the more or less coordinated efforts of the whole are directed—without regard to the harm they may do to individual members, even the majority. This means, in effect, that in those societies controlled by a dominant class which has the power to determine the direction of the coordinated efforts of the society, the goals of the society are the goals of this class."[2]

The way I explain it in Egypt is that in the U.S., the so-called dominant class is made up largely but not exclusively of a "mosaic of special interests" representing large and small chunks of the population. They compete, accommodate each other, and make deals and compromises as they pursue their special objectives. Sometimes they clash. Sometimes they are unable to reach or even pursue their special goals. In this structure, the likelihood for error on a national scale is lower than in the old monarchies and authoritarian countries, where one small clique or one person rules unopposed. "The people" can have a voice, particularly on issues they understand and which affect them directly: employment, inflation, and so on. Most importantly, the system has a much larger capacity for self-correction than elsewhere. The Jews have a strong influence, particularly with regard to Middle-Eastern issues, but no, they do not control America, let alone "the world." Like other powerful groups, they must be very careful not to become a target of national ire. They will back down when necessary. I usually add that Jews are democratic among themselves: there are those who support Sharon and the Likud, and there are others who very much against, and say so loudly and eloquently.[3] I sometimes add that when we have our own democracy, we too will be able to properly pursue our interests and resist our enemies. Usually such pronouncements are followed by silence and a change of subject.

---

2 Lenski, *Power and Privilege*. Lenski's ideas are a synthesis of two older theories regarding the interplay between individual interest and social interest.

3 See, for example, <http://www.jewishvoiceforpeace.org> and <http://www.jewsagainsttheoccupation.org>.

"Wherever I Go, 'They' Try to Manipulate Me"

Who is "they"? Everywhere I have been where I could understand the language, I have seen that the best way for the elites to achieve their goals while minimizing coercion is to persuade a majority of the people that the chosen goals are in the interest of society as a whole. Persuasion often looks very much like manipulation. The Roman statesman Marcus Tullius Cicero (106—43 BC) believed that the laws, attitudes, and values of a people are structured to suit the rulers and elite. Jean-Jacques Rousseau (1712—1778) also recognized this phenomenon.[4]

In the old absolute monarchies and in modern dictatorships, a ruling minority can use violence against those who stray from the imposed "consensus." Those whose beliefs differ are "enemies of the people" and may receive cruel and grotesque punishments. A kind of "double-think" sets in among oppressed people: publicly adopt the "truth" as laid out by dictators. Different ideas must remain private and must not be expressed. To be completely safe, don't even have any different ideas or thoughts. A slip of the tongue can bring big trouble. "The walls have ears."

In modern free democracies, elected governments are limited in their ability to use force against dissenting ideas peacefully expressed. I can see that the only way for the elite to have their way is to win the support, or at least the acquiescence, of a sufficiently large proportion of the population. Sometimes, support for the elite is well-deserved. Occasionally, reasonably honest leaders in an enlightened political system can serve the people well, even as they cater to their own self-interests.

The leadership elite in the United States has guided the country to victory in the Cold War—one of the greatest victories in history, achieved with negligible casualties on both sides, considering the fantastic destructive power available. It created an economy which generates unprecedented wealth. Though there are questions about the fairness of distribution of that wealth, most Americans love their country because (with some exceptions) it provides well, or at least adequately, in terms of universal human needs and goals.

As part of its overall competence, the dominant class is skilled at "manufacturing consent" to pursue certain objectives. In my view, though there is room for criticism, the U.S. elite has, on the whole, done

---

4 In *The Social Contract*.

much better for their people than other large powers (in addition to doing very well for themselves.) The communists had the genius of Marx, the brilliance of Lenin, the shrewdness of Stalin, and the enthusiastic obedience of millions of hopeful workers formerly oppressed by the czar. That leadership managed to maintain wretched living standards for their peoples and to establish conditions that in the end destroyed the U.S.S.R. The National Socialist German Workers Party (the Nazis) had their charismatic Führer, a most advanced military technology and the unflinching support—in the face of great hardship and horrendous losses—of many millions, including low-income industrial and rural workers. They committed monstrous atrocities and destroyed Germany, which ended up under foreign occupation for years. By comparison, the U.S. leadership elite has done very well indeed. In spite of whatever abuses and errors anyone may wish to point out, it has developed and adheres to a system seen as successful by most Americans. It is not my place to pronounce judgment on the U.S.'s ruling elite. It appears that the majority there feel that the American leadership collectively deserves their trust.

Obviously, however, not all actions by leaders and opinion shapers in even the best democracies are without selfish motives. The famous professor Noam Chomsky excels at showing how the elite in democracies use the mass media to manufacture consent and to manipulate public opinion to their advantage:

> "The major media and other ideological institutions will generally reflect the perspectives and interests of established power."[5]

The "truth" (perspective) that ordinary citizens learn to accept, in many cases, is the one that suits the rich and powerful. I was first introduced to how established power spins events to further its interests when I was about ten years old, well before I followed news reports in any media. Like many boys my age at that time, I had a stamp collection and greatly enjoyed the international flavour of my album. My father occasionally brought me additions for my collection and one day gave me a very handsome stamp. It was a large, monochrome green, ten-piastre stamp commemorating the entry of the Egyptian army into Palestine in 1948. It showed a very long, neat, and precise column of soldiers disappearing on the horizon into a map of Palestine. It had a

---

5 Chomsky, *Necessary Illusions*, p 10.

portrait of King Farouk in the upper left corner, young, handsome, and serene, appearing to preside over his army embarking on a noble effort.

I asked my father, "Where were our soldiers marching to?"

My father answered that they were going to Palestine.

"Why?"

"Because there was a war."

"Are they still there?" I asked.

"No, they left Palestine," he replied.

"Is there a stamp of them leaving Palestine?" I asked hopefully, with a view to enlarging my collection.

"No, there isn't."

"Why?" I asked.

"Because," my dad said, "when they were entering Palestine, they were winning. When they were leaving, they were losing."

In this case, the manipulation was done by omission: issue a beautiful stamp when we are winning and don't issue a stamp when we are losing.

That stamp attempted to increase the cooperation and national group cohesion of Egyptians by boosting their pride, reminding them that they had a brave army. It reflected nobility, since the army was helping a people in need. It further boosted their pride due to the fact that their army was winning. The cameo portrait of King Farouk was intended to associate all these good feelings—courage, pride, nobility, power, victory—with His Royal Highness. There was no stamp covering the humiliating retreat.

"The Evildoers Are Solely Responsible for 9-11"

Truth is the first casualty of all wars, including the "War on Terrorism" and the new global class war. Quite naturally, the "dominant class mosaic" in the U.S. pursues its interests partly through promoting the "right" perceptions among the public.[6] Within that structure, a number of special interest groups in the U.S. have an interest in my old part of the world, the Middle East. For example, there are special interest groups concerned with the aerospace industry and armaments. There are companies with fine expertise in engineering and infrastructure projects, such as water plants and airports. These can be very big-ticket items worth tens or hundreds of millions. Such

6 Chomsky, *Necessary Illusions*, p 10.

specialized lobbies can benefit handsomely from the ability to influence an administration. As far as I can tell, the biggest, but not the only, such influences come from two skilled and powerful special-interest groups with enormous stakes in the Middle East. I call them p^2, or "p-squared": Petroleum and Palestine.

For decades, these two special interests have pursued their goals on the backs of Middle-Eastern societies. They have been largely unopposed by other players in positions of power in the U.S. The p-squared players within the dominant class, pro-oil and pro-Israel, have collaborated, compromised with each other, and occasionally been at odds, as they used their influence in the system to achieve their goals. Whenever their interests converge—as in "keep them weak, keep them divided," etc.— they bring the economic and military power of the U.S. to bear. The 2003 aggression on Iraq represented such a conversion of interest: the petroleum group wanted to seize Iraq's oil, a great prize, and the pro-Israel group wanted to improve Israel's strategic position. There has not yet developed a Muslim or Arab component within the "dominant class mosaic," able to block such actions.

When there are setbacks and pain among the people, dominant classes all over the world will go to great lengths to shift responsibility away from themselves. Manufacturing consent is especially important in times of difficulty and pain. Since 9-11, it has been very important for p-squared and other special interests to deflect any hint of blame from themselves with regards to that disaster.[7] Whether or not or to whatever the degree the United States is to blame, the leadership class must strive to ensure that the majority of Americans never come to believe what the majority of Canadians believe: that the United States is at least partly, if not principally, responsible for the deaths and destruction at home. If there are deficiencies, they must be seen to be of a technical nature, such as a failure in intelligence gathering and coordination. I agree with Chomsky when, in one of his bestsellers, he writes:

> "It is convenient for Western intellectuals to speak of 'deeper causes' such as hatred of Western values and progress. That is a useful way to avoid questions about the origins of the bin Laden network itself, and

---

7 In November 2003, as President Bush was visiting Britain, two murderous truck bombs struck British interests in Istanbul. At the same time in London, some of the tens of thousands of protestors against the war in Iraq blamed the policies of America and Britain. British Foreign Minister Jack Straw responded, that the responsibility for the atrocity must never be shifted away from the terrorists. That is important, for the most likely place it would shift is to himself, his colleagues and predecessors, and their American counterparts.

about the practices that lead to anger, fear, and desperation throughout the region, and provide a reservoir from which radical terrorist cells can sometimes draw. Since the answers to these questions are rather clear, and are inconsistent with preferred doctrine, it is better to dismiss the questions as 'superficial' and 'insignificant' and to turn to 'deeper causes' that are in fact more superficial, even insofar as they are at all relevant."[8]

Sophists[9] and sycophants in the service of the dominant class denigrate and ridicule what they call the "root-cause crowd." Their message is simple: "Don't think too deeply and accept only our truth: we are always good and the other guys are always bad. The timid and the appeasers among us are a danger to our national security."

Linking Chomsky's words with Samantha Power's thesis about the gap between American values and American policy, the task of Western sophists and sycophants, is to disguise that gap and render it invisible to at least the majority of the population. The "deeper causes" presented to the American public must explain the reasons for killing and abusing people overseas in a way that fits comfortably into the framework of noble and fair values of ordinary Americans. One of the reasons I am proud to be Canadian is that we are collectively more able to detect and resist the gap and are more inclined to try and influence our foreign policy according to our values. Living in Canada, I find opposing viewpoints galore on topics of interest to me without having to visit the local library or research the Internet. For example, programs such as "counterSpin" and "Hot Type" on CBC television present a wide range of opinions. The daily national newspaper, The *Globe and Mail*, regularly prints articles and opinion pieces representing opposing viewpoints. Such a level of media service to the public is not to be found in every country.

Envy Is Not a Motivator for Murder

One explanation for 9-11 has been particularly effective in deflecting blame away from the architects of United States policies that attract hostility: envy. Simply put, the argument is: "They envy us because we are rich and they are poor." The conclusion to be drawn from this skillfully constructed illusion is that there is really nothing that can be

---

8 Chomsky, *9-11*, p 77.

9 The Sophists of Ancient Greece reasoned like some corporate lawyers today, who may say, "Tobacco products do not cause cancer, but even if it they do, some people would die earlier, relieving pressure on the health system at great savings to the public."

done to placate those who hate us. There is no reason for their hatred except our success, of which we are justifiably proud. We are rich and good, for we are competent at creating wealth and have harmed no one. They are poor and evil, for they are incompetent and obsessed by the sin of envy. The only option we have is to defend ourselves by hitting them hard, while bearing the inconvenience of increased homeland security. Nobody explains why Switzerland, today the most successful and prosperous country in Europe, is not the target of envy-related terrorist attacks, or any terrorist attacks.

Having grown up in a small privileged class in a vast ocean of poverty, my experience compels me to agree with Prime Minister Jean Chrétien when, in a CBC interview on September 11, 2002, he linked poverty to terrorism. I also agree with some hawkish supporters of p^2 that poverty is not in itself a motivator for violence. It would seem contradictory to agree with the proponents of two opposing perspectives. The explanation is that in the case of the p^2 group, we have a fine example of manipulation by omission, reminiscent of my old stamp collection.

Many formative years spent in an environment severely polarized between rich and poor should qualify me to comment on the psychology of envy. It is an emotion which very rarely, if ever, leads to murder. Even more, it is certainly not known to lead to sufficient desperation to motivate the envious to give their lives in order to kill the envied. The outcome of envy is not suicide and murder, but *Schadenfreude*[10] whenever the envied suffer losses.

I also learned that the overwhelming majority in many developing countries is very religious and fatalistic: there is a widespread belief that God distributes wealth and power as He sees fit. In Muslim countries, if the rich are perceived to be noble and just, they are seen to have been favoured by God. There will be admiration for them. The poor will seek to emulate their success, cultivate their friendship, and perhaps hope for charity. Only when the rich and powerful are seen to be oppressive and unjust do they become hated. Injustice alone is seen as beneath contempt. The greatest emotion and determination occur when the rich and powerful engage directly in killing the poor and weak. Then it becomes the duty of the brave, just, and virtuous, whether rich or poor, to fight against injustice. Individuals from any social and economic class

---

10 *Schadenfreude* is the experiencing of pleasure at the misfortune of others.

might take up the cause of resistance against injustice. (Ernesto "Che" Guevara—who condoned violence by the poor against injustice by the rich—was a physician.) Poverty alone—with or without envy—is insufficient to generate widespread, systematic terrorism.

Conservative politicians such as Brian Mulroney and Stephen Harper attacked Jean Chrétien's linking of poverty and terrorism as "disgraceful" and worse. Those in the mainstream media who propagate the "preferred doctrine" of the political right came up with angry rebuttals. In the U.S., many media editors and reporters who work for the rich and powerful studiously avoid mentioning the part about injustice and oppression of the poor as catalysts for terrorism. Manipulation by omission is probably the safest kind, since no outright lies need be told. I see in it a sophisticated form of corruption. Nothing in my family background, education, or career inclines me to lean away from the political right and towards the left. However, using wealth and influence to manufacture a consensus so that we may use our advanced technology to safely (or so we thought) drop bombs from a great height, or inflict malnutrition and disease on poor defenseless people in faraway lands, is where I draw the line. Clearly, I will not be voting for a party of the right until there are changes. Other immigrants I know share my view. This is one way that the increasing numbers of Canadians from former colonies will have a growing impact on Canadian politics.

Can the War on Terror Be Won?

To my knowledge, the 9-11 attack was the first occasion when terrorists from a weak and poor region struck so viciously and dramatically at the heart of what they saw as an oppressor-nation. The continued ability of the poor to strike at the rich is uncertain, even in the age of globalization. It is too early to tell whether 9-11 was an opening salvo in an enduring new ability of the poor world to strike at the rich world. I am no expert on how to pursue our interests through the global use of military and economic power. I cannot gauge how far we can safely go in enraging others and how well our superior technology and organization can combat their passionate hatred and apparently bountiful source of recruits. I hope and pray that the "War on Terror" will stop such attacks entirely. Perhaps giving up some civil liberties for the sake of "homeland security" will make attacks like 9-11 too rare to make matters even worse. But I feel a knot in my stomach every time I think of the course the U.S. leadership has apparently decided to pursue. Even though it has often generated success in the past, my concern this time is that we can only win the war against terrorism if we also fight oppression, injustice and poverty.

Only extremely important benefits can lead to actions and policies which enrage people enough that they are willing to die in order to strike at us now, or in some years from now, or when their children have grown enough to take up the cause. We can take our cue from the state of Israel, which, more than half a century after its creation, can have neither peace nor security and says it must still fight for its very survival despite mounting cruelty and casualties. It must continue to war against those it wronged so long ago as well as their descendants, who have not forgotten.

Of course, not everything that special-interest groups do is against the common good. Honest lobbying is a legitimate part of democracy. Also, when one special interest goes too far, another often rises up to act as a political counterforce. Whatever the case, the dominant class in the U.S. does not have to convince every last American that its way is the right way: in democratic systems, a majority is enough. Intuitively, I think that about 25% of Americans have a good understanding of various viewpoints and are difficult to manipulate. Others are ambivalent. What matters is that the establishment be competent and able to forge a consensus in the voting public.

Many in this voting public I call "jaywalkers," after Jay Leno's thoroughly enjoyable "Tonight Show," presented on weeknights on NBC. In some segments, Jay walks around asking members of the American public—sometimes on university campuses—questions like, "Who were the enemies of the United States during World War II?" and "What country is on the other side of our northern border?" Answers can be hilarious and great fun to watch. The downside of all this is that too many jaywalkers in a society enable the dominant class to unfurl flags and banners, sound the bugles, and point at anyone they dislike, creating support against a hand-picked "evil target." It does not help vulnerable peoples in faraway lands that Americans are on the whole decent, moral, and fair-minded if so many of them are so easily manipulated.

Since about the end of the Cold War, America has been called a rogue state. In my view, this is correct if the definition of a rogue state is one that thinks it is so powerful it can act with impunity and abuse others, whether for perceived self-defense or for gain. (The line between the two is subject to interpretation.) If I were to compile a list of modern states by degrees of "roguery" over the last century or so with the worst at the top, the U.S. would be some distance down, nearer to the bottom. I am disappointed that one of the two best countries in the world (the other being Canada) behaves much like any other country when it perceives it has a military advantage. I am reminded yet again that we all belong to the same species. Something Nietzsche said comes to mind: "The more I understand humans, the more I come to respect animals."

Philosophy aside, I saw the wrath of the poor early in my life. It was not pretty. By coming to Canada, I thought I had escaped such conflicts for the rest of my days. However, for the second time in my life, I am being adversely affected by the obsession of the poor to get back at the rich. The outcome is not easily predictable.

Can I Hope to Be Wrong about U.S. Intentions?

Anything that does not fit into the awful perception of the United States comes as a confusing shock. When President Bush and members of his administration—Secretary of State Colin Powell, Deputy Secretary of Defense Paul Wolfowitz, and others—say the purpose of the 2003 invasion of Iraq was to bring democracy to the people, practically no one in the Muslim world believes a word they say. Those with even minimal knowledge might scrutinize the name "Wolfowitz": "Sounds Jewish. He is a hawk who was active in pushing for the illegal, immoral, and unjustified attack against our brothers in Iraq. He must be a Jew. Of course, his principal aim is to smash any country that has the potential to one day threaten Israel. Iraq has a substantial population with significant education, and wealth in oil. It could one day become a danger to Israel." Middle-Easterners are not alone in this kind thinking. Some "self-hating Jews" agree. From Joe Klein:

> "A stronger Israel is very much embedded in the rationale for war with Iraq. It is a part of the argument that dare not speak its name, a fantasy quietly cherished by the neo-conservative faction in the Bush

administration and by many leaders of the American Jewish community. The fantasy involves a domino theory. The destruction of Saddam's Iraq will not only remove an enemy of long-standing but will also change the basic power equation in the region. It will send a message to Syria and Iran about the perils of support for Islamic terrorists. It will send a message to the Palestinians too: Democratize and make peace on Israeli terms, or forget about a state of your own." [11]

Therefore, Iraq must be smashed. Mr. Wolfowitz uses his position in the Bush administration to keep the Ay-rabs weak and divided.

One day the spring of 2003, it is fleetingly reported, Paul Wolfowitz said that the United States must promote democracy in the Middle East even if it is against its short-term interests, because it would be in its long-term interest. I reacted with surprise:

"What? He said that? No way! The man is a Jewish hawk and probably a friend of Prime Minister Sharon. It can't be true. His words don't fit with the record of U.S. aggression. It's a ruse. But what if it is true? Is the U.S. really becoming interested in spreading real democracy in the world, even if it means that these democratically-elected governments might have interests contrary to those of the U.S.A.?"

Other tidbits of intriguing ideas surface here and there. A prominent and generally reliable American "capitalist" business publication presented an article about the "challenges [of] planting the seeds of democracy in the Middle East."[12] Something new seemed to be happening. Then in November 2003, as things were going badly in Iraq, President George W. Bush made the clearest statement yet that appeared to indicate the United States might now genuinely prefer democracy in the Middle-East.

> "President Bush challenged Iran and Syria and even key U.S. ally Egypt to adopt democracy and declared past U.S. policy of supporting non-democratic Arab leaders a failure. … [He said] 'Sixty years of Western nations excusing and accommodating the lack of freedom in the Middle East did nothing to make us safe, because in the long run stability cannot be purchased at the expense of liberty'."[13]

11 *Time Magazine*,, 5 February 2003, online edition: <http://www.time.com/time/columnist/printout/0,8816,419688,00.html>

12 Cover story, *Business Week*, 21 April 2003.

13 Terence Hunt, White House correspondent, Associated Press, "Bush: Mideast Must Move Toward Democracy", 5 November 2003. From Yahoo News: <http://story.news.yahoo.com/>.

Initially, it all seemed too wonderful even to contemplate. Upon further reflection, it is not completely unthinkable. It would not be a first in human history: something similar has happened before. For a time after their revolution, the French became idealists about their "liberty, equality, fraternity." In the late eighteenth and early nineteenth centuries, their armies went around Europe defeating and deposing royal dynasties and establishing republics.[14] They laid the foundation for a democratic Europe. Could the U.S. assume a similar role in the forlorn countries of the world that still have no democracy, even though the governments that initially came to power democratically could be anti-American?

If so, it would begin to close Samantha Power's "gap between U.S. values and actions." I could once again see the U.S. as I did in my early youth. It almost seems too much to hope for, except that now there is a good reason for a tiny glimmer of optimism: self-interest would motivate United States support for genuine democracy in the Middle East and elsewhere. Self-interest or not, in the unlikely event that it proves to be true, my admiration for America would again rise. Before long, the War on Terror would be won, because too few people would see a need for terrorism. I would even be willing to stop quoting Nietzsche...

---

14 My involvement with classical music sometimes gives me a unique insight into historical events. The French had so many sympathizers among the oppressed European citizenry that "La Marseillaise," the anthem of the French Revolution, was banned by a fearful emperor within all territories of the Austrian (Hapsburg) Empire. Some subjects managed to find creative ways to express support for the French. Composer Robert Schumann wrote a piano piece describing a "Carnival in Vienna." It consists of melodies representing the various fun-filled activities of the carnival. Suddenly, out of the blue, there appear a few bars that sound suspiciously like the "Marseillaise."

Chapter 11: To Plague the Inventor

Muslim Arabs see a cruel policy in which the U.S. pursues its self-interests abroad at great cost to their societies. In sheer frustration at their inability to influence the U.S. through peaceful means, some have turned to extreme violence. An invasion by foreigners is one thing—formal warfare is quite common in human affairs. But some of those involved in the 9-11 attack had apparently been living in America for a long time. It is base, the height of treachery, to live and work among a people for years, accept their hospitality, be treated as equals, earn a living and benefit from their prosperous socio-economic environment, then turn against them in this vicious and appalling manner. According to my education, there is nothing Islamic about such behaviour. It was immoral and very wrong. In addition, even though some have despaired about stopping malicious and often violent intrusions in the Muslim world except through violence, killing civilians crosses the line.

What Should North American Muslims Do?

When I am asked, "What, then, should Muslims do to help their brothers in such dire straits in Palestine, Iraq, Chechnya, and elsewhere?" I believe my answer does not seem compelling and cogent to many of the deeply troubled and impatient. I acknowledge the U.S.'s unsavoury role but also point out that a substantial part of the troubles in the Middle East are results of the debilitating legacy of European colonialism, not of U.S. wrongdoing. Another reason for their troubles, I must admit, has its roots in the region itself. Then I suggest patience and hard work in order to turn the tide of public opinion in the United States, as has now happened in much of Europe. Bin Laden's call for violence, in contrast, is inspiring and exciting for millions who pine to strike back at the aggressors from abroad, who seek gain from the weakness and misery of the Muslim world. Millions adore him. Many more would flock to his banner if they could. Some of these tend to write off people like me. Some extremists, though not all, see us as having run away from the problem and moved to Canada to pursue the good life. Some see people like me, who chose to become Canadian, as sell-outs.

Religious fanatics who write off North American Muslims are making a mistake.

I have seen a number of reports that Islam is the fastest growing faith in North America. In my opinion, North American Muslims will exert the best influence on Islam in the coming years due to the interaction of two elements: the populist and benign but pragmatic nature of Islam, which responds so very well to the human condition; and the widespread values of freedom, tolerance, justice, and respect for every human being. These are values preached by Islam. However, at this time in our history, I don't know where in the world they are practiced.

North America seems to hold the best hope. As a "new North American," I can confirm to Muslims all over the world that I have found these characteristics here. I sometimes say that, to the best of my knowledge, Canada adheres more to Muslim values than any country I know well enough to be able to judge. The United States comes in second, due mainly to its relative neglect of its own poor. There are flaws and lapses and some injustices, but these do not damage the overall texture, at least so far.

Slowly, peacefully, as the Muslim community establishes itself, it will be able to develop its fair share of influence on policy. I doubt that rivals or enemies of this growing influence will be able to crush it. That would be difficult to do without damaging these free and democratic societies themselves, potentially threatening the security of all ethnic and religious groups. The North American Muslim community some day should be in a position to help Muslims worldwide, by example and through mediation and the bridging of cultures. This can be done by peaceful means, so that even the likes of Bin Laden will find it unnecessary to ignore the rules of their faith and kill civilians. This is the type of solution I point to if asked what should be done to help Muslims under duress. At this time, my view seems implausible and whimsical to more than just impatient fanatics. It does not compare to spectacular views of fireballs engulfing buildings and causing thousands of deaths among the "evildoers."

Violence against American civilians seems all the more unfair because the U.S. gives its Muslim citizens the freedom to practice their faith and express their opinions peacefully and securely. In spring of 2003, at my niece Nora's wedding in Cairo, I had the good fortune to be introduced to Mrs. Azmeralda Alfi by another niece, Sherein (the very same with whom the discussion took place a year earlier regarding "how an individual comes to know that something is true".) Mrs. Alfi is administrator of the Bureau of Islamic and Arabic Education (BIAE) in Los Angeles, California. We even managed to have a little chat in the midst of the festivities. She confirmed what I already knew: she could practice her faith in the U.S. in complete freedom. At one point I asked, "How do you get along with the Jewish community? Is there hostility?"

"I would say the contrary," she responded. "There is cooperation with Jewish educational institutions. We face similar problems in educating our respective children in our languages (Arabic and Hebrew), which are not common in the U.S. We exchange ideas and learn from each other's experiences. But we make it clear that when we communicate, we will not discuss politics."

Back in Canada, I visited BIAE's Web site and found a presentation of a number of the essential ideas of Islam, freely and eloquently expressed. Some of what I found:

> Our mission is to secure the future of Islam in America, with Muslims, as part of the American pluralism that is distinguished by positive contributions that set the example for others.
> O you who have attained to faith! Be ever steadfast in upholding equity...
> There shall be no coercion in matters of faith.
> Peace should not be violated unless the alternative will be tyranny and oppression that cannot be stopped by other means...[1]

In my mind, the conduct and contributions of North American Muslims can be very valuable in promoting mutual understanding and respect and in reducing the chances of violence and a prolonged "clash of civilizations."

A Nation-State Cannot Defeat a Religious Faith

The U.S. is officially doing its best to treat the American Muslim community fairly and to protect it from belligerent citizens who have been manipulated by groups hostile to Islam. In addition to adhering to its values, the U.S. is acting astutely by insisting that its "War on Terrorism" is not a war against Islam or Muslims. To demonstrate this, President George W. Bush made a well-publicized visit to a mosque. He

---

1 <http://www.biae.net/>

and high-ranking members of his administration repeat often that this is not a war against Islam. I find that to be wise, for I believe that no nation-state can defeat a well-established, timeless faith such as Islam.

The Soviet Union had the power to destroy the world. It was ideologically driven to eliminate Christianity. Churches were destroyed. Clerics and religious figures were severely abused or killed. Ordinary citizens who showed any sign of religiosity were mistrusted, denied advancement, and kept to remain forever on waiting lists for Ladas and even the most humble apartments. All this was supported by a carefully-crafted ideology that was attractive to many. Ideologues carried out a "scientific," well-thought-out and persistent campaign of "exposing" religion as the "opium of the masses."

In the end, the Communists could not even eliminate Christianity within territory they controlled completely. Now the U.S.S.R., the terrible superpower that terrified everyone for decades, is gone. Churches have been rebuilt and Christianity is back.

The Soviet Union also tried to suppress Islam. While a student in Zurich, I remember being invited to a dinner party organized by the Soviet embassy for dozens of students from various countries. It was the height of the Cold War, and I was president of the Arab Students Association. Although the main purpose of the event was public relations, it was also an attempt to recruit students, who would eventually go back home to their various countries as Soviet agents. I asked one of our Russian hosts about Islam in his country.

"Some old people still practice it," he responded ever so diplomatically. "But the young, educated ones prefer a new ideology and the modern ideas that make us a great power." We know how all that turned out.

(A few months later, the U.S. embassy countered by also inviting me to supper, also as one of a group of students. It was a relaxed affair, organized differently. After meeting somewhere for aperitifs and introductions, we broke up and went to the individual homes of the embassy staff to dine with their families, including their kids. It was the first time I had been in an American home and I remember enjoying the friendly, informal atmosphere. After supper, the kids went to bed. What started out as a friendly chat about our respective homelands eventually turned to a heated but polite conversation about Israel. Essentially, my hosts wanted to know why we Egyptians didn't like Israel, while I explained in no uncertain terms. At one point, the lady of the house said, "You know, the U.S. wants to be friendly with your people."

"I would like that too," I said. "Let's be friends and let the Soviets support Israel." I deduced from their reaction that they had never heard of such an absurd idea.)

Nazi Germany declared war on Judaism. For a while, it was invincible and could rely on diligent, efficient, and competent professionals to implement systematic plans to wipe out the Jews. The Nazis are in the garbage can of history and the Jews, after some terrible losses, are doing fine.

Similarly, after what I hope will be a long time, when Canada and the United States have ceased to exist as sovereign nation-states in their present forms, Islam will continue to be a powerful force in human affairs. Regardless, the backlash from religious persecution should not be underestimated. The Roman crowds cheered when Christians were thrown to the lions. However, every time lions devoured a Christian, a few of the spectators left the Coliseum in a mood of thoughtfulness and discomfort. Many were intrigued. More and more subsequently converted to the faith of the victims. Islam is a universal and welcoming faith, centered on the individual. In my view, persecuting Muslims because of their religion will lead to the same effect in open-minded North America. In the United States, this effect could be especially powerful among the large underclass, which sees itself as marginalized and neglected. Along with the undesirable characteristics of human behaviour, there are noble and kind traits. Among these is the propensity to empathize with and help the victims of abuse.

In spite of the efforts of the U.S. to remain true to its values and not to go to war against Islam as a whole, many Muslims believe they are doing just that.[2] America apparently desires a weak and passive form of Islam that cannot serve as a universal rallying cry for resistance against intrusions in the Muslim world. A tiny minority of Muslims see it as their duty to strike at America, its allies, its military, its economy, and even its civilians. A tiny minority of about 1.2 billion Muslims still adds up to a very large number.

---

2 And not without reason: President George W. Bush is a "born-again Christian" with close ties to fundamentalist evangelists, who rallied their congregations to vote for him. His immediate response to 9-11 included a call for a "crusade" and a Biblical declaration that "He who is not with us is against us."

Learning from the Rich and Powerful

I must confess that I am puzzled as well as distressed when radical Muslims kill civilians and must condemn such attacks in the strongest terms. It seems that 9-11 was designed to change the behaviour of the U.S., largely the same reasons the U.S. bombed Vietnam. The attackers on 9-11 apparently were all devout or fanatical Muslims. From what I can tell, such people generally have the same goals and desires as most people, regardless of faith. This might include dignity, material belongings, a good life for their families, and so on. For the very religious, however, the pursuit of worldly objectives must never interfere with the highest objective of all: to enter Paradise.

I am no Islamic scholar. Still, I have been taught that Islam sternly prohibits the killing or abuse of civilians and other non-combatants, such as prisoners of war. There are certainly no exceptions to exonerate the deliberate mass killing of civilians. Attacking armed and hostile forces in wartime is one thing—losing one's life for such a righteous cause will be rewarded in Paradise. After 9-11, I wondered what could have justified the killing of thousands of non-combatants in the minds of these apparently pious Muslims, and how they still believed that they would not incur the wrath of God and would not jeopardize their place in Heaven.

I can think of only one explanation. All over the world, in many cultures, peoples copy useful and advanced aspects of Western culture. They often enjoy participation in harmless Western-style fun. They also sometimes internalize ugly components of the West's civilization. The "sacred warriors" of 9-11 in their zeal, rage, and desperation somehow felt justified in deviating from the rules of Islam in order to copy a most abhorrent technique of the rich, powerful, and successful West. For, in modern times, the mass killing of civilians to achieve military and political goals is indeed an invention of the West.

Deliberately making war on civilians is a relatively recent invention.[3] What today is routinely accepted as "collateral damage" was once seen as conduct unbefitting a gentleman-warrior. During World War I, American aviators refused to participate in air raids over Europe that might endanger civilians. At the beginning of that same war, German submariners gave warning and time for crews to escape their ships

---

3 Without taking into consideration atrocities committed many centuries ago, such as when the Mongols slaughtered the entire civilian populations of a number of cities they had conquered, including Baghdad in A.D. 1258.

before they torpedoed them. However, the concept of "honour" declined swiftly thereafter. Among Western innovations is the mass bombing of large cities, first used by Hitler in Spain then enthusiastically adopted and expanded upon by the likes of the RAF's "Bomber Harris." Near the end of World War II, the German cities of Hamburg and Dresden were attacked by bombers dropping alternating waves of high explosive and incendiary bombs, an attack designed to kill as many civilians as possible. The genocide of concentration camps is a Western invention.[4] Other notorious examples are the nuclear attacks against the civilian populations of Hiroshima and Nagasaki. These were deliberate, calculated attacks designed to massacre tens of thousands of civilians, with the political goal being the surrender of Japan. As usual, Western apologist "scholars" invoke noble reasons and explanations. They say this act probably saved the lives of many more American and Japanese by ending the war quickly. Perhaps this was indeed so. But Islam accepts no excuses or justifications for deliberately killing civilians.

The only explanation I can posit is that 9-11 was the result of years of torment and rage, blinding some people to the values of their faith and heritage. They copied the very worst aspects of Western behaviour in their desire for similar success:

> "...that we but teach bloody instructions, which, being taught, return to plague the inventor."[5]

There are millions in the West (whom I naturally consider to be knowledgeable and informed) who at least understand the reasons for my perspectives. But I do understand and sympathize with the millions of those in the West who might shut out such ideas and refuse to recognize or countenance that their beloved nation-states led the way and, by example, taught others to engage in the mass killing of civilians, as a way to achieve political or economic gains. Referring to Morgenthau,[6] there is an "abstraction" (my country) with which we are inculcated since early childhood and throughout our lives, and to which our identities and self-esteem are closely tied. That abstraction may not

---

4 The British are generally credited with inventing the concentration of civilian populations in special camps during the Boer War in South Africa. As they made no progress in the war and suffered heavy losses, they rounded up the families of Afrikaans fighters and incarcerated them in concentration camps. Conditions were so bad that many women and children died, which became a major factor in the eventual surrender of the rebels.

5 Macbeth, Act I, Scene vii.

6 In chapter 1.

encompass anything ignoble or reprehensible. In the West, to acknowledge that the mass killing of our civilians is a result of others copying our own techniques, is strictly taboo.

Part III

Quebec and Immigrants: Reduced Mutual affinity

Chapter 12: Coercion and Failure

Taboos

There exist taboos in most countries and societies, about things that must remain unsaid and topics that must remain unbreached. One such topic, seldom spoken about, is the sometimes uneasy relationship between immigrants and Quebec. Statistics Canada has determined that Quebec is losing in relative demographic weight every year. A fundamental reason is that proportionately fewer immigrants come to Quebec and stay here than go to other parts of Canada. Being an immigrant myself, I am all too aware of the reasons why this is the case. The reasons are primordial and relate to the needs of our species.

Whenever I bare my soul and try to articulate these reasons—a difficult and gut-wrenching process at the best of times—I find that many Québécois shut out my concerns and begin to explain the legitimate and good reasons Quebec has to "defend itself." I know these reasons. I was born in a downtrodden colony of the British Empire. My grandmother was shot and wounded by the occupying British army during an Egyptian intifada in the 1920s. Foreigners—Europeans—dominated the economy and discriminated against and disrespected Egyptians until the oppressed drove them out. I do empathize with what Quebec has had to face. Conversely, it seems many Quebecers do not understand the difficult and anxious process of crossing cultures. Most seem unfamiliar with the obsessive drive of immigrants, first to survive and then to succeed. These priorities marginalize many other considerations.

I am fortunate to have a good choice of places in the world to live. Quebec has been, and is still, my choice. Yet, most immigrants do not feel as I do, and in my view, this endangers the future of French language and culture in North America. It is not for me to tell Québécois what to do, but I am qualified to inform them as to why too few immigrants have come over the last decades, and why this is dangerous. Whenever I try, it is often interpreted as "Quebec bashing."

The purpose of this discussion is to show how the thinking of immigrants differs from that of native-born Québécois. Following are some of the conclusions I have drawn based on conversations with others as well as my own observations. If I were to as address the issue from a native-born Quebecer's perspective, my message would be almost useless, since it would not reveal anything about the special mindset of immigrants or explain why they might be drawn to, but also repelled by, Quebec.

Having become familiar with a number of countries and societies, I know of none that have no flaws, even though they may have other wonderful attributes. Even the words "flaw" and "wonderful attribute" are subjective and can cause disagreement. There is no shame in any of this. Still, it is common for populations to be sensitive about what others call weaknesses, to paper them over and to make discussing them taboo. For decades there have been certain taboo subjects in Quebec. Attitudes towards many have relaxed, but some still remain, making it difficult to share my perspective with others, and making it difficult for many other immigrants to do the same.

Some nationalists and separatists might think that I "don't really understand" and that I haven't made "a proper assessment of Quebec-Canada relations." That in itself raises an interesting question. How is it that an immigrant who is fluent in French, who prefers living in Quebec, and who has been here many years still "doesn't understand?" Perhaps it is time for Quebec to make a genuine effort to learn about the anxieties of immigrants instead of making self-centered arguments about injustices of the past or the plight of Franco-Ontarians. In any case, by taking a stand and being honest about an immigrant perspective, perhaps I risk being denigrated and mocked as "too influenced by the English media," just as fine federalist Quebecers are insulted as *vendus*. Still, I have no ill will against Québécois, and feel that I can best serve my country and province by presenting my views honestly.

Distinct Impositions

Immigrants are expected to adapt and conform to the order that exists wherever they decide to settle. Most of them are eager to do so, to learn the dos and don'ts of their new home and to blend in. For this to happen, they must feel that the dislocation they go through and the efforts they expend are justified because their self-interest is better served in the new location. All individuals must make sacrifices for the common good. It behooves immigrants to find out as much as possible about the impositions and rewards in what may become their new country. They must feel that such impositions are justified or at least acceptable when weighed against the advantages. The impositions by Canada on its citizens are easy to accept and are lighter and fewer than in most countries I know.

In the 1970s, the Québécois embraced their nationalism and accepted special impositions on themselves because this served their interests at both the emotional and material levels. Nationalism eliminated the nasty "dees and dose" bias. It removed the emotional discomfort of domination by anglophones. It opened up new opportunities for material gain by filling the economic vacuum created by anglophone departures and by making French the official language of the workplace. To most Quebecers, these impositions, inspired by nationalism, were justified and acceptable. To many immigrants they were not, so they avoided Quebec.

Today, an increasing number of Quebecers find these nationalistic impositions more and more at odds with considerations of individual, material self-interest. To the extent that this trend reduces the distinct impositions Quebec places on all its individuals, the province can become more attractive to immigrants.

Everywhere I have been, most individuals accept the impositions placed upon them by society. Other individuals resist them when they clash with their self-interest. The purpose of coercion is to force adherence to the rules when persuasion fails. It is a grave and difficult responsibility, even for the most honest and benign leadership, to guide individuals through a combination of coercion and persuasion. Errors can be costly. In my view, societies that use less coercion are the better for it.

Over the years in Montreal, I learned that many Franco-Québécois have difficulty considering any viewpoint which suggests that an error was made any time in their history or that any aspect of their culture has not served them well compared to *les anglais*. That is taboo. In the early 1990s, I wrote a letter to the editor in which I bemoaned media reports that the high school dropout rate in Quebec's French school system was about 40%. I pointed out that the rate in the English school system was much lower (as a special example, the anglophone Lakeshore School Board had a dropout rate of less than 10%.) Before sending the letter, I sought the opinion of a bright young Québécoise, a professional working for a prominent financial institution. She did not like my letter.

"This is no good," she said. "You are saying the English are better than we are."

"Of course not," I said defensively. "How can you say that? All I am doing is quoting verifiable figures..." But it was no use; she was already walking away, shaking her head in vigorous disapproval. The centuries of exasperation were showing. I was sorry.

I changed the letter. It still bemoaned the high French dropout rate, but this time compared the forty-something percent to the 0.5% dropout rate in Japan, which was much lower than both the English and French. There was no mention of the English school system. I showed her the letter again, and this time it was all right. It did not matter that I was saying that the Japanese were much better than the Franco-Québécois in this specific respect. She didn't care about Japan or that the rate there was almost one-hundredth that of what it was here.[1]

As the 90s passed, there followed a degree of relaxation as the scars continue to heal. I noticed more willingness in the French media to address sensitive questions. By 2000, "the right questions" were being asked freely. An excellent article by Jules-Pascal Venne outlines how conditions in Quebec have changed and how he felt that his party, the Parti Québécois, should "re-evaluate its option,"[2] in other words, it should reconsider the impositions it wishes to place on people. Venne writes that the success of the "Quiet Revolution"[3] has made Quebec nationalism and the separatist option obsolete. The self-interests of many Quebecers are no longer served by politics and policies based on nationalism. I am sure such ideas are still heresy to die-hard separatists. But Venne's article gave me a moral boost and increased my feeling that I was "a real Quebecer." At last, questions near to my heart were being asked by at least one heavyweight intellectual of the PQ. Quebec's impositions were becoming less distinct.

---

1 Perhaps just a coincidence: though *The Gazette* published my letter, *La Presse* did not publish the French version.

2 Jules-Pascal Venne, "Le Parti Québécois devrait réévaluer son option," *La Presse*, 8 April 2000. The author is described as a former platform advisor and member of the executive of the Parti Québécois.

3 The "Quiet Revolution" designates the transformation of Quebec society after World War II from a primarily agricultural and insular society dominated by Anglo-Saxon-owned business and the Catholic Church to a secular, urbanized, and industrial society dominated by a Franco-Québécois business and political elite open to contact with the outside world.

Losing New France

Why did the once-great and apparently well-established colony of New France fail? Someone, at some time, must have made mistakes for such an historic catastrophe to have occurred. When I arrived in Montreal, though I was keenly aware of English-French rivalry in many parts of the world, I knew little or nothing about the history of the conflict between the two empires in North America. I looked into it and reached my own conclusions: two coercive measures contributed mightily to the loss of France's North American colonies: mercantilism and xenophobia. Though their two empires behaved similarly in many ways, England did do something better than France. While the English fostered population growth and economic prosperity in their North American colonies, New France continued their coercive measures, stifling prosperity and inhibiting population growth despite the high birthrates of the French settlers.

There is an opinion to the effect that "history is bunk."[4] I disagreed until I understood that this comment was referring to the highly subjective process of historical interpretation. Historians routinely spin events to favour their peoples, perspectives, or personal interests. In studying the fall of New France, having no particular affection for either empire, I had no personal interest in making either the English or the French look better than the other. I do, however, have a special interest in two serious flaws in New France that contributed to its fall and that still have a faint echo in modern Quebec, affecting me and other immigrants. In my view, they weaken Quebec as they weakened New France.

When Europeans and other immigrants began to come to the Americas in substantial numbers, many came as individuals or small groups of settlers. However, four sovereign nations came to the New World as formal powers and were able to establish enduring colonies, linked to their mother countries for many years. These are England, France, Spain, and Portugal. (Other colonies, founded by Sweden and Holland, disappeared after a brief existence.)

Today, it would be stating the obvious to say that the English language is doing very well in North America and indeed the rest of the world. Though vast territories originally claimed by Spain were lost to the United States, Spanish is the mother tongue of hundreds of millions

---

4 A maxim of Henry Ford, car-manufacturer and inventor of the Automotive Revolution.

in North, Central, and South America.[5] It is jostling the mighty English language in parts of the U.S., where the concept of language laws to protect English from Spanish is gaining acceptance. In South America, there are about 120 million people in Brazil whose mother tongue is Portuguese. That language will be around for centuries to come. Meanwhile, French has practically disappeared from the Americas, except for a small presence in the North East, in Quebec and New Brunswick. In the seventeenth and eighteenth centuries it would have been difficult to believe such a disaster could occur.

Self-Interest versus Collective Interest

To understand the "big picture" and sort out its complexities, I have found it useful to try and break it down to the motivators of individuals, both in current events and in history, which lead to the current environment. In my view, self-interest at the individual level is a very powerful human motivator and of great importance in shaping history. The technique of viewing big events, past and present, through the lens of individual self-interest has served me well. In looking at the rivalry between the British and French empires in the New World, I naturally fell back on viewing events from the perspective of the self-interests of the people involved.

Belonging to and cooperating with a socio-political grouping is clearly a matter of self-interest. A national collectivity protects its people and presumes to foster their interests, stroking their egos and giving them a sense of identity and belonging. In exchange, it demands loyalty, cooperation, the acceptance of a certain social structure, and the surrender to the collectivity of some personal freedoms, all ostensibly for the common good. According to this view, even loyalty to and cooperation with "our collectivity" and adherence to its customs and laws is very clearly a matter of self-interest. Today's powerful grouping, the sovereign nation-state, increases group cohesion through various time-honoured techniques, such as giving individuals the feeling they are better than others. This helps regulate cooperation within social hierarchies and structures.[6]

---

5 However, like many others, I consider North America to end at the U.S.-Mexico border.

6 The nation-state is a new development and even today does not have a complete monopoly on loyalty everywhere. In Afghanistan, tribal loyalties can supersede national priorities. Sometimes, religious affiliations transcend group cohesion based on nationalism.

Immigrants, by definition, exchange one collectivity for another. I have found them to be more sensitive about questions of self-interest versus collective interest, than are citizens who live in one society all their lives. Those questions can strongly affect their decision about where to settle, adapt and try to integrate.

Immigrants are individuals who reach the conclusion that cooperating with their old collectivity is no longer in their self-interest. Something happens to weaken the bond. They are looking for a new, more suitable grouping to join. This is not a new phenomenon. In my opinion, one of the most important reasons for the fall of New France is that too few immigrants came looking for a new home, even as they streamed to the English colonies. Even French Catholics in many cases were not interested in New France.[7]

To keep its people, attract immigrants, and obtain the loyalty and cooperation of its members, a national grouping must develop customs, traditions, and laws that cater to and foster the self-interests of its citizens—including the need for identity and feeling of belonging—as well as the interests of the nation as whole. But the self-interests of individuals often diverge from the collectivity to which they belong and to which they are expected to be loyal. Gerhard Lenski[8] is a social scientist who developed ideas dealing with self-interest versus social interest.

> "When men are confronted with important decisions where they are obliged to choose between their own, or their group's interest, and the interest of others, they nearly always choose the former—though often seeking to hide this fact from themselves and others."[9]

Therefore, the state, controlled by the individuals or groups in power, must apply some coercion to keep self-interest in check for the common good.

> "Any government which cannot suppress each and every forceful challenge to its authority is overthrown. Force is the foundation of sovereignty."[10]

---

7 Many of the English-speaking immigrants to "the colonies" were seeking an environment of religious and political freedom they could not find in their countries of origin, as much as they were looking for opportunities to escape poverty and become independent landowners. In contrast, New France was established as a semi-feudal society, ruled by French aristocrats and the Catholic Church.

8 Lenski, *Power and Privilege*.

9 Ibid., p30.

10 Ibid., p50.

Anarchists propose a society without a centralized state or any authority with coercive powers. It is an interesting idea, reminiscent of ancient hunter-gatherer societies where property and authority in the modern sense did not exist. But I don't see how it could work in practice. I have not seen a viable, realistic alternative to an elected, responsible government with adequate powers to enforce rules. I do not believe that in our democracies the state is fundamentally a tool for the powerful to oppress the weak, as the anarchists maintain.

My *Weltanschauung*, however, points to a complication: the self-interests of the leadership elite are not always the same as those of the people; however, the direction society takes is influenced disproportionately by the elite. Repeating a quote by Gerhard Lenski,

> "We are obliged to define as the goals of a given society those ends towards which the more or less coordinated efforts of the whole are directed—without regard to the harm they may do to individual members, even the majority."[11]

A question often arises as to whether those in power are applying coercion for the common good or for their own self-interest. I decided to come to Canada not because I did not wish to cooperate with my old collectivity, but because the dictatorial regime of the time set goals that were more concerned with protecting their own power than serving the interests of the population.

Thus, there is often a discrepancy between the perceived interests of society as a whole and those of its individual members, regardless of how the society is stratified and to which strata individuals belong. These perceived interests of society are often heavily influenced, if not actually manufactured, by individuals in the higher strata—the rulers and elites. Once alerted to the phenomenon, I was able to closely observe and detect the mechanism at work in a number of societies with different political systems. It is much more flagrant in non-democratic societies than in democratic ones. Powerful groups in democracies have been forced to develop ways to "manufacture consent"[12] to further their objectives.

Often, population and government agree to the need for collective coercion. Henry David Thoreau (1817—1862) wrote:

---

11 Ibid.

12 A now-famous expression proposed by Chomsky to describe the deliberate manipulation of public opinion; see his book *Manufacturing Consent*.

"The people must have some complicated machinery or other, and hear its din, to satisfy that idea of government which they have. Governments show thus how successfully men can be imposed on, even impose on themselves, for their own advantage."[13]

Thus the people will accept certain amounts and types of coercion if they believe it to be for the common good or in the interest of a majority of the population. The great difficulty is looking into the future and predicting which short-term coercive measures will not, in the long term, lead to a collective disadvantage. For these reasons, it is my view that coercive measures designed today must be as mild as possible and limit as little as possible the individual's freedom to pursue his or her self-interests.

One of the reasons I enjoy living in Canada is that its people, more than those of any other country I know, have access to such a wealth of information that they are able, with confidence, to form opinions contrary to those of the government.

Coercion in New France

In the eighteenth century, English was limited to an area at most one tenth that of French. Two coercive measures would set the stage for the expansion of English at the expense of French, mercantilism and a xenophobic immigration policy.

The first destructive, coercive measure, the policy of mercantilism, was imposed by Louis XIV, King of France during the French colonial regime. The king was free to define policies that were in his own interest, regardless of the interests of the people of New France. Mercantilist policies, which focused on the enrichment of the French state, were developed and implemented by a skilled administrator, Jean-Baptiste Colbert, with the support of Cardinal Richelieu. In the 1660s and 1670s, Colbert brought efficient accounting procedures and order to the finances of the kingdom. Imports of manufactured goods were to be reduced and exports increased so as to accumulate wealth (much of it in the form of silver) in France. Raw materials were needed from the Americas and other colonies to create employment in France's manufacturing sector. Manufacturing in French colonies overseas was seen as a threat to jobs in the mother country.

---

13 Henry David Thoreau, *Civil Disobedience,* downloaded from <http://www2.cybernex.net/~rlnat/civil1.html> and available elsewhere on the Internet and in print.

France imposed strict laws and regulations to control economic activity in French North America. France determined at what times on what days markets would be open. Trade was permitted only in products manufactured in France. Draconian price controls were put in place. Worst of all, industrial activity was completely prohibited except for the construction of ships and forges, which were deemed essential for the survival of the colony. In 1704, a royal decree prohibited all activity that could "compete with the manufacturers of the kingdom (France)" and explained that "the colonies exist to provide raw materials to the mother country...not to become independent of it."[14] When, in 1736, dynamic French entrepreneurs in Montreal and Quebec set up manufacturing facilities to produce fur hats, they were closed by order of the king. Over the years, other businesses, including a textile factory in Montreal, suffered the same fate. In all of New France, there was little profitable business activity going on.

An exception was the fur trade. That trade was controlled by a large elitist monopoly, the Company of New France, established with the support of Cardinal Richelieu and also known as La Seigneurie des Cent Associés. A French gentleman-officer who finished his tour of duty here more often than not had nothing to stay for. The self-interests of French pioneers in the North American colonies were not catered to. Through coercion, most economic life in French America was limited to simple rural transactions. The "right question" for the king was a "wrong question" for New France and its people. The monarchy in France imposed laws that were in its and the aristocracy's self-interest but contrary to the interests of the people of New France. However, these settlers did not rebel against the elite in Paris or the king.

The second excessively coercive measure was a xenophobic immigration policy based on religious and racial intolerance. Only Catholics from France were allowed to settle in New France. Catholics from other countries were not welcome. Even prospective immigrants from France who were not Catholic were banned.

The history of French Protestants deserves special mention. Known as the Huguenots, they were severely persecuted in France. An edict by King Henry IV in 1562 allowed them some leeway; however, the monarchy at the time was too weak to enforce it, and Protestant lives and property were taken all over France. On St. Bartholomew's Day in

---

14 Trudel, *Nouvelle-France*. Translated by the author.

1572, thousands of Huguenots were massacred. Among those killed were the Protestant leader Admiral Gaspard de Coligny and his lieutenants. Catherine de Medici, the Queen of France originally from Italy, had known about and not opposed plans for the assassination of Coligny. In 1598, the Royal Edict of Nantes endeavoured to protect the Huguenots again. The edict granted them the "freedom of conscience" and the right to practice their religion in public (in certain areas) and to hold public office.

Eventually, the Protestants lost their military power, but for a while they were still able to practice their faith. Then, in 1685, Louis XIV revoked the Edict of Nantes. He decided that two churches in his kingdom were one too many and proceeded to destroy the Protestants. More massacres followed. Persecution was brutal. Churches were burned and children of Protestant parents were taken away to be brought up as Catholics. Many of the best Huguenots, perhaps 250,000 people skilled in industry and commerce, were expelled or fled. Protestantism in France was practically wiped out and never recovered.

The surviving Huguenots pleaded to be allowed to emigrate to New France. Even though they would still be subjects of France and its king, they expected there would be no massacres of Protestants in the Americas. They were refused, even though in today's perspective—stripped of religious considerations—they would have made fine immigrants. One of the obligations of the Company of New France was to keep the French colonies Catholic. Also, the Jesuits were specifically charged with keeping the Huguenots out of New France.

I cannot help but wonder how the history of the French language in the Americas would have been affected by the arrival of a large, well-educated, and skilled French-speaking population which would likely have contributed handsomely to the colony's prosperity. There is reason to expect that the French-speaking population of modern Quebec would have been larger, its territory bigger, and its language less fragile.

Britain's American colonies developed differently. While New France was controlled directly by the monarchy and the aristocracy in an autocratic fashion, in the English colonies, much political and economic power resided in the hands of local colonials. Like France, England pursued a policy of mercantilism, perhaps to an even greater degree. It also used coercion to impose its will and benefit England at the expense of "the colonies." While colonists in New France placidly obeyed the laws of the rich and powerful back home, the Anglo-American leadership was headstrong in pursuing its own and the colonial community's interests. English colonists did not easily accept the laws made in England: they were unruly and rebellious, and thus able to improve the ability of ordinary citizens in the colonies to pursue their self-interest. Again in contrast to the French, in the English colonies there was religious and racial tolerance, thus the population grew. Scots, Irish, and others came in large numbers. Starting in the early 1700s and lasting over a period of about fifty years, up to 250,000 German immigrants arrived. These alone were about three times as numerous as the entire "pure" population of New France. Many Huguenots came too. It was noted at the time that they were generally above average in terms of education, skills, and affluence. The children and grandchildren of all these races learned English because they wanted to.

In the seventeenth and eighteenth centuries, there were similarities between the North American colonies of the British and French empires. There were also differences: more acceptance of coercion and less tolerance by the French, less acceptance of coercion and more tolerance by the English. The results of these respective policies were decisive. Prospective immigrants were less attracted to New France because Colbert's policies meant few economic opportunities—even talented French Catholics saw no future here. On the other hand, immigrants from various nations flocked to the English colonies because independent-minded settlers had resisted coercion from England and created economic opportunities. In addition, there was tolerance for religious and racial diversity.

By the time of the Battle of the Plains of Abraham in 1759, the huge territories claimed by France contained a population estimated at 70,000 to 100,000, most living in a simple rural seigneurial economy. The estimate for the much smaller territories of the English colonies at that time is 1.7 to 2.5 million. It was multiethnic and engaged in bustling industry and commerce, in addition to farming. Well before the first shot was fired on the Plains of Abraham, New France was lost. Even had France won that particular battle, it would have only been a matter of time before the small numbers of Catholic French—who, incidentally, were feared as brave and skilled fighters—were overwhelmed by the exploding multiethnic, English-speaking population of the Americas.

I do not buy the argument espoused in francophone circles that the bold exploration and geographic expansion of New France happened too quickly, overextended the colony, and was harmful. Had New France also created an environment to foster prosperity and rapid population growth, it might have had much more stamina, power, and resources to use against the English. Large territories could have been an advantage.

Ironically, the English also lost their North American colonies due to coercion and the denial of individual self-interest. The English population of the Americas rebelled against mercantilist policies not dissimilar from the ones imposed on New France. Taxes were considered unfair and too high. The famous cry was: "No taxation without representation." By that time, however, the English language was well on the way to establishing a strong foothold in North America. It also gradually pushed into and took over former Spanish territories. France's coercive measures and lack of tolerance had resulted in a failure of historic proportions, one whose ramifications would reverberate for centuries to come. New France was gone and would never return.

Coercion in Modern Quebec

I am sorry to say that, in my opinion, modern Quebec is still making some of the same mistakes as its forefathers. Centuries after New France was lost, when my trusty notary was a young child, he tried to enter into the Quebec French school system in the 1949/1950 school year. He was born in Montreal of Italian Catholic immigrant parents. He was refused. At about the same time, according to media reports, Adrienne Clarkson, who became Governor General of Canada, also tried enrolling in the French school system and was also refused. The fact that the parents of these two children—and I suppose many others—perceived it in their children's best interest to be educated in French carried no weight with the decision-makers at the time.

A couple of decades later, language laws were passed to coerce the children of immigrants in a diametrically opposite direction. Over one generation, allophones saw Quebec go from "You may not enter the French educational system, no matter how much you want to, because you are not one of us" to "You must enter the French school system, whether you like it or not, so that you may become like us."

Centuries ago, Richelieu and Colbert were pleased with the short-term results of their intolerant and coercive policies in New France. The king was amassing wealth and the population of New France was homogeneous, faithful, and loyal. Everything seemed fine. The end result was the loss of New France.

In the mid-twentieth century, authorities felt that the short-term results of the coercive policies of the French school system had been successful. They were pleased that the student body was pure and that French culture was being protected. They felt the exclusionary rules were necessary. The long-term result was that many allophones and immigrants, prevented from integrating into and strengthening the francophone majority, went over to the English.

More recently, those responsible for the coercive language laws, policies, and attitudes in Quebec have been pleased with the short-term results. Many anglophones left the province. Fewer immigrants came. French seems to be doing much better than before and the English school system has shrunk even more than the French. However, as in earlier times, the long-term results are not yet clear.

The impositions in Quebec draw my attention because they affect immigration and have kept friends and acquaintances away. There are also historical parallels with New France. Quebec's coercive measures may look good to some, but in my view they also constitute a danger.

Firstly, in New France many immigrants were kept out due to their race, religion, and language. In modern Quebec, immigrants are also repelled because of race and language. It seems to me that, despite apparently sincere protestations to the contrary, the issue of race is particularly important to the separatist movement, whose mandate is based on the aspirations of a portion of one race only: old-stock Québécois.

Secondly, in New France prosperity was subjugated to the "higher purposes" of enriching the king and favouring employment in France. In modern Quebec, prosperity is adversely affected by giving priority to the "higher purpose" of nationalism.

Apparently, so convinced are some hard-liners that all this is for the good of Quebec and its regular folks that they still occasionally call for more intense coercive measures, perhaps partly motivated by a desire for revenge. Just like elites everywhere, separatist leaders and politicians don't like their manufactured consent to be challenged or disturbed.

"Across a broad spectrum of articulate opinion, the fact that the voice of the people is heard in democratic societies is considered a problem to be overcome by ensuring the public voice speak the right words."[15]

"The system protects itself with indignation against the right of deceit in the service of power and the very idea of subjecting the ideological system to rational inquiry elicits incomprehensible outrage."[16]

In a fit of rage, former Premier Lucien Bouchard once said that federal Intergovernmental Affairs Minister Stephane Dion "does not exist." The separatist leadership despises the federal minister, who has steadily chipped away at the doctrine painstakingly built up by separatist intellectuals over decades. Federalists behave not much differently. At the height of the Quebec "language wars," the minister responsible for the protection of the French language, Louise Beaudoin, was often represented in Aislin's cartoons in the anglophone Montreal *Gazette* as a kind of "Louise of the SS." She was decorated with Nazi-like emblems and a peeled banana resembling a fleur-de-lys, presumably suggesting the efforts of separatists would amount to nothing more than a banana republic. Former Premier Lucien Bouchard was sometimes accused of being an unprincipled opportunist.

Old-Stock and Newcomers: Converging Motivators

Over the decades in Quebec, the population has been exposed to the rhetoric of two diametrically opposed establishments, federalist and separatist. Each establishment has its political leadership, budget, intellectuals, journalists, and opinion-shapers. All are trying to sell their viewpoint and undermine the opposing viewpoint. Each side has consistently worked to create a consensus among the population of Quebec that their vision is for the common good while their opponents' are wrong or outright dishonest. With regards to these issues, the population thus has a democratic menu of options to choose from, as is not the case when only one establishment is manufacturing consent according to its own interests.

Many immigrants and allophones[17] understand both English and French but belong to neither of the two principal ethnic communities of the province. They are, in my view, more intellectually free to weigh their own self-interest in the light of the arguments of both sides. If the

---

15 Chomsky, *Necessary Illusions*, p 19.

16 Ibid., p 9.

17 The Canadian term (in both languages) for anyone whose mother-tongue is neither English nor French.

majority become federalists, it is unlikely to be due solely to manipulation by the media. Pressure is growing on the influential "old guard" in Quebec. In today's world, flexibility and the ability of a society to change with the times is of utmost importance. In his article, Jules-Pascal Venne writes,

> "All movements or projects which give priority to the collectivity are being abandoned in favour of projects based on the primacy of the individual."[18]

Well, at last.

Thirty years ago, the political and economic contexts of Quebec made it easier for the collective-sovereignty project to appeal to the blossoming of Quebecers. Today, this is not the case.

Thirty years ago, the self-interests and motivators of Franco-Quebecers were very different from mine and those of other immigrants, allophones and anglos alike. Today, a convergence of self-interests has occurred. The motivators that fostered the nationalism of the 1970s are being replaced by new and different motivators, more like those of other Canadians.

Abraham Maslow proposed the existence of a now-famous "hierarchy of needs" that influences the perception of self-interest and determines motivation.

Human needs arrange themselves in hierarchies of pre-potency. That is, the appearance of one need usually rests on the prior satisfaction of another, more potent need.

The strong attraction of the Parti Québécois in the 1970s was based on its ability to satisfy the needs of Franco-Québécois, at not one but two levels of need in the hierarchy.

At one level, many Québécois were motivated by the need for economic safety. Separatist politicians promised them this through the ability to work in their own language, French. This need was satisfied through language laws. At another level, having been "conquered and humiliated," Franco-Québécois were motivated to support the PQ by their need for self-esteem, self-confidence, and respect. This second need was satisfied by the threat of separation and the reasonable response of the rest of Canada. The Parti Québécois was successful in serving its supporters and largely satisfying these fundamental needs.

---

18 Translated by the author.

However, "a satisfied need is not a motivator of behaviour." A growing number of Franco-Québécois are motivated by new needs at a higher Maslow level, such as personal self-fulfillment and a better standard of living.

> "Human nature is not nearly as malleable, nor as free from inherent tendencies to promote self-interest, as Marx and many other theorists since the Enlightenment have imagined…Moral incentives have proven no match for material incentives."[19]

Efforts to create the "New Nationalist Man" in Quebec were successful decades ago because the moral incentives were accompanied by material incentives. With the success of the "Quiet Revolution," materialistic motivators are increasingly taking precedence over idealistic motivators, and nationalist-specific coercion is becoming ever less acceptable.

Changes seem to indicate that the interests of Quebecers are converging with the interests of immigrants. Such changes, once firmly established and visible to the world, will encourage more immigrants to come to Quebec and participate in its society and economy. As for me, these on-going changes have given me the feeling that my children and I are less likely to be coerced and freer to pursue personal success. They make me feel even more at home in Quebec.

---

19 Lenski, *Power and Privilege*, preface, p ix.

Chapter 13: How to Alienate Immigrants

It's easy. Stimulate their anxieties and dim their hopes by threatening their priorities.

Each immigrant is a universe unto him or herself. Yet, even though they come from many different countries and social environments, the difficult process of crossing cultures creates a commonality among all these newcomers. Like everyone else, they are seeking to satisfy fundamental human needs. Displacement and uncertainty make them more sensitive or aware of three important aspects of their lives in their new destinations.

Three Priorities of Immigrants

First, except for the very wealthy, immigrants want a fair opportunity to earn enough to maintain dignity and an acceptable standard of living. Second, there is a keen desire among immigrants to belong equally and fully to their new country. Third, they must perceive that their new country is on the right track for a prosperous, secure, and stable future. For native-born Canadians, these aspects of ordinary living are important but might be taken for granted, or at least may not always be at the forefront of their conscious thinking. For immigrants, they are a vital part of planning and decision-making.

Immigrants hope that there is at least one destination that caters to their priorities better than their current countries. Secondary immigration, resulting in more dislocation, is a result of immigrants arriving at one destination only to discover an advantage to moving again. My cousin Ismail, an architect, came to Toronto then moved on to New Jersey.

These three priorities are interrelated: for example, the degree of belonging and integration into the new society affects equality in job opportunities. They also have different timelines. The first, sufficient earnings, should be satisfied as quickly as possible; except for a few rotten apples, most immigrants desperately want to pay their own way. The second is the feeling of belonging. This is medium-term, as the immigrant comes to understand and adapt to the new environment. The third priority, perception of where society is headed, is longer-term and a matter of individual judgment. It is based on things like level of education, past experience elsewhere in the world, and personality. Immigrant parents extend these priorities to include the futures of their children as well as their own.

I do not know of a country that has the potential to satisfy the priorities of immigrants as well as Canada and the U.S. do. Quebec is special and contains elements of both North American and European postures regarding immigrants. Statistics Canada demonstrates that proportionately too few immigrants settle in Quebec. Why?

This is where the taboos kick in. Whenever I have expressed my concern about the future of Quebec and the French language in North America, instead of listening to what someone with a different perspective has to say, even some very well-educated francophones have become defensive and condescending:

"Who are you, Mr. Immigrant, to say that the entire francophone people of Quebec, with their democratically elected government, are wrong?"

"Mr. Immigrant, you don't understand the policies of the Federal Government."

"Paradoxically, you agree that the French language is in danger but are against measures to protect it."

It is gratifying that no one here ever gave me the standard European response:

"If it is so bad here, why don't you just go away?"

Quebecers are indeed better. I would have a ready answer, if ever I were to be confronted with such a question. I would respond that I find living with the fine people of Quebec to be wonderful; otherwise I could indeed have moved away, and still can, but won't. I would agree that many immigrants indeed "don't understand the policies of the Federal Government." Why not explain these policies in terms of the anxious immigrant's own self-interest, rather than in terms of injustices against francophones? Having been thoroughly exposed to the interaction and competition between languages, I would say that I have reason to worry about current strategies to protect French in North America. (There is more on this in a later chapter.) I would add that I humbly apologize for hurting anyone's feelings, but the stakes are high, and I feel compelled to describe my perspective as it really is, with no offense intended.

With regards to my personal priorities, like all other immigrants, I am entitled to gauge what impact some nationalist policies may have on the future of Quebec and how my third priority is affected. Having broken off from my old collectivity, I will not blindly follow another. To the best of my ability, I will reach my own conclusions and make my own decisions. So far, I have easily decided that it is quite all right for me to consider Quebec my home—and a privilege to be permitted to do so. I ask that my comments on these problems not be seen as an attack on Quebec but simply the result of the way I think, a result of my different experiences and mindset. I have observed that more than just a few other immigrants tend to think in a similar way. We must ponder important questions in our own way. We are entitled to ask questions, from our perspective, regarding the policies of Quebec today and how they may affect our future.

Asking the Right Questions

Asking the right questions is so very important. According to popular proverb: "If you ask the right question, you are halfway there." In business management, educators stress the importance of asking the right questions. The first component of business strategy, or any strategy, consists of asking clear and realistic questions regarding missions and objectives. However, the "right question" is a subjective matter. In situations where there is no quantifiable measure, such as profits or point scores, asking the right questions is much more difficult.

> "A clear strategic mission and vision are particularly important in a not-for-profit organization, because these types of organizations are driven by their duty to the community and society. Translating the mission and vision into a clear statement can be very messy..."[1]

Governments are "not-for-profit" organizations. The consequences of not asking the right question can be wasted years and undesirable outcomes. With regards to seventeenth—and eighteenth-century New France, for the good people of New France, the forefathers of today's French-Québécois, the right question should have been, "How can we strengthen our French colony in America, insuring its growth, long-term viability, and prosperity?" Instead, the king of France pursued his own "right" question. For a time, the monarchy accumulated wealth. As for

---

1 Beamish, *Strategic Management*.

the French colonists in New France, their right question was never even asked.

In modern Quebec, it is generally accepted that separatists, on the one hand, and federalists of all backgrounds, on the other, tend to engage in a dialog of the deaf. Therefore, let me humbly suggest what I think is the "right question" for myself, which may possibly be acceptable from both federalist and separatist perspectives.

"What are the factors that, in the modern world, make a society, people, or independent nation confident, prosperous, and respected?"

Does the answer lie in the possession of valuable raw materials and natural resources? No, for if this were so, the Sudan would be one of the world's leading countries. Is independence and a seat at the United Nations the "magic wand" to gain respect and achieve a better life? Laos, Ecuador, and many African countries have a seat at the United Nations. Is it the possession of a terrible arsenal of nuclear weapons? No, for then Russia would be an enviable place to live.

My answer to the question of how power, confidence, prosperity, and respect might be achieved anywhere in today's world is twofold. The first component relates to widespread education, encompassing formal training in schools and universities with a solid informal education, with instruction in democratic values, a good work ethic, and a "critical mass" of integrity. The second component relates to population size. The larger the population of a society, the more weight and importance it can have regionally and in the world, provided the population is sufficiently educated. Many good things can flow from the weight of numbers of a large, well-educated population. Therefore, the larger the population of Quebec and the higher the overall level of education, and thus the more likely it is to achieve prosperity, confidence, and respect in North America and the world, the better my priorities are served.

Chapter 14: English Words and Arabic Numbers

Knowledge of English Is Very Desirable

Pragmatic immigrants seeking to efficiently pursue their priorities—including the best possible standard of living—understand that a good knowledge of English is essential. Other languages are important too, particularly French in my family's case. Living in Quebec, the presence of the French language in our environment contributes handsomely to our adaptation and our joie de vivre. Nevertheless, I don't really care whether commercial signs are in English, French, or both. It matters not whether doctors and nurses in our hospital system speak to me in French or English. In fact, I have also received medical services in German and Arabic, and things went very well in each case.

With regards to my priorities for my children, I cannot stress enough that they must be completely fluent in English and master it as a first language. Some immigrant friends and acquaintances with children in French schools are not dissatisfied. Their children pick up English in the French-language school playground, at home, and watching TV. Later they expect an anglophone CEGEP (junior college) and university to give them formal training in English. That is good enough for many. It is not good enough for us. We wanted our children to be formally very well educated in English, starting in early childhood. As they progressed, we wanted them to write essays in English and learn about Keats and "The Ancient Mariner." Not that Schiller, Molière, and Al Manfaloti did not have interesting and valuable things to say. It is just that they did not say them in English, while our purpose is to help them build a solid platform in that language. We want our children to be able to use English as eloquently as the limit of their natural linguistic abilities permits. As insecure and often embattled immigrants, we wanted to give them the tools to be real North Americans and to open doors all over the world. There was a time when we owned property in both Ontario and Quebec. Back in Canada after spending time abroad, the plan was to sell one and build on the other. We pondered these alternatives for a while. Finally, it all came down to whether our kids could be educated in English in Quebec. They could. We sold the property in Ontario and decided to live in Quebec.

One Way Language Laws Can Backfire

In the case of our family, it is ironic that had a coercive language environment not existed in Quebec, our children might have gained a deeper knowledge of French than they have now. The reason their French is acceptable but not as strong as it might have been is partly a result of my own wary mindset, formed through previous exposure to a government filled with fanatics pushing an ideological agenda.

I clearly remembered how an ardent collective ideology could overrule self-interest and ruin lives. I remembered a story in Egypt of how a government had broken its promises and severely hurt those who had trusted it. My parents told me about how an Egyptian government pursued its ideology regardless of fairness. A few years after Nasser took power in Egypt, it became clear that military rule was not just a temporary phenomenon, one to be tolerated only until we were rid of the British imperialists. Authoritarianism was in Egypt to stay, and soon Nasser gained the confidence to act as he pleased. The dictatorship came to be driven by an ideology inspired by the now-defunct Soviet Union. There was a fanatical resolve, couched in noble slogans, to build an "ideal socialist state," using extreme coercion as needed. In this environment, the revolutionary government once issued "guaranteed" savings certificates at a good interest rate. Many individuals with some savings used them to buy these attractive certificates; by no means could all the buyers be called wealthy. One day, completely out of the blue, Nasser simply declared these certificates worthless. The money of the "bloodsucking rich" would go towards building the new utopia and helping the poor.

As my parents told it, one of their acquaintances at their club "lost his mind" as a result of this treachery by the government. Dr. Moustapha Enawi apparently had used most of his savings to invest in these government certificates. After the blow, he went around the club shouting to himself, "My money! They took my money! Why? Why? I did not steal it. I worked hard for years and earned it through endless hours of helping my patients. Where is my money?" Dr. Enawi closed his clinic and disappeared. He became a recluse for a number of years. The majority of Egyptian people, too poor to have invested in these certificates or anything else, did not care about the fate of Dr. Enawi and thousands of others like him. Some of those who had been particularly downtrodden before the revolution cheered.

When a couple of our children had an opportunity to go into French-immersion schooling in Montreal, we thought it might be an interesting idea. We began to ponder the pros and cons, evaluating whether the quality of their English could be adversely affected and so on. Our evaluation process was cut short by a dark, stirring suspicion that became a sudden realization. What if we put our children into French immersion and the government later took away their right to send their own children to English schools? What if those who had received anything other than a 100% English education were not allowed to go on to an English post-secondary school? What if…? What if…? Would the majority Québécois voting population attach importance to what immigrants wanted for their children and rush to defend them, or would they simply go along with a change in rules by the government they had elected? Would they even cheer as poor Egyptians had done when the "rich" were dispossessed? I had to answer that no, most would not care and yes, some would cheer. Thanks for the offer of French immersion, but no thanks. We would take no chances and the kids would stay put in the English system. Later, they could always build on the basic knowledge of French they would inevitably acquire growing up in Quebec.

French Is Not Equal to English

In my view, nationalist Québécois often make a mistake by seeking to equate the importance of French to that of English. They expect some kind of "equality." The reality is, French is not equal to English. More precisely, no language is equal to English; it is the most attractive language in the world. Its use is growing by leaps and bounds everywhere. More people of neither French nor English mother tongue prefer English as a foreign or second language to any other and look to it as their passport to the world and to self-betterment. French is still respected in many places, but English is overwhelming. In Germany, French, English and some other languages are taught as foreign languages in school. English is first and French a distant second. In "Schools of General Education" (primary and secondary schools) between 1993 and 1999, the ratio of students learning English to those learning French has remained steady at just under 4 to 1. In German vocational schools, legendary for their ability to produce technicians and craftsmen of the highest caliber, the ratio in favour of English has gone up from about 7 to 1 in 1993 to about 9 to 1 in 1999.[1] In

Holland, there three are types of secondary schools, only one of which can lead to university studies. At this highest level of secondary education, 99% of pupils study English versus 35% who study French. In other words, practically all study English, while about one third of these presumably brightest of Dutch youngsters also study French. In the two other types of secondary schools, 98% study English, while 21% and 25% respectively also study French. These are ratios of 5 to 1 and 4 to 1 in favour of English.[2]

When a once-powerful culture declines, its language becomes less attractive to others. In the long history of the region where I was raised, a good example is the Arabic language. For some centuries until the thirteenth, it was the foremost language of learning in the world. It was very attractive: if you wanted to be thoroughly educated and up to date, you had to learn Arabic. Then, in the thirteenth century, came a precipitous decline caused by a number of factors, including bad rulers and the catastrophic destruction wrought by the Mongol invasions. Over a period of some decades, Arabic ceased to be the universal language of learning.

Something similar happened to the Turkish language. Today Arabic and Turkish are important only to Arabs and Turks. It seems that the same fate might be overtaking French. Having been raised in a country with a very long history of six or seven thousand years, I take it for granted that languages come and go. French flourished, was very attractive for a while, and is still important. But now it is declining. I'm sorry, but *c'est la vie*. As the worldwide attraction of French declines, its position in Quebec will become ever more precarious.

It does seem to me, however, that there are also positive factors favouring French. For one thing, it gives millions a sense of identity and makes them feel "distinct" (in some cases "better") in this huge, multicultural continent. A substantial portion of these people will put an effort into preserving the continued use of French. This is probably the best thing French has going for it. Nationalism and a sense of identity are powerful emotions and language is a pillar of both. Nevertheless, populations are fickle; values and priorities can change, especially if the price of nationalism, measured in dollars, is perceived to be too high.

---

1 German Office of Statistics. 4 May 2000. < http://www.statistik-bund.de/basis/e/biwiku/schulsttab15.htm>.

2 Central Bureau for Statistics. Ministry of Economic Affairs. Voorburg, Netherlands. 10 May 2000. Courtesy of Mr. Frank Blom. Sector Educational Statistics. E-mail: fblom@cbs.nl/tel.: (070) 337 5345/fax: (070) 337 5978/

There are also many rural areas in Quebec where English is remote and life goes on very well without it. Many monolingual francophones make satisfactory or very good livings and will continue to speak French only for a long time. These individuals are able to lead productive careers provided they are not involved in high-tech fields, exports, the knowledge-based economy, or symbolic-analytics. They must also be easy going and patient enough to wait for the translation from English of many of the new developments in topics of interest to them.

Helpful also is that many Canadians outside Quebec value the presence of the French language and culture in Canada. It helps them define and distinguish their country from the U.S. In addition, in Britain, the U.S., and among many non-francophone Canadians, a knowledge of French is seen as prestigious, perhaps a sign of having been to an expensive private school. Among upscale anglophones, a knowledge of French can often have snob appeal. This seems to be a leftover from days gone by: French is still often respected as a global language of culture and refined living. It adds ornament to any non-French education.

A further source of support for the French language comes from francophone immigrants.

I cannot tell whether all these positive aspects of the language situation are enough to protect the French language in Canada over the long term.

Separatists' continuous warnings that French is fragile and endangered, though they may rally nationalist feelings among old-stock francophones, serve to make the language appear less attractive to allophones. What, educate our kids into a language that is in danger and could disappear? We come all the way to a continent dominated by the powerful and wealthy English language, then teach our kids some other language that is in danger of disappearing? Who is kidding whom? Besides, though it is none of my business, I see that many francophones are themselves giving higher priority to comfort and material advantage than the preservation of their language, culture, and nation. In the perception of many immigrants I know personally, francophones are not willing to make the really serious "sacrifices" required, such as maintaining stable families and having many more children.[3] (Many immigrants come from conservative societies where the family is paramount.)

---

3 In some cultures, children are considered to be a gift and blessing from God, the most beautiful ornament in life, rather than a "sacrifice" by their parents.

Decades ago, a day before attending my first lecture of the first semester at the Federal Institute of Technology in Zurich, new students were given a welcoming speech by Professor Saxer, head of the department of mathematics. The speech was in German. Having only recently arrived in Switzerland, my German was still inadequate; there was much I did not understand. One phrase, however, I understood perfectly, because Professor Saxer said it in English. At one point in his speech, he looked into our eager fresh young faces and said:

"If you don't know English, you cannot become a real engineer."

In a German-speaking city, in a country which at that time had three official languages, none of them English, a professor in that prominent European university was warning us about the dire consequences of not speaking English. As far as I could understand, Professor Saxer did not even mention the two other official languages, Italian and French. In 2001, there erupted a controversy in Switzerland regarding the second language taught in schools. Some in German Switzerland are seeking to replace French with English as their second language. Some in French Switzerland are seeking to replace German with English as their second language. Swiss parents are very attracted to English for their children. Swiss nationalists are resisting.

Dr. Butros Butros Ghali, visiting Quebec for a francophone Summit, felt it necessary to say that if the purpose was to do battle against English, then the cause had been lost in advance. The following was written in the mid-1980s:

> Three quarters of the world's mail, and its telexes and cables, are in English. So are more than half the world's technical and scientific periodicals: it is the language of technology from Silicon Valley to Shanghai. English is the medium for eighty percent of the information stored in the world's computers. Nearly half the business deals conducted in Europe are conducted in English.[4]

Since then, events have further strengthened English; there seems to be no limit to its growth and attractiveness. The collapse of the Soviet Union left the United States with an enormous influence in the world, which it exerts in English. The explosive growth of the Internet was an English phenomenon.

---

4 McCrum, *The Story of English*, p 20.

Everyone Wants Arabic Numbers

The phenomenon of English dominance is not unique in history and should not upset anyone. It has often happened that the product of one culture is adopted by other cultures everywhere and becomes "universal." When I listen to the music of Mozart, I don't think of Austria. Mozart belongs to all humankind. The discovery of vaccines (by Louis Pasteur) and the use of vanilla flavouring originated in France. Heartfelt thanks France, but these ideas belong to all of us now. In the same way, the universal use of the English language has become disassociated from its country of origin, England. I know of another tool of immense value to mankind, originating with one people, that has displaced other, competing forms: Arabic numerals and numbers. The numbers on the pages of this book, on your bank statement, in arithmetic classes in school, and in writing used to describe the trajectory of interplanetary probes, are Arabic.[5] The numerals and number system of the Arabs have been universally adopted by humanity. Except for the fact that this way of writing numbers is originally Arabic, it no longer has any kind of special relationship to the Arab people.

In a chat with an amiable colleague from London, I had the temerity to gently criticize the British Empire (though not as blatantly as in this book.) He acknowledged some of my complaints, but I could feel he was holding something back. Finally it came out.

"You learned our language very well. I believe we gave the world a shared language that improved mankind's ability to communicate and share knowledge of all kinds. I'm sure you benefited from the English language. I can see you enjoy it." Luckily, I had a ready answer.

"Absolutely, I could not do without it. Nevertheless, I propose a deal: I will stop using English forever if you promise never to use the Arabic numbers we taught you. You can fill out your tax returns and ask for your bank statements in Roman numerals, or perhaps in numerals from the pre-Roman system used by Queen Boadicea."

We laughed, and that was that.

To push this analogy further into the absurd, what would one think of the leaders of a collectivity that "doesn't like the Arabs" and that

---

5 It has been suggested that Arabic numerals actually originated in India. If you think so, just replace "Arabic" and "Arabs" with "Sanskrit" and "East-Indians." One former Egyptian professor at Cairo University told me that he thinks modern Europeans are using Arabic numerals while the Arabs are using Indian numerals. I am fairly certain that the idea of a symbol for "zero" is purely Arabic.

"wants to protect its identity" trying to legislate the use of Roman numerals? Instead of writing 24, a law is passed so children must learn to write XXIV. How long would it take for the people to rebel against such a law? The rich and well-educated would be the first to teach their children Arabic numerals. For a while, everyone might agree to continue learning the old numerals for use locally when not communicating with the outside world. There would be a kind of unofficial "binumeralism." Everyone would pay lip service to the "official" Roman numerals and most correspondence with the government would, as far as technically possible, use Roman numerals. There might even be a numbers police, or Office des Numéros Romains. Gradually, the use of Arabic numerals would overshadow the other. Eventually, having to learn Roman numerals would become a nuisance. This analogy is weak and farcical when applied to the relationship between Russia, China, or Italy and the English language. But for the tiny Quebec population, situated right in North America, where the English language is simply overwhelming, the analogy has merit.

French Is Endangered But Nonetheless Important

There are a number of reasons we think French is important and want our children to learn it. We want them to belong and be real Montrealers and Quebecers. They cannot properly integrate into Quebec society without a reasonable knowledge of French. We want them to know the two official languages of their country, Canada. We want them to respect common courtesy and learn the language of the majority here.

Even though still young and engaged in entry-level hi-tech jobs where they do not really need it, later on when they are ready to advance to higher positions or start their own businesses, they will be much better off if also fluent in French. Even if they move to other parts of Canada, a good knowledge of French will set them apart and give them an advantage. If they move to the U.S., knowledge of French is prestigious—an indication of refinement and a good education.

Some important parts of the world are French speaking. Their mother is Swiss so they have very close ties to Switzerland. French is an official language there and gives our children better access to that culture.

I would not like to see the French language suffer the same fate as New France. Even anglos who are labelled "extremists" do not appear to desire the demise of the French language. They say their struggle is about equality for their own language. (Something I admire about Anglo-Saxons is that in their culture the importance given to individual rights is legendary: they will not be easily sacrificed for the sake of some collectivity, not even their own. This attitude has served them well and has enabled them to successfully balance the interests of individuals with those of society.)

Possibly, no solution will be found to stop the gradual decline of French in Quebec. Its long-term future is uncertain. The first step in finding a solution is going back to basics and asking the right questions. To me, this means giving the self-interests of individuals appropriate weight.

Why Is French Not Sufficiently Attractive?

Because it is in the self-interest of everyone in Quebec, whether they realize it or not, to be fluent in English. For most immigrants, this is a straightforward matter. For more and more Québécois, self-esteem has been restored, old grudges are forgotten. As the population moves up the hierarchy of human needs, an increasing number of individuals will be motivated to become fluent in English. It is thus that the coerced predominance of French interferes with the self-interests of more and more individuals. The current formula could be a losing one.

Chapter 15: Education

Educational considerations are closely linked to the fundamental priorities of immigrants. This chapter looks at three important ways education impacts on the immigration process. The first is the education of the immigrant, learning many new things necessitated by the changes the immigration process brings to the lives of those who venture into such a demanding project. The second deals with how alert immigrant parents wish to see their children educated. The third is linked to the second and relates to how the future of a society may be judged by its competence and priorities in matters of education.

Immigration Means Adaptation, Which Means Education

Immigration necessitates large-scale changes; this demands substantial adaptation. Adaptation means learning, which means education. The education may be formal or informal, organized or haphazard. It has been my observation that individuals who make the decision to immigrate, on the whole, are more willing and able to engage in learning and adaptation. Individuals who are averse to risk, dislike change, and have difficulty adapting are more likely to stay in the old country.

For a time both before and after the actual physical move, immigrants must go through an intensive period of learning. In my case, most of it was of the type educators call "self-directed learning." The phases I went through before and after my arrival in Canada are very accurately described in the literature. I wish I had been aware of Alan Knox[1] while I was engaged in the process of immigrating to Canada. It would have helped a great deal and reduced my stress and anxiety immeasurably. I would have been conscious of moving from one phase to the next instead of being hit and jolted by each change as it came along. In a chapter entitled "Adjusting to Change Events," Knox writes,

> "Most change events can be described as a sequence of time periods during which there are changes...Five time periods typically occur..."[2]

---

1 I learned about this prominent adult educator at Concordia University during the fall semester of 2002 in a core course called "Adult Education as a Field of Study in Quebec" given by Professor Riva Heft.

2 Knox, *Adult Development and Learning*, p513.

I remember each of these periods clearly in my own case. Knox continues, "The first [period] is the prestructure, which consists of a period of relative stability ..."[3] I was engaged in scientific research, had a convertible sports car and an impetuous youthfulness. "The second is the anticipation period..." I knew that I did not want to return to Gamal Abdel Nasser's military dictatorship in Egypt, nor did I wish to stay in Switzerland, which was less than welcoming towards foreigners. My motivation to continue my formal studies was impaired. I applied for landed immigrant status to Canada and waited anxiously. At that time, I started two self-directed learning projects, "The American Business Environment" and "About Canada," by managing to find books on these subjects.

"The third period is the actual event change. This period is usually quite brief..." In my case, it was not brief. I was hired by a high-tech multinational corporation shortly after my arrival and immediately sent to the U.S. for an extended period of training. I had to adapt to the Boston area. Then I came back to Canada and had to adapt to Montreal, which I had previously visited for only a few days. In addition, my change had three components, all requiring much learning, simultaneously. First, I changed not only residences within a city, or cities within a country, or even countries within a continent, but actual continents, each with completely different languages and cultures. Second, I changed careers radically, from scientific research to business. Third, my marital status changed overnight. I engaged in a huge amount of learning during this time.

"The fourth period is the disorganization period..." It did not seem so disorganized to me, since I seemed to know what needed to be done. It was more a period of stress and anxiety and more intense learning.

"The fifth period is the poststructure period of relative stability..." It took me almost two years to achieve this. There was less self-directed education during this period, since I had started evening courses at McGill University and was also swamped with employer-related technical and business courses, seminars, and informal guidance and instruction by management. Though it was tough, I am glad to have had that experience, since I believe it made me more competent at "lifemanship" (the ability to make one's way through life and to try to maximize the expected utility of problem formulation and decision-making.)

---

3 Ibid., p536.

At about age twenty-five or twenty-six, shortly after having obtained a Master's degree in Electronics Engineering, I read *The Revolt of the Masses* by José Ortega y Gasset. It created in me the desire to avoid being a mass man. Ortega y Gasset has been criticized as elitist. His book has been called brilliant yet flawed.

In a chapter entitled "The Barbarism of Specialization," he writes:

> "The scientist has been gradually restricted and confined into narrower fields of mental occupation. Enclosed within the narrow limits of his visual field, he does actually succeed in discovering new facts and advancing the progress of science. Science has progressed thanks in great part to the work of men astoundingly mediocre, and even less than mediocre...The specialist 'knows' very well his own tiny corner of the universe; he is radically ignorant of all the rest...previously, men could be divided simply into the learned or the ignorant...But your specialist cannot be brought in under either of these two categories...He is not learned, for he is formally ignorant of all that does not enter into his specialty, but neither is he ignorant, because he is 'a scientist' and 'knows' very well his own tiny portion of the universe."[4]

That was written in 1930 in Spanish and first published in English in 1932. It has been said that Ortega y Gasset wrote these words seventy years too early, and that today everyone should read this book, despite its flaws.

Having read this, I certainly did not believe that all of the world's bright scientists, who expanded human knowledge, were "mediocre." Still, I decided that very narrow specialization was not for me. Ortega y Gasset made me decide that a broader education would help lead to better life. Yet, I was on the road to being "gradually restricted and confined into narrower fields of mental occupation." I was happy with the science and engineering I had learned thus far. They gave me a better understanding of the workings of the universe. Mathematics and the techniques of modern engineering are powerful mental tools. Gradually, though, I decided to change. One motivator, I must admit, is that personal incomes in business were substantially higher than in research and development. I also decided to continue learning as much as possible about the arts, the world, and our species.

In addition to self-directed learning, formal education in a recognized institution is of great value to immigrants. My primary motive for studying business at McGill University was related to career change. These studies contributed to my rapid advancement in my

4 Ortega y Gasset, *Revolt of the Masses.*

corporate setting. In a number of cases, I was able to apply directly to my work the knowledge gained in class. Furthermore, the depth of academic knowledge I received helped me articulate complex and advanced ideas in meetings. It was noticed, and I was promoted rapidly. This helped satisfy a priority of all immigrants: good earnings.

Formal education also helped fulfill my social priorities: belonging, integrating, and gaining respect in my new country. These needs are primordial and seem to be underestimated by many everywhere who have never crossed cultures. It requires first, understanding of and adaptation to the society in which one seeks to integrate and, second, recognition by the new society of the worth and desirability of the immigrant. A formal degree greatly contributes to both of these. On the one hand, attending classes and mixing with students most certainly helps one understand the culture, manners of speech, and attitudes. On the other, having a Canadian degree is invaluable in earning the respect of other Canadians. I urge all immigrants who are able, to try and pursue a formal degree at a recognized Canadian educational institution. Your priorities will be well served and you will find Canada attaches great importance to fostering the education of adults, including immigrants.

Globalization and Our Children's Education

There must be some, but I do not know any immigrants who are not keenly interested in the education of their children. The best of them will give careful consideration to their destination country's education system. By seeking good educational opportunities for their offspring, they are responding to the priority of helping them achieve a good standard of living. At the same time, they are also addressing their desire to settle and grow in a society where the future looks prosperous. If their children can be well-educated, then so can all children of the society. In today's knowledge economy, a well-educated workforce is the greatest asset. Immigrants can expect their children to do well in a society that places a strong emphasis on education.

Widespread education among a population has not always been essential for economic power. During the so-called Industrial Age, even the lack of a high school degree did not mean economic hardship. The industrial revolution saw the main engine of wealth creation in society shift from agricultural production to manufacturing. At first, the knowledge used in manufacturing was still acquired mainly through the old method of trial and error. Gradually, as scientific knowledge grew, scientific theories could be applied more systematically and rigorously to the manufacturing process. Industry progressed in leaps and bounds. Many new scientific theories came from the discoveries of a relative handful of geniuses, some of whose contributions preceded the beginning of the industrial revolution. By geniuses I mean people like Lavoisier, Newton, Faraday, Joule, Marconi, Edison, and Pasteur through to Einstein, Schrödinger, and de Broglie. Together with those of other famous scientists, their discoveries and inventions eventually changed the world beyond recognition. A pattern emerged in the Industrial Age whereby a relatively few highly-educated scientists and engineers built on the brilliant discoveries of the very few geniuses. These highly-educated scientists and engineers were supported by highly-educated financiers, bankers, and others. A legal and moral structure (for example, Calvin of Geneva) emerged to support the values of the industrial revolution. Products of the Industrial Age, such as automobiles and electric generators, were designed and built. These goods were then produced by factories that relied on millions of semi-skilled workers performing repetitive tasks.

The bulk of the population moved from the rural areas to cities and industrial areas. With minimal training, they were able to work productively in factories and share in the new wealth. They protected their interests through trade unions.

> "The well being of citizens was linked to the success of the national economy, which depended in turn on the success of its giant corporations."[5]

The concept of "the nation" was central to economic development. Self-centered nations competed fiercely with each other and went to war for the scarce resources needed to feed their industries. In the "national economy" of the Industrial Age,

> "The only prerequisites for most jobs were an ability to comprehend simple oral and written directives and sufficient self-control to implement them...Well-paying factory jobs awaited high-school graduates and non-graduates alike...."[6]

These changes did not occur uniformly all over the world, or even in different regions or provinces within the same country. In many

---

5 Reich, *Work of Nations*, p34, 59, 61.
6 Ibid.

countries, including my birthplace, Egypt, the transition from an agricultural to an industrial economy did not fully occur, or occurred in some places in a spotty and warped manner. Though there are first-rate engineers and scientists in the country and though some industrial workers are diligent and focused, the society as a whole has not really made the transition from agriculture to industry, and most working individuals have not adopted the self-discipline and rigorous attitudes of an industrial environment. The result is a strange and whimsical relationship between people and machines.

One example of this mismatch occurred when vacationing with my family in Egypt. To get from Cairo to Hurgada on the wondrous Red Sea, I chartered a minivan and driver from a reliable company we knew and had dealt with before. We had never had problems or complaints. The vehicle was new and highly polished. The driver, Fawzi, was clean-cut, courteous, and looked eminently competent. We started out late on the 400-kilometer trip.

The sun soon set and it became dark while we were still far from Hurgada, but the driver did not turn on any of the vehicle's lights. We were on a desert road on a dark night with no lights whatsoever. The dark, asphalt two-lane road ahead was barely distinguishable from the desert sand on either side. I said to the driver, "Fawzi, why are the lights off? Please turn on the headlights."

"It's all right, sir," he replied, "I can see very well."

A small truck whizzed by, also without lights. Since both vehicles were doing over 100 kilometers per hour, the relative velocity was at least 200 kilometers per hour.

"The lights are not just for you to see; they must be on for others to be able to see you from far enough away. Please turn on the lights right now."

"Honestly, sir," he said politely and patiently, "everything is all right. I don't need the lights."

I thought I would try one more time, and if he refused, I would order him to stop the vehicle until he complied. If it came to that, I thought, he would have to stop the minivan off the road in the sand to the side. Since our lights and the lights of much of the traffic on that road were turned off, we would not be visible from a sufficiently safe distance. My wife Heidi and our three youngsters were all with me on that trip. I was becoming angry and he could sense it. I said, "Please listen to me for a minute, Fawzi. Machines like automobiles were invented by foreigners and come from abroad. They have much more experience with machines than we have. If we use their machines, we should also listen to what they say and do as they do. It's for our own good. Abroad, where cars were invented and are manufactured, the lights must be on at night by law. Please turn on the lights now."

He didn't like that at all, but he turned on the "little lights," as they are called in Egypt.

"No," I said, "I want the big lights—the headlights—on now, please."

He finally turned on the headlights but was unhappy all the way to our destination. Other vehicles we crossed flashed their lights when they saw ours on. Fawzi cheered up when we arrived and I gave him a tip much higher than he expected. I think he understood that I had not meant to annoy or offend him. However, where the safety of my family was concerned, there would be no flexibility. Later I asked my brother Aziz, who lives in Cairo, why drivers in Egypt often do not turn their lights on at night. He didn't really know but thought perhaps it had something to do with saving money on automotive light bulbs.

Immigration from pre-industrial countries to countries like Canada entails a move not just between geographic locations, but also between eras of human existence.

The West has left the Industrial Age behind and moved on to the next era. As always, things changed again, and the industrial economy evolved into a "knowledge-based" economy. For a nation to prosper in today's knowledge-based economy, education and advanced skills must be widespread among the entire population.

Wealth, prosperity, and growth depend on the advanced education and skills of the working-age population. At the individual level, a high school degree is not enough any more. Robert Reich is an influential economist and former U.S. secretary of labour. He was also a policy maker in the Ford and Carter administrations and is a member of the faculty of Harvard's John F. Kennedy School of Government. Reich explains how the "high-volume" national economies of the Industrial Age have been replaced by a global "high-value" economy.

> "The standard of living of a nation's people increasingly depends on what they contribute to the world's economy—on the value of their skills and insights..."[7]

---

7 Ibid., p154.

"In the high-value enterprise, profits derive not from scale and volume, but from continuous discovery of new linkages between solutions and needs."[8]

There has emerged a "global web" of industry and commerce. Whereas in the past corporations and products had distinct nationalities, today

"[...] fewer products have distinct nationalities. Quantities can be produced efficiently in many different locations, to be combined in all sorts of ways to serve customers in many places."[9]

The modern company "... knows no national boundaries, feels no geographic restraints."[10]

The fanatical nationalist emotions that engendered momentous wars, zealous self-sacrifice for the "fatherland," and a monstrous level of casualties during the Industrial Age appear to have abated. In Europe, where nationalism and chauvinism were invented, there has been a steady increase in the willingness of countries to give up aspects of their Industrial Age-style sovereignty in exchange for greater prosperity.

Reich believes that most modern jobs fall into one of three categories, which he calls routine-production services, in-person services, and symbolic-analytic services. Routine-production services are similar to the jobs of the Industrial Era. They consist of repetitive tasks that do not require much education and can be performed practically anywhere in the world. In-person services are described as those which require the service to be rendered face-to-face, in person, such as in the retail trade. These cannot be exported; they remain purely local. A requirement here is a pleasant demeanour and patience with customers.

The third type of work, symbolic-analytic, is the most crucial. In the modern era, it offers good to great financial compensation, as well as other rewards. The symbolic-analytic workforce is engaged in "high-value" enterprises, where the driving force is knowledge and brainpower. There are many opportunities. Examples of symbolic-analyst services are numerous and range from design and software engineers, to financial

---

8 Ibid., p84.
9 Ibid., p112.
10 Ibid., p124.

and energy consultants, to journalists and corporate headhunters.[11] Work related to the Internet is a good example of the new workplace, which knows no boundaries. In addition, the Internet itself enhances the scope of symbolic-analytic work. It facilitates the creation of an inexpensive and efficient virtual workplace where individuals located anywhere and everywhere in the world can form a task force or workgroup to pursue certain objectives. Once the task is terminated, individual symbolic-analysts can move on to a new project, with or without some of the same people. In the early 1990s, Reich felt that the gap in rewards between highly-remunerated symbolic-analytical work and the other two work categories would grow. He was right. Symbolic-analysts are among the group of rich who are getting richer, while the other two categories contain the poor who are getting poorer.[12] Reich described the advent of globalization a decade before it became a big issue and prompted large and often violent demonstrations.

I believe most immigrants, especially skilled workers, are not likely to be attracted to anti-globalization rallies. Most are far too busy and anxious to be concerned about such esoteric topics as the problems of globalization and its unfairness towards the poor. Besides, many immigrants come from countries where the poor are really wretchedly poor. Canadians officially classed as poor may not appear all that poor to them. The focus of newcomers is to avoid joining the ranks of the poor themselves. They try to anticipate where the world is going, then position themselves and their families to do well. I remember my own early years in Canada, when I used to work hard all day to pay for food, lodging, and other necessities, then have a hurried snack before rushing to evening classes at McGill University, which sometimes went from 6 p.m. to 10 p.m. Many evenings and weekends were consumed by assignments or exam preparations. I did this even though I already had a post-graduate degree in electronics engineering from a world-famous university. I most certainly had no interest, time, or physical or mental energy to worry about issues that were the target of rallies and demonstrations, let alone actually participate. If the world is to be divided among high-income and low-income populations, I most certainly want to be among the former.

11 See Reich, pages 177 and 178 for a longer list of symbolic-analyst professions. Pages 182 and 183 give many interesting descriptions for these jobs, which "may seem mysterious for people who work outside the enterprise web..."
12 Ibid., Chapter 17: "Why the Rich are Getting Richer and the Poor, Poorer".

"The Education of the Symbolic Analyst"[13] extends beyond graduation. In addition to good basic knowledge and skills, four additional skills must be refined: abstraction, system thinking, experimentation, and collaboration.

There is one more necessary skill Reich takes for granted and does not mention. I would like to add to his list of four skills this essential fifth skill: thorough knowledge of English.

Trade unions will be far less able to protect their workers than during the Industrial Era. Some workers will make it to the in-person economy, which is generally better but often limited. In May 2000, the first automated McDonald's restaurant opened in the U.S. Though this specific idea may or may not catch on, people's jobs in the in-person services are in increasing danger from technological advances, such as e-commerce and automatic bank-teller machines.

During the Industrial Age, the sovereign nation-state took on a mystical allure to its citizens, almost of all of whom shared a "common destiny." In the new age, elite workers in Canada will have more in common with other symbolic-analysts worldwide (ones who can communicate in English) than with the remainder of the local workforce.

I have done my best to guide my children so they may do well for themselves in the new knowledge-based economy, each within the limit of their individual abilities. I am ever mindful of the five skills they need to have: abstraction, system thinking, experimentation, collaboration, and English.

Education and Terrorism

My children and I have always talked about the gap between the well-to-do and the less fortunate. We concluded that eventually everyone loses if the rich continue to get richer and the poor poorer, ad infinitum. My children, all born Canadian, should realize that in order to protect what they have, moral considerations aside, there should be no unfairness towards the poor. The worst kind of situation occurs when the poor perceive that their prosperity is being prevented by obstacles built into the system. Almost inevitably, they will rebel through mass demonstrations, strikes, and other disruptive tactics. In the extreme, depending how the rich and powerful respond to defend their wealth and privilege, the rebellion can take the form of terrorism or massive social upheaval.

---

13 Ibid., chapters 18 and 19.

I saw this happen in Egypt, where wealth and poverty were determined by a rigid class system. Something similar has happened before in Quebec, though on a smaller and milder scale. francophones perceived that their language and race were obstacles to advancement. The English were dominant and prosperous and were perceived as prejudiced against the French majority. Rebellion punctuated by violence began to build. There were mail-bombings and kidnappings—terrorism was beginning to appear. Canada solved this problem admirably, with maturity and justice. The majority of countries have large populations of poor. In the West, including Canada, there are proportionately much fewer poor. There are fears that, due to globalization, the proportion of poor in rich countries may increase. In keeping with my third priority, I wish my country and province a stable and prosperous future, free from destructive rich-poor conflicts. Therefore, in my perspective, Canada, including Quebec, must prevent a growth in the proportion of its poor and ensure that the entire country is able to receive a high standard of education. Looking at it from the perspective of narrow self-interest, failure to do so will impact negatively on my family's third priority: a secure and prosperous future.

One night I had an awful nightmare. In it, a world emerged with a cohesive, well-educated, high-income class of symbolic-analysts. A class war was in progress, where the upper class was attempting to keep the low-income, uneducated workers "under control." In my nightmare, the global wealthy class was quite large, not a small "aristocratic" percentage of the population, as in old traditional societies. The income gap continued to grow, as Reich's writings suggest it might. This triggered the emergence of a truly global terrorist class—with leaders themselves well-educated and perhaps wealthy—encompassing rich and poor countries alike. "Domestic terrorists" from rich countries like Canada and the U.S.—resentful people who were becoming poorer and felt excluded and manipulated—had found a common cause with enraged terrorists from poor countries. Organizations like Al-Qa'ida emerged everywhere spontaneously and found natural allies and collaborators from many ethnicities, races, and religions, many right here in North America. The FLQ, squads of McVeighs, and clandestine cells of Bin Laden admirers were drawn together to coordinate their efforts. Desperate and outraged Hispanics in Central and South America, as well as in the U.S., joined in too. Criminal gangs from

Moscow to Los Angeles lent a helping hand whenever it suited their purposes. Some individuals engaged in the War on Terror began to accept bribes; others simply sympathized with the "struggle." I woke up startled from my agitated sleep, so I don't know how the nightmare might have ended. Had I slept on, this mother-of-all class wars between rich and poor would perhaps have ebbed and flowed over the decades. The bright and well-educated upper-income classes could never have been secure. If the dream had continued and the world's rich tried to protect a provocatively large and growing gap between themselves and the poor, they would have to resort to repression of Stalinist proportions. In my nightmare, individual rights and freedoms were fading into a distant memory.

According to a 1997 article by Ralph Peters, written four years before 9-11:

> "We have entered an age of constant conflict...Those of us who can sort, digest, synthesize, and apply relevant knowledge soar—professionally, financially, politically, militarily, and socially. We, the winners, are a minority...Those who cannot understand the new world, or who cannot profit from its uncertainties...will become the violent enemies of their inadequate governments,...and ultimately of the United States.
> ...the future is bright—and it is also very dark. One of the defining bifurcations of the future will be the conflict between information masters and information victims.
> The laid-off blue-collar worker in America and the Taliban militiaman in Afghanistan are brothers in suffering.
> ...These discarded citizens sense that their government is no longer about them, but only about the privileged. There will be no peace."[14]

This excellent article does not consider the costs and benefits of bringing education—and by extension, prosperity—to the poor against the costs of ongoing violent conflict. The two processes are not mutually exclusive, and it is probably desirable that they not be. Perhaps the optimal approach for the rich would be to offer a genuinely helpful, respectful, and kindly hand, and at the same time maintain the ability— rarely seen and applied—to defend themselves.

Also, the article was written before 9-11, the anthrax attacks, and the Washington D.C. sniper. It does not address the question of the now-exposed vulnerability of the North American economy and quality of life. My family is fortunate to have the potential to join the ranks of the

---

14 Peters, "Constant Conflict."

well-to-do in the "defining bifurcation of the future" between educated and uneducated. But I have been there before. I do not want my kids to spend their lives on a restricted, fortified island of prosperity, in a world of conflict where no quarter is given, where they are continuously threatened by a pervasive fear of the wrath of the have-nots, the large majority in the world. Discarded citizens do not have to defeat the awesome power of the privileged. They need only sufficiently hurt the economy and cause enough fear and misery to make us think again about our approach.

Perhaps we might add yet another requirement for a modern education to Reich's list: an understanding that, for everyone's well-being, it is important to educate the poor.

An "Elitist" Perspective?

During the British occupation, the colonial authority advised the Egyptian elite not to educate the masses, lest they rise up to overthrow their benefactors. The "rabble" rose up and changed the system anyway. The new global elite, the wealthiest and most powerful top bosses, do need a large class of talented knowledge workers to generate wealth and develop new technologies for use in the War on Terror. But is it worthwhile for them to encourage and assist widespread education throughout the world?

First, they might point out that I myself admit that I cannot tell which side will prevail in the War on Terror. Today's leaders are bright and alert and able to hire the best talent, unlike the effete and incompetent former elite in Egypt, which was overthrown by the masses. It seems, they might say, that experience has left me with a trauma irrelevant to the here and now. In balancing the expected rewards to the elite of the new global class structure with the potential impact of global terrorism, the expected returns from the former might outweigh the risks of the latter. It is a business decision.

I have noticed that in the U.S. the elite is already taking a similar approach. Taxes for the rich are low while many of the poor are deprived of a safety net, health services and so on. The rate of violent crime is high, but its impact is mostly felt among the poor themselves, as the rich can afford to isolate themselves from this kind of trouble. Such an approach might work just as well on a global scale, in the War on Terror.

Another rebuttal to my argument might be that I keep repeating my observation that we are a cruel species. Therefore, the poor, being of the same species, can be just as greedy and vicious as the rich. Among all classes there are the kind and generous as well as the dishonest and brutal. I must admit that I can see how some lower-income people can be just as obnoxious as those with high incomes. I remember how, during the construction of the Montreal Olympic Stadium, workers and rich contractors cooperated to gouge the tax-paying citizens of the city.

There is much worse. Throughout history, the poor have sometimes been brutal in the extreme. During the French Revolution, formerly downtrodden peasants massacred all the landowners they could catch. They also slaughtered all their children, including babies. These merciless killings might appear to have been depraved and mindless atrocities by ignorant peasants, but in fact, they were carefully calculated. Having seized the land of the aristocracy, the new owners wished to eliminate any possibility of claims by the heirs if ever circumstances changed sufficiently to make such a reversal possible.

It should also be remembered that Hitler and Mussolini came from low-income, working-class environments. They created and led workers' movements, originally to defend the poor against the unfettered capitalism of the arrogant upper classes. The Nazis developed a network of popular educational workshops where low-income citizens were taught about their rights, and also that Jews must be hated and the Aryan race was destined to rule the world. They taught that good Germans must not shrink or be inhibited from inflicting brutality and death on subhuman peoples, for the sake of the Fatherland.

So, the new global elite might say, if the whole human race shares the same characteristics, why knock only the rich and privileged? It is arguable that the rich and powerful do not engage in more evil acts than the poor. A world where everyone is educated is a fantasy. I might be asked: why not focus on joining the wealthy and doing well for yourself, since you seem to be saying that humanity as a whole is terrible anyway, despite the presence of kind and noble people? There is kindness and nobility among the very rich, too. Would it not be better to pull yourself together, overcome the wimpy "knot in your stomach," and do what is right for yourself?

Although I try to resist this self-serving mentality, I admit the prospect of living guilt-free among the elite has a certain allure to it that most people would confess they are attracted to from time to time.

Chapter 16: Population

Population size and growth rate are the other factors that combine with education levels to determine the importance and weight of a people. For a given society and its distinct culture and language, the bigger and better-educated the population, the more importance it will be given by others, the more opportunity for innovation and creativity, the more capital can be created and attracted, the more important its market opportunities, the more people are motivated to learn its language, the more attraction to bright young individuals to come and participate, the more funds will become available for health, education, and research.

Put another way, the larger the actual number of individuals in a given population who are well-educated and who can participate in the global web, the more the population will be confident, prosperous, and respected. It will also have a greater impact and more importance, regionally and in the world. Today, the largest number of symbolic-analysts concentrated in one country is found in the United States. Canada's economy is fortunate to be able to benefit and grow from a close association with such a large, skillful, and rich open market. As a bonus, we appear to be doing better with the distribution of the wealth we create and in slowing the growth of the rich and poor divide. (Unfortunately, in the society I left behind, the socialist dictatorship endeavoured to reduce the rich-poor divide by making the rich poorer, instead of the poor richer, even at the cost of a sharply decreased ability of the nation to create wealth.)

Needed: More Procreation and Immigration

Alas, as far as my third priority is concerned—my concern for what the future may bring—Quebec is not doing well in terms of population growth. For my province merely to maintain its population, it requires a rate of 210 live births for every 100 women. Instead, we have less than 150 births per 100 women. Every year, the number of francophones with French ancestral roots shrinks, and I don't know when it will stop doing so. In addition to the shrinkage in numbers of "real, original" Québécois, every year the overall population of Quebec has declined as a proportion of the population of Canada. In 1961, the population of Quebec was about 84% of that of Ontario, a province comparable in size. In 2001, it had declined to just under 63%.[1] The two reasons for this decline are low birthrate and low levels of immigration.

Former Quebec premier Lucien Bouchard once expressed disappointment that women of his race had the lowest reproductive rate of any "white" society. He was immediately chastised and to my knowledge, never publicly mentioned the subject again. Nor am I aware that he publicly raised the question of how the number of immigrants coming in to strengthen Quebec might be increased. The number of francophone immigrants coming to Quebec is still not sufficient to turn the tide of demographic decline.

The well-being of the French language in Quebec still depends primarily on the declining old-stock population. For decades, the intellectual and political elite has been aware of the demographic decline but unable to persuade Québécoises to return to anywhere near pre-Quiet-Revolution, pre-sexual revolution birthrates. Apparently, faced with the insoluble dilemma of wanting population growth while refusing to be outnumbered by people of other cultures, they turned their attention to hypothetical questions like the divisibility of Canada and the non-divisibility of Quebec. These are not the right questions: the strengthening of Quebec will take a meaningful increase in its population.

To be fair, Quebec is only one of many societies experiencing low birth rates. In much of Europe, for example, birthrates are about the same as they are here. In Japan, we read news items like,

> "Percentage of under-fifteens declines for twentieth year. The number of children aged under fifteen as of April 1, 2001, was 18.34 million, 240,000 less than a year earlier, making this the twentieth consecutive year-on-year fall. Government officials said the number of children is expected to decrease for some years yet."[2]

Some other provinces of Canada are also in trouble with regard to population growth. All this is of no help to Quebec, which is declining compared to Canada as a whole. We cannot blame Quebec's leadership for not having a solution to this problem. In the context of present economic

---

1 Statistics Canada Internet site, 12 March 2002,
<http://www.statcan.ca/english/Pgdb/People/Population/demo02.htm>
2 *The Daily Yomiuri*, 5 May 2001, "Kyodo News".

conditions and culture, there may be no solution. But with over 120 million people, the language of Japan is not in danger of disappearing anytime soon. Nor are the languages of Italy or Spain. Unlike Quebec, the populations of these countries are neither small enough nor shrinking quickly enough to be in imminent danger of assimilation by some giant powerful and advanced neighbouring culture. Though the "incredible shrinking population" phenomenon is not limited to Quebec, its impact on this small society's future can be serious. Quebec simply must find a way to increase its population, especially its population of symbolic-analysts, or it risks a gradual decline towards insignificance. I am quite fond of Franco-Quebecers and their culture. It bothers me to see it may fade away.

Canada as a whole is increasing its population though, ironically, the original English population is shrinking, too. While the old-stock Québécois population declines, what it calls "English Canada" is exhibiting continuous growth. Predominantly English-speaking Canada, has allowed the number of citizens originally from outside Canada to increase through immigration to maintain its growth. Collectively, English Canadians no longer allow ethnic considerations to dominate immigration issues. In fact, there are no serious impediments to increasing their population, and thus also their significance and prosperity, through a substantial increase in immigration. Descendants of the original French population in Quebec are afraid of doing the same. In 1998, despite having almost 25% of the population of Canada, Quebec received less than 14% of its newcomers, who were classified as "skilled immigrants."

"Secondary immigration" refers to newcomers who arrive in one province then move to another within Canada.

"In the case of Quebec, over the period 1980 to 1995, there was a net loss of one out of four English-speaking immigrants and of approximately 17% of those who spoke neither language."[3]

Grim Statistics

Until the trends noted above are reversed, the situation regarding population growth in Quebec will remain grim. Compared to Ontario, its neighbour and a good reference point, Quebec is consistently declining every year, at the rate of about one half of one percent[4]:

3 Jedwab, Immigration, p19.
4 *The Canadian Global Almanac*. Toronto: John Wiley and Sons Canada.

Table 1: Population of Quebec as Compared to Ontario, 1971-1996 (as at July 1 of each year)

Population in thousands	1971	1981	1991	1996
Ontario	7,849	8,811	10,428	11,101
Quebec	6,137	6,584	7,065	7,274
Quebec as % of Ontario	78.1%	74.7%	67.7%	65.5%

After the 2001 census, postcensal estimates show the trend continuing and that the rate of growth of Quebec's population is about one third that of Ontario.[5]

Table 2: Population of Quebec as Compared to Ontario, 2001-2003 (as at January 1 of each year)

Population in thousands	2001	2002	2003
Ontario (and percentage increase)	11,777	11,964 (1.6%)	12,109 (1.2%)
Quebec (and percentage increase)	7,395	7,435 (0.5%)	7,467 (0.4%)
Quebec as % of Ontario	62.8%	62.1%	61.7%

I found the following figures interesting. They show that in 1996, the immigrant population of Ontario was proportionately two and a half times greater than Quebec's, that for the following three-year period (1996—1999) the growth rate of the Quebec population was about one-third that of Ontario, and that in 2001 Ontario received almost four times as many immigrants as Quebec.

5 Statistics Canada's Internet site, 27 June 2003.

Table 3: Received Immigrants and Immigrant Population, Quebec versus Ontario

	Quebec	Ontario
1996[6]		
Immigrant population	664,500	2,724,490
% of total population	9.1%	24.3%
1996-1999[7]		
Population increase (3 years)	77,800	408,600
Growth % over 3 years	About 1%	3.7%
Year ending June 30, 2002[8]		
Immigrants received	38,984	152,825
Total population (thousands)	7,455	12,068
Immigrants received as % of total population	0.52%	1.26%
Growth rate for total population 2001-2002	0.5%	1.5%

With regards to the weight of the French language in North America, it does not help that the population of Nova Scotia is growing even less than Quebec's or that the population of Newfoundland and Labrador has been declining for years.

Quebec fears either immigrants or what it must do to attract immigrants. For decades, separatists have placed less of a priority on bringing immigrants in to increase the population and help the economy than on keeping them out, so that "control" remains in the hands of the majority race, the descendants of the original settlers from France. (I remember similar motivators in New France.)

It remains uncertain whether Quebec will be able to attract and keep more immigrants as long as its current priorities remain in place. In any case, as Jedwab notes, "The recruitment of francophone immigrants is apparently not that simple."[9] It is not enough for bright bureaucrats in Quebec City to declare that immigration will be increased. Even their

6 Statistics Canada's Internet site, 16 May 2000:
<http://www.statcan.ca/english/Pgdb/People/Population/demo35a.htm>.

7 Statistics Canada, Demography Division. Report on the Demographic Situation in Canada 2001, edited by Alain Belanger. Catalogue No. 9-209-XPE.

8 Statistics Canada's Internet site, 27 June 2003:
<http://www.statcan.ca/english/Pgdb/demo33b.htm>.

9 Jedwab, "Immigration", p17.

theoretical targets are not sufficient to reverse the decline of Quebec's demographic weight in Canada and the Americas. Even Canada as a whole, which is more attractive than Quebec in particular, is not able to meet its immigration targets.

"The real number of immigrants who came to Canada each year failed to reach the annual target established by the Federal Ministry of immigration."[10]

Immigrants are under no obligation to come to Quebec simply because the good minister said he wants to increase their number. Conditions must first be made more attractive, necessitating changes that many nationalists fear.

Some Immigrants Prefer Quebec

Having at one time partnered with a friend who was a lawyer and immigration consultant, I have a good feel for the kinds of immigrant that might be attracted by Quebec in the new century. I will mention just two kinds, at opposite ends of the spectrum, who may decide to settle here when they first arrive. The first is the immigrant who is very well-off financially and wants to live a life of leisure. For decades, a person with three or four million dollars has been able to come to Quebec and buy a magnificent waterfront estate for not much more than a million dollars.[11] Living in luxury on such an estate, with no mortgage, would still leave two or three millions with which to live a comfortable existence. With that kind of money, a family can educate its children in any language it likes. No one can force rich immigrants—or rich francophones for that matter—not to give their kids a superb English education if that is what they want. In Toronto, the same luxury estate would perhaps cost two to three million dollars, leaving "only" about one or two million dollars to live on. Toronto is nice, but no more nice or fun than Montreal. Some of these millionaires might feel "squeezed" in Toronto (though the extremely rich would not feel squeezed anywhere.) For decades, the relatively depressed state of the Quebec economy and lower prices here have suited millionaires well: their money can go much further.

Another class of immigrant is the one who speaks at least some French and no English. Such immigrants can improve their economic

---

10 Ibid.

11 A similar estate near Geneva, Switzerland could cost four or five million dollars.

situation quickly by coming to a francophone province. This is precisely the same reason motivating protests by monolingual Quebec francophones in the 1960s and 1970s, who wanted jobs in French, because they could not speak English. The language laws of Quebec are structured to "ensure" that monolingual francophones can work in French, to the extent that jobs are created here that do not absolutely require knowledge of English. Many monolingual francophones migrated to Montreal from rural areas of Quebec in pursuit of such jobs. Immigrants from former colonies of France, like Morocco and Algeria, who often speak French and Arabic but little or no English, can come and join the monolingual francophone workforce. Like local monolingual francophones, they mostly, but not exclusively, pursue routine-production and in-person service jobs.

The same environment that is unfavourable for symbolic-analytic workers can be favourable and attractive for routine-production workers. Lower costs in Quebec attract factories, which can employ monolingual French workers. Even though Third-World wages may be substantially lower, in many cases there are clear business advantages to operating in Quebec rather than in Third-World countries. The infrastructure in Third-World countries can be inadequate to support anything but the least sophisticated forms of manufacturing. The bureaucracy may be (and usually is) corrupt, inefficient, and very intrusive. Currency and other controls make life difficult. Qualified local management and technical expertise may be in short supply and bringing in expatriates may be difficult and very expensive.

The Best Immigrants Can Choose

Skilled immigrants have the ability to pick and choose the destination that will best meet their priorities. Too often they do not choose Quebec. Among the most valuable immigrants are those who have a good, expensive education paid for by someone else. These can function in the modern workplace in any physical location and can come and go more or less as they please. Fanatical Quebec nationalists should know that all immigrants, but especially upscale, bright, and well-educated ones, possess a powerful weapon. They can simply not come, or once here, if jostled and aggravated, can simply pack their bags and leave Quebec. No one should assume that immigrants are fools.

I am personally aware of a number of cases where skilled immigrants left Quebec via secondary immigration. One sold his small factory in Egypt and came to Montreal with his wife and three children in the late 1980s. His English was barely passable and his French was weak. He complained to me that a couple of times, when he asked directions in Montreal, francophones became very rude when he could not express himself in French. (He could not express himself well in English either.) He and his family are no longer in Quebec.

A wealthy investor-immigrant, with a petroleum-engineering background, a good knowledge of English, and a little knowledge of French, came to Montreal with his wife and four children in the mid-1990s. He stayed at an expensive hotel in Montreal for about two weeks then moved to Toronto. I was told by the immigration consultant who helped him come to Quebec that this skilled and wealthy immigrant subsequently invested several million dollars in a business in Ontario. My brother Mo, who lives in Toronto, knows of other immigrants who have deliberately avoided Quebec, because their priorities were better served elsewhere.

I would have liked these families, and others like them, to have stayed in Quebec. I feel a sense of loss when good people I know avoid Quebec. Some separatists may think that my loss is their gain, that they are helping the "yes" vote in some future referendum by keeping my acquaintances and many others away. But the big loser is Quebec. If immigrants really are vital, then separatists who feel they are "winning" by helping to keep them away are actually hurting Quebec.

Why We Stayed in Montreal

Fortunately for the population statistics in Quebec, there are immigrants who come and stay. Why are my family and I still in Montreal, and why do I consider it home and enjoy living here? Because the environment here responds to our major needs and priorities and because we enjoy the flavour and lifestyle. In addition, it is because my family and I are in the fortunate position of having been able to deflect or avoid, to a sufficient degree, the adverse effects of Quebec's special priorities on our own priorities. The fact we were able to do this is a tribute to Quebec's democracy: it allows fanatic nationalists some leeway, but it blocks their excesses.

I have frequently spoken to potential immigrants about coming to Canada. I always praise Canada very highly and support such praise with reasoning. About Quebec, I say that it is a great place with a couple of well-known drawbacks. In recent years, I have been saying that the probability of separation has been declining and that, for the foreseeable future, the risk is very low. The election of an anti-separatist Liberal government under Jean Charest in April 2003 gives credence to my argument. To prospective immigrants, I say that if their specific personal and family circumstances are such that these special circumstances do not adversely affect them, then Quebec is one of the best places in North America—or indeed the world—to live. The more so if they speak French or can at all manage to communicate in French.

My family's first priority, my children's ability to develop a modern and strong earnings potential, has been well-satisfied. Educational facilities in Quebec are able to produce knowledge workers of the highest order. Even compared to expensive private schools my children have attended overseas and in Montreal, I am satisfied with the quality of education they have received here in public school,[12] CEGEP, and university. (It is ironic and sad that while we as immigrants avail ourselves fully of this fine system, too many Quebecers forgo this opportunity for a good education.)

I am troubled by pressures on the French language. The decline of the original francophone population is worrisome. Low birthrates and tepid immigration figures are a danger to prosperity and of concern to everyone in Quebec. However, these dangers should frighten de souche Quebecers more than they frighten us. They are endangering the future of their own collectivity more than my family's. I hope that they succeed in overcoming the problems of population and education. As immigrants, we can help to solve both.

Finally, though I think that Franco-Québécois have not always pursued priorities that suit me, it is so easy to like them and enjoy life among them. They are kind, gentle, warm, and humorous people. I very much agreed with the polls that showed Quebecers to be the least belligerent of all Canadians. They are the most uncomfortable Canadians when it comes to the thought of going overseas to kill

---

12 In my view, English, science, and mathematics are taught quite well in the school system here. The weakness, compared to expensive international private schools overseas, is in subjects such as history and geography. As parents, we have been able to overcome some of these weaknesses through travel to various countries and our own international experience and outlook.

defenseless human beings. The majority—highly educated or not—are diligent and conscientious in their work. The fact that I perceive their collective priorities to be changing to suit me better impacts positively on my second priority, belonging and integrating.

However, the question remains: does all this make me a real Quebecer?

Chapter 17: Am I a Real Quebecer?

Integrating in Quebec: A Special Case

As an immigrant, one of my priorities is to belong genuinely in Quebec. If Quebec wishes to attract, keep, and effectively integrate a good number of skilled immigrants, it must structure itself so as not to contradict the following rule: Integration into Quebec and integration into the rest of North America must not be mutually exclusive.

It is more difficult for immigrants to integrate into Quebec society than it is to do so in other parts of Canada. It is easier for newcomers to become part of a multiethnic Canada, where no one race has an overwhelming majority. It is easier to internalize the priorities of Canada, which relate to universal and fundamental human values and needs common to many cultures. It is more difficult to relate to some of the important priorities of Quebec, which for decades have been based on the needs and aspirations of one race. While it is easiest for outsiders to feel that they genuinely belong to Canada or the U.S., it is difficult or impossible to genuinely belong to most other sovereign nation-states in the world. The degree of difficulty for newcomers trying to belong to Quebec lies somewhere in between North America and the rest of the world.

During a meeting with members of the Jewish community in May 2000, while he was still deputy premier of Quebec, Bernard Landry said, "Quebec is a nation. Quebec is not a distinct society. Quebec is not a simple province of Canada. Quebec is a nation, just like Israel is a nation or Greece is a nation or France is a nation." He repeated this message on several occasions.

It is exactly what I do not want to hear. This is precisely the kind of talk that alienates many immigrants. It scares them away from Quebec. If they do come and stay, it helps make them feel like outsiders and motivates them to resist the separatist project any way they can. I am not at all interested in a Quebec that would be like other sovereign nation-states. France is for the French. I have relatives who live in France. They went there to study and stayed on. Some of them have obtained citizenship. They enjoy Paris, the most beautiful and cultured city in the world. But they are not "real French." Greece is defined by the race of its population. I cannot change my race and could not become a "real

Greek" and neither could Premier Bernard Landry. The driving force behind the creation of the state of Israel is the Jewish people. By living in Israel, Premier Landry would not belong to the Jewish people. He goes on to say, "Who belongs to the nation? People who are living in Quebec. It is not an ethnically-based nation or exclusively ethnic nation. It's an open nation. Everyone is welcome."

This statement makes me feel better, though I am in partial disagreement. The Quebec nation envisioned by separatists is most certainly ethnically based. On the other hand, he did say that everyone is welcome. By saying so, the Premier favourably differentiated Quebec from many nation-states. "Everyone" is not welcome in France, Greece, Israel and the majority of nations in the world. I would have felt much better if he had said, "Quebec is a nation not like France, it is a nation like Canada and the United States," which of course an independent Quebec would not be, not quite. It would, however, be better than Europe and the second choice for many immigrants not accepted into Canada or the U.S. (or perhaps Australia?) This is due primarily to the kinder, gentler, and broader-minded attitude of its people. This is the conclusion I have reached after living in Quebec and several European countries. Outside Canada, Quebec would be less attractive than it is as part of Canada; even fewer well-qualified immigrants would choose an independent Quebec over the U.S. and Canada than do now.

"A Good Quebecer of Egyptian Origin"

In the early 1990s a very good friend of mine, Alain Rouleau, introduced me to his uncle Mr. Jean Campeau, at the time a PQ government minister. The minister kindly agreed to meet with us to give us his opinion on a possible high-tech start-up venture. He invited us to his home. After the meeting, we chatted a little and, as we were leaving, he shook my hand and said, "You are a good Québécois of Egyptian origin." So, I thought not for the first time, not all separatists are against "outsiders." For Alain, it went without saying, but I was comforted that a minister with the political party that was trying to create an independent country of Quebec would make a point of making me feel welcome. It reminded me of the corporate environment in the U.S. and the American policeman in Boston who had made sure to do what he could to make me feel welcome in the United States. It made me feel like a real Quebecer. However, it seems that every time something happens to make me feel included, something else happens to alienate me. More than once, xenophobic nationalists came together to define "who is a real Quebecer." By definition, this included a consideration of who is not a real Quebecer.

There is much preoccupation in Quebec with the problem of the integration of immigrants. It is an important goal of the province that immigrants adopt and internalize the language, values, political objectives, and other aspects of the lives of old-stock francophones. An important factor that favours this objective is the keen desire of most immigrants to belong to their new home. It is a powerful force, motivating them to understand, sympathize with, adapt to, and contribute to their new culture. But there is an essential condition to make this happen: the prospective new home must reciprocate and treat immigrants like family.

Quebec does try hard to integrate immigrants, though this is done within the constraints of its distinct priorities. There have also been signals discouraging to "New Quebecers."

The splashiest and most sensational occurred when then-Premier of Quebec, Mr. Jacques Parizeau, ranted against "money and the ethnic vote" upon losing the 1995 referendum on separation. If only he had said "money, the ethnic vote, women, and people over fifty-five years old," things would have been much less bad, because he would have spread his wrath more widely and not appeared to be against all groups not of his race. Such signals are not the way to bring newcomers "into equal membership of a community." They dampen the momentum to integrate and make immigrants more cautious and reserved when adapting to their new culture.

Integrating with a Kind and Gentle Majority of a Different Race

There is a difference between really integrating and feeling at home in one's new society, and merely affecting integration and adaptation in the eyes of the dominant majority. Immigrants do not usually arrive to create an emotional wall between themselves and the local population. If there is such a barrier, it is created by the existing population whether deliberately or inadvertently. In Canada as a whole, there is no formidable state-sponsored, legal, social, or political wall. There may be localized pockets where the majority favours their own. Such pockets can be easily bypassed in everyday life. The exception is within Quebec, where the barrier is clearly present (although not as impermeable as in many other places in the world where immigrants are not really desired at all, e.g., much of Europe.)

Quebec nationalism is based on one kind and gentle race. Though American society is very nationalistic—some would say aggressively nationalistic—nationalism in the United States is not based on one race. The moral code there is that individuals and organizations must strive to make everyone from every background a member of the American family. Not all adhere to that code, and there are examples of racism. After 9-11, fear and anxiety among the general public have resulted in racial profiling. However, other than in special circumstances such as these, I find an embracing attitude to newcomers to be second nature to the American people as a whole and one of their most important sources of power and continuous rejuvenation. Canada also embraces newcomers as equals. In contrast, in Quebec, since the "Quiet Revolution," there appears to be a moral code which says, "Take care of the interests of our own race first and foremost." Another moral code says, "At all costs, let us keep control in our own hands." This is the primary reason I have felt that most Québécois I know, though they individually appear to resemble typical North Americans, sometimes collectively exhibit traits common to those in chauvinistic sovereign nation-states.

Ironically, after 9-11, I feel that Quebecers are more prone to defending the human rights of Muslims and Arabs. They are also less prone to focusing suspicion on this group, simply because the U.S. inclines that way. I don't have a clear explanation for this apparently contradictory but welcome behaviour. Probably, on the one hand, Quebecers at the individual level are fundamentally tolerant and have gentle, humanitarian instincts. This aspect is a positive factor; it helps all immigrants to belong and feel integrated. On the other hand, perhaps an excessively self-centered group attitude is a result of the long period when francophones where treated by some anglos as second class-citizens. Perhaps injustices in the past have left scars and created a siege mentality that is manifesting itself as a defensive attitude towards outsiders. Whatever its origin and whoever is to blame, that works against integration. Fortunately, there is also an effort to welcome immigrants.

Of course, some in Quebec are overtly xenophobic. For example, in February 2001 the youth wing of the Bloc Québécois produced a document to the effect that French Quebec must not dilute itself and that pluralism and inclusiveness are undesirable. Prominent author Paul Ohl writes of francophone "linguistic anxieties caused by ethnic forces on Quebec territory."[1] He is clearly referring to me and people like me as the cause of anxieties. This is strongly reminiscent of Europe and its anti-integrationist attitudes.

"Ethnic forces" sounds alien, sinister, and menacing. The phrase "on Quebec territory" makes it sound as though we do not belong here. My first reaction was to be angry with Mr. Ohl personally. After calming down, I took a step back and reread the article. I concluded that they probably did not represent Mr. Ohl's personal opinion. He was saying that some Quebec politicians were maintaining and fostering anxiety among a segment of the population of Quebec to further their own political objectives.

Whatever the case may be, having been rubbed the wrong way and my hostility provoked, I will be frank about my own conclusions. First of all, Quebec's anxiety has nothing to do with ethnic forces. It is due to the loss of New France, which immigrants had absolutely nothing to do with. As I wrote in an earlier chapter, the French monarchy, together with Cardinal Richelieu and the ancestors of today's francophones, achieved this partly by keeping the population of New France too small, due to their obsession with racial and religious purity. New France was unable to withstand the exploding multiethnic population of the English North American colonies. The elite in Paris and the people of New France at the time showed unrelenting antagonism towards all racial, religious, and ethnic groups except their own. Second, I am not an ethnic force on Quebec territory. I am a Quebecer and Canadian citizen at home on Canadian territory. Tabernac!

Furthermore, these so-called ethnic forces represent a growing and prosperous segment of society. Without them, Quebec faces a shrivelled and aging future. However, we do not like to be coerced or manipulated. In December 2000, during the estates-general on language, Jean-François Lisée, a leading separatist guru, author, and former top advisor to Lucien Bouchard, considered highly intelligent by friends and foes alike, proposed what he suggested would be a reasonable and balanced

---

1 Ohl, Paul, "La peur entretenue," *La Presse*, 15 March 2001.

compromise. He proposes to strike a deal with the Quebec anglo community. As a goodwill gesture, since that community has been shrinking for decades, children of immigrants from English-speaking countries would be allowed into the English school system. The withering English school system in Quebec would receive a much-needed boost. In exchange, the children of allophone immigrants in the French school system, who now may switch to English when they graduate from high school, would have to continue their post-secondary education in French institutions.

To suit his own people, Mr. Lisée proposes a deal with *les anglais* on the backs of everyone else. Give something to the anglos and take something away from the allos. Quebec wants to be loved and wants immigrants to integrate willingly, so let us be illogical and restrict their choices even further. The lack of empathy is jolting. As far as I know, Mr. Lisée gave no suggestions as to how strong immigrants can be forced to attend French post-secondary institutions when they can simply leave the province or not come here in the first place.

Genuine affection and the positive feelings and desire to belong are balanced by the need to be as disengaged as possible from the coercive measures of the majority, which we immigrants may deem to be against our self-interests. Few alert and agile immigrants are likely to wait in trembling anticipation of a favourable outcome in the debate among others. We know our particular circumstances and what is best for us better than any government or think-tank consultant.

Genuine Belonging or Opportunistic and False Integration?

The question of integrating newcomers into Quebec sounds complicated, because it is. Integration is different from adaptation. The latter usually means coming to understand new conditions and adjusting behaviour accordingly. I was happy to live in Rome, Italy, and became well-adapted, but not integrated. To complicate matters further, there is a phenomenon I call opportunistic integration. I do not necessarily mean opportunistic in its negative connotation, meaning unprincipled. In a sense, much human behaviour is opportunistic. When Canada accepts immigrants, it acts opportunistically by taking in good people who want to leave their homes. However, it does not later turn away from them for some perceived gain.

There is at least one very good immigrant friend of mine who is completely integrated and who really feels for Quebec nationalism. He is a professor in the engineering department of a French-language university and very highly educated. The fact that he is married to a beautiful and charming francophone must also play a role in his integration.

Insecure and struggling to pursue their priorities and make a place for themselves, some immigrants feel compelled to opportunistically adjust their level of integration for maximum gain. At certain times in some environments, such as Quebec's public service, that could mean volubly supporting separatism. The most common examples are to be found among those who work in public Quebec institutions with a heavy concentration of de souche Quebecers, such as in the government, schools, universities, and other public organizations. Because they are treated well and constantly rub shoulders with separatists and hard-liners, over the years some have genuinely internalized these perspectives. Others only appear to have done so. Such an effect occurs because many sense that they are not quite equal to "real Quebecers," for example in matters such as hiring and promotion, or perhaps due to something in their mentality carried over from their old countries. If they were to change jobs from the provincial government to a private sector company full of federalists, would they change sides politically? The response of some immigrants to real or imagined "anti-integrationist" signals in Quebec is a kind of non-committal, opportunistic integration.

This question brings us to what I call false integration. I know only one immigrant who I am certain is falsely integrated. This person works for a branch of the Quebec government, speaks fluent French, and behaves as if nicely integrated, but cannot wait to leave and do something else.

"I don't like them," this person says about the majority of the province. Apparently, in a meeting some years ago, someone said that people like the person above did not really belong in Quebec. The uncertain and vulnerable sometimes resort to subterfuge. The behaviour of some Franco-Québécois towards immigrants resembles that of the "dees and dose" English manager of decades ago. That kind of behaviour, even by a few, can bring dislike upon a whole race. The attitude of some narrow-minded francophones is reminiscent of the regulations that govern "temporary foreign guest workers" in European countries. This is not why I crossed the Atlantic.

In the 1980s, I was surprised that the PQ was trying to attract large numbers of immigrants and allophones to the separatist cause. To me that was a fantasy. Some francophile immigrants may be persuaded, but certainly not most immigrants. As the years went by, I was even more surprised that many separatists continued not to understand why immigrants do not flock to their banner. I hope this book helps explain the reasons for the schism between the desires of many newcomers to Canada and those of Quebec separatists. It is not a matter of malice by either side.

When I decided not to go back home to Egypt, Canada became my new home. A very important reason for this is that, in Canada, no ethnic grouping constitutes a majority. Neither the English, French, Italians, Hungarians, nor any others constitute fifty-percent-plus-one of the population. We are therefore all minorities. As the late Pierre Trudeau put it in 1971[2]:

"Canada's population distribution has now become so balanced as to deny any one racial or linguistic component an absolute majority. Every single person in Canada is now a member of a minority group."

There is an interesting phenomenon related to our mixed marriage. We left Canada and returned to live in Egypt for a few years. My relatives and old friends warmly welcomed my Swiss wife, Heidi. As they got to know her, they grew to like her and enjoy her company. But despite the warmth, kindness, and hospitality of the Egyptians, there was simply no question of her ever becoming a "real Egyptian." In Switzerland, Heidi's family and friends are very nice—they spoil me and treat me as one of their own. But there is no expectation on any side that I can be a "real Swiss." In Canada, the question never arises: Heidi and I are both 100% Canadian. We are both at home. My wife, children, and I are "real Canadians" no matter what. We are real Quebecers because Quebec is part of Canada. We can shrug off anti-integrationist currents. We can genuinely belong.

---

2 During a Ukrainian-Canadian congress in Winnipeg.

Part IV

An Immigrant's Wish List

Chapter 18: Two Wishes for Canada

In stories from my old culture, a genie, or jinn, is a member of a distinct non-human species, as angels are also considered to be. Often, a jinn appears—famously, from an ancient lamp, but possibly from somewhere else—and offers to fulfill the wishes of a human, usually in exchange for something or other. Like folktales all over the world, these stories are a reflection of the values and accumulated wisdom of a people. They serve to pass down in verbal form their cultural heritage and give the listener food for contemplation. The wish—how it is formulated, fulfilled, and the consequences and repercussions thereafter—serves to shed light on the fears, desires, strengths, and weaknesses of individuals and their relationships with people around them and with their societies. Myths are a reflection of the culture that produces them.

I think stories about genies in my mother-culture are in some ways equivalent to those of magic wands in Western culture. One difference is that while a magic wand is itself usually lifeless and under the control of its user, genies can be petulant and even mischievous at times. They can become angry or vindictive. It appears to be more difficult to deal with a genie than to handle a magic wand, and there is a higher element of uncertainty. We can imagine that I actually did meet a genie and managed to persuade him to grant my wishes. Of course, I started by wishing for lots of money and other personal things (which surely would come as no surprise to any genie experienced with humans.)

When I got around to making wishes for Canada, my first wish was for the Canadian people and governments to maintain their calm and national poise in the face of terrorism and continuing global conflicts. We should not be frightened, manipulated, or pressured into either joining unwarranted aggression overseas, or allowing the unique relationship between our diverse ethnic, racial, and religious groups to degenerate into internal turmoil.

The source of immigrants to Canada has been shifting ever more away from the former colonial powers of Europe. More and more immigrants are coming from formerly subjugated and oppressed colonies of the same European countries that supplied the bulk of immigrants in the past. Many of today's New Canadians are sensitive to injustice by powerful post-industrial countries—with their weapons that can inflict widespread death and destruction from a distance—against weak societies still struggling to grasp the fundamentals of the Industrial Revolution. However it is presented and explained, there is something wrong when we reach the point that the wealthiest country in the world, our ally, feels compelled to bomb some of the poorest.

Most of us know that "peace is the dream of the wise" and not much more. Wars will continue to be commonplace. There is, however, an element of human decency in our species that seeks to avoid inflicting suffering on others. My wish is that this noble emotion continues to dominate the foreign and domestic affairs of Canada. Though I know that it might sometimes be necessary to participate in the violence of a harsh world, let it be a rare misfortune.

Included in my wish is that governments, the Canadian power structure, and regular folks of every racial, religious, and ethnic origin neither favour nor disparage any grouping as a result of conflicts abroad. In the diversity of our society, it is only natural for people to sympathize with troubles related to their "other home" and try to help the old country. However, the behaviour of individual cultural groups should not reflect troubles abroad in a way that harms Canada and other Canadians. Of course, violence must never occur within Canada. We must all learn from the example of passionate federalists and separatists in Quebec who, on the whole, dealt with a difficult and tense relationship in a decent and civilized manner. Canada is comprised of many ethnic groups who have chosen to journey through life together. No group should instigate serious hostility, conflict, manipulation, or social and political pressure and injure our delicate mosaic. If many ethnic groups were to pursue the interests of some foreign cause on the backs of other Canadians, we would not have a country for long. Also included in this wish is that Canada always find a way to balance good relations with the U.S. with the need to uphold our own moral standards and pursue our benign foreign policies.

My next wish for Canada was indirect, a wish primarily for our neighbours and friends, the Americans. It is not for me to tell Americans what to do. But our destinies are inextricably linked. When America is safe, so are we. When America prospers, so does Canada. I can say that, as a Canadian, I will be comfortable again when I see the rare and admirable self-correcting capabilities of the American system do three things.

First, please stop the boastful nonsense about predominance in the world. Setbacks in Iraq and Afghanistan alone should warrant a rethinking in more modest terms. Furthermore, it has become clear that attempts at global hegemony will inevitably result in long-term countermeasures among the not so weak, those who cannot be defeated or controlled except possibly at a cost out of all proportion to what might be gained. At the time of this writing France, Germany, and Russia have pulled together to quietly pursue their own interests in opposition to the U.S., which has chosen to go its unilateral way. Russia, China, and India have strengthened their cooperation with one another to counter U.S. ambitions.

More dangerously, talk of a mighty "American Empire" ignores a critical aspect of the New World Order: the world has learned that America is vulnerable. One adult, with one rifle and the assistance of one minor, for weeks terrorized the capital city of "the most powerful empire the world has ever seen." After the Taliban were routed, Bin Laden was mocked as a fugitive hiding in a cave somewhere. Yet, the president and vice-president of the greatest power the world has ever known also had to be hidden away in "undisclosed locations." For all we know, there may have been a cave or two among these locations, perhaps fortified relics of the Cold War. In the American Empire, insecurity affects everyone from the top leadership to the ordinary citizen. The blackout affecting 50 million people in the U.S. and Canada in August 2003 demonstrated the frailty of our way of life. With the unprecedented military and economic power, there is also unprecedented vulnerability. In my view, this is the most important way the world has changed since 9-11.

Second, as a logical conclusion of the above and as a component of strict security measures against terrorism, at the very least I would like to see our friends south of the border stop participating in the torment of Third-World peoples. Everything possible should be done to be fair, just, and, if possible, compassionate. The gap between American values and American actions should be narrowed as much as possible, while remaining relevant to the reality of our world.

Third, do all that while still carrying a big stick.

Other than these two, I don't think I would have any wishes to make for Canada directly, even though there are many things wrong with my new country and much room for improvement. To borrow from Winston Churchill: Canada is the worst country in the world, save all the others. Given our characteristics as a species and regardless of the U.N.'s "quality of life index," I don't believe any large group of humans can live together in a modern, complex society and do any better than we have done here. I don't want to tamper with a good thing. If it ain't broke, don't fix it.

When I had finished with the first two wishes, the genie raised one eyebrow ever so slightly. "Be careful with your wishes, human," he said in a cold, stony voice. "Your second wish sounds too much like a wish for world peace. You should know better. That would require that characteristics of your species be changed. I would not do such a thing even if I could, even if I were allowed to. Think carefully and be realistic."

I had heard that the jinn are an irritable and impatient race. At least this one seemed quiet enough. Still, I resolved not to let myself get carried away, and from then on to focus my wishes on my direct environment in the city and province where I live.

Chapter 19: A Wish for Montreal

My next wish, O perspicacious and forbearing genie, is to rescue beautiful Montreal from the dominance, priorities, and politicians of the rural regions of Quebec and allow it to reach its full, world-class, glittering potential.

Perhaps the results of the 2003 Quebec elections will prove to be a first step in fulfilling this wish.

Cities Are Economic Motors

Many centuries ago, cities overtook rural areas as generators of wealth. Economics teaches us how the armed caravans of itinerant merchants, which very slowly rendered the old closed manorial economies obsolete, represented an important factor in the emergence of the modern city. Apparently, starting in about eighth-century Europe, these traveling traders were neither lords nor peasants and were free. Gradually, permanent trading places established themselves around fortified sites, such as castles. Almost imperceptibly, urbanization was born. It progressed gradually over the centuries until a new class of merchants surpassed the traditional feudal lords in wealth and power. Revenues of the feudal aristocracy, based on the surpluses produced by downtrodden serfs and peasants, could not match the riches amassed by the new merchant classes. Prominent trading families established their networks over great distances and brought desirable and advanced products from the Middle East and the Orient. Even well before the industrial revolution, cities became the centers of a new economy that produced never-before-seen wealth. Such urban centers became largely independent of the old power structures of feudal-rural societies.

Cities created great wealth through (in modern parlance) business activities on a large geographic scale. The Industrial Revolution magnified the effect, and wealth creation in and around cities took another quantum leap. In modern times, cities and their surrounding areas are enormous creators of wealth. The output resulting from the synergy, creativity, and concentration of talented and educated workers cannot be matched by rural areas.[1] Not surprisingly, since the

---

1 Some predict that with new inexpensive means of rapid communication such as the Internet, the physical concentration of talent and resources will be less important for wealth creation.

emergence of the earliest cities there have been differences in mentalities and priorities between urban and rural populations. War has sometimes resulted from the dissonance between urban centers and rural regions.

A Tale of Two Basels

One city which in the past has clashed with the countryside around it is the small Swiss city of Basel (or Bâle.) It is a beautiful, prosperous, and cultured city. However, when I first visited it I was not interested in and did not visit any of its many museums. Nor did I pay much attention to its dozens of captivating fountains, some of them veritable works of art. I did not know or care that this city had emerged in the usual way—in the case of Basel, around Roman fortifications—or that the first settlement had been Celtic. I knew that it was at the intersection of Germany, France, and Switzerland, but it did not register that this was an important factor in its historic ability to trade and amass riches. It didn't matter that the city boasted Switzerland's first university, founded in 1460. Nor did its very high proportion of superbly-skilled workers mean much to me. I was just a young student and all my attention was focused on the reason that had brought me to Basel in the first place: the annual Fastnacht, or carnival, which turns the otherwise serious city, usually intensely focused on wealth creation, into one giant uninhibited masked ball.

Being wealthy, the citizens of Basel spend freely on the most magnificent costumes. Particularly fascinating to me were the extremely sophisticated bands of fifes and drums.[2] The drums beat complicated and beautifully intricate rhythms while the melodies from the small, shrill flutes soared high above, seemingly free and detached yet completely integrated. Each of the multitude of bands had its own musical style and its own distinctly fascinating costumes and masks. As they moved slowly through the streets I stood transfixed and watched in fascination. At the time, in my rash and immature youth, the only thing that could compete for my attention with these exquisite bands were the exquisite young ladies enjoying the festivities.

Then, I also knew that there were two Basels, Basel Stadt and Basel Landschaft. The first is the canton of Basel City and the second the

---

2 Apparently, this type of band was introduced to America during the War of Independence. It was brought across the Atlantic by the Hessians, who learned about it from the Swiss.

canton of Basel Countryside. A canton in Switzerland can be compared to a province in Canada. Both countries are quite decentralized and Swiss cantons, like Canadian provinces, have many powers and freedom of action in their fields of jurisdiction. There was a time in the past when there was only one united canton of Basel: until about 1830 the city and rural areas of Basel formed one canton. In what was probably the last serious violent civil conflict in Switzerland, the formerly-united canton of Basel was partitioned into two half-cantons, each with a separate constitution. The priorities of the city and of rural folks were just too different. The city was located on the river Rhine, a major artery, and its prosperity depended on openness and trade. It was open to the world and relied on its skilled traders and craftsmen for its wealth. It prospered. However, in the early 19th century, there were commercial, economic and old socio-political problems that had to be resolved.

Though Napoleon had been brought down earlier, the ideas of the French revolution had strongly influenced the Swiss Confederacy. Everywhere the ideas of nationalism and fraternity, still new at the time, were replacing the old conservative political structures. A few Swiss cantons, including and especially Basel, held out and resisted the changes. The conservative elements were in the city of Basel, whereas the new "radical" ideas were steadily permeating the countryside of the canton. The city dominated the countryside, the relationship based on the old, unfair structures and ideas. As historian Karl Weber wrote, "The internal politics of Basel were reactionary. This weighed heavily on the citizens of the rural areas."[3]

Though rural residents outnumbered the city's population by two to one, the ruling council had more voting representatives from the city. The laws and regulations for the whole canton were heavily influenced by the city's priorities. For years, the countryside requested that representatives be elected to the ruling Grand Council of the Canton of Basel in the same proportion as the rural and urban populations.

> "The city refused not simply out of narrow-mindedness, but because its politicians believed it would not suit the city's commercial interests to give the majority vote in the Grand Council to representatives of rural areas who had such different interests."[4]

---

3 Weber, *Revolution*, p8. Translated by the author.
4 Dürrenmatt, *Schweizer*, p464. Translated by the author.

Finally, in November of 1830, citizens from the country presented a petition to the Grand Council of Basel, again requesting equal representation. The council refused.

The civil war in the Canton of Basel began in January of 1831. A troop of armed men from the country advanced on the city. Troops from the city confronted them and suppressed the rebellion, temporarily. A second battle followed, and then a third in which the city was defeated. Alienated and bitter, the countryside held a referendum in which it proposed a constitution that would serve its own people and be completely separate from the city. It was a winning referendum: the partitioning of the Canton of Basel was accepted by the rural population.

The outcome was rejected by the city. It sent out yet another army for a fourth battle. It was defeated decisively. Partition became a reality. The federal government of Switzerland helped set up a commission to arbitrate and helped with the technicalities of separation and the division of assets. The dividing of territory did not present a big problem:

> "The border between the two new cantons corresponded to the city limits...The partitioning of the population was also a simple matter."[5]

Citizens belonged to one canton or the other depending on where they lived. Of course, they all remained Swiss citizens since neither of the partitioned parts wanted to separate from Switzerland.

Partitioning the assets of the formerly united cantons presented the biggest legal and technical challenges. The binding arbitration commission judged that the assets should be divided according to population: a third for the city and two thirds for the rural regions. The rancour and continuing political tensions meant that only the few easiest and least-important assets could be agreed upon quickly. The bulk of the process was complicated, difficult, and acrimonious. Citizens of Basel City were enraged at proposals to physically divide their beloved university as well as its movable and immovable assets. There were cries of derision about what a bunch of peasants were going to do with valuable books they couldn't even read. Finally it was decided that the university, with all its assets, would remain intact and stay within the canton of Basel City, but that Basel Countryside would receive monetary compensation in lieu of its share.

---

5 His, *Staatsteilung*, p76. Translated by the author.

A Rich Montreal Benefits All

Basel City was unfair to the countryside in the formerly-united canton of Basel. Residents of the rural areas wanted to get away from the political power of the city. In modern Quebec, it may be the other way around. It seems to me that many Montrealers would not object to removing themselves from the political influence of the countryside, known as the "regions." I do not support partition in Quebec. Still, the example of Basel serves as a reminder of what could happen in a stubborn environment. Fortunately today's Quebecers are neither stubborn nor insensitive so that the idea of partition is far-fetched. Furthermore, twenty-first-century Montreal is far removed from nineteenth-century Basel: there will most probably be no civil war here. A point to be made is that, in the conflict of interests and priorities between the Greater Montreal area and the regions, the majority of immigrants tend to side with the city.

Immigrants in Canada as a whole tend to settle in large urban centers, with Toronto attracting the lion's share of new arrivals. They are attracted to the Montreal area for the same reasons. Many of Quebec's high-tech jobs are concentrated here: skilled allophone workers, sorely needed in this sector, are more likely to find employment here. Few such workers do not speak English (they probably would not be as skilled and up-to-date if they didn't), and a weakness in French does not disqualify them from many good jobs.

Furthermore, the city is obviously more likely to enable immigrants and allophones from each origin to find and socialize with groups from the old country. There is more opportunity to speak the soothing language of their childhood. They may more easily find restaurants that serve nostalgic dishes from the old culture. There are more likely to be community centers and language classes for those who want to pass on as much as possible of the old culture to their children. Immigrants who settle in Quebec overwhelmingly prefer do so on the island of Montreal, or very nearby.

Many urban and suburban francophone Quebecers are federalist and value the presence of allophones as an indispensable "ethnic force" to help counter the rural-based separatist forces. Shortly after the defeat of the 1995 referendum on sovereignty and the negative remarks attributed to Bernard Landry and Premier Jacques Parizeau, it seemed to me that on more than one occasion when I interacted with francophones in Montreal, they were even more pleasant and warm towards me than usual. I remember thinking that they were perhaps trying to placate me and compensate for the hostile statements of prominent politicians. If I am right, then that was a fine example of North American behaviour, such as one would expect to encounter in Canada and the U.S. I am thankful for the presence of federalist de souche Quebecers in Montreal. I would like to take this opportunity to extend my compliments and thank these francophone Canadians here and wherever else they may be in Quebec and Canada. They are open-minded and advanced—even if they may give importance to nationalism, they give at least the same importance to equality between races. They have to put up with verbal abuse from the narrow-minded Quebecers who call them *vendus* or *collabos*. But these are the Canadian Quebecers with whom I and other immigrants are happy and proud to integrate. Without them, Quebec would be a far less attractive place, perhaps even an unbearable place for many of us.

Rural Quebec needs the city. The city needs its current mostly federalist immigrants—its ethnics—and many more new ones for its future prosperity. The city can do without rural Quebec for its prosperity. Taking this a step further, there is an opinion that Montreal would be better off without the regions. (A similar opinion has been expressed in Greater Toronto regarding relations with its own Ontario rural hinterland.) Montrealers know that the forced mergers of municipalities, on which they were not consulted, was imposed by a government that came to power by virtue of the rural vote.

My wish is that Montreal be set free to grow in population and soar in prosperity, while remaining part of Quebec. There would be a great deal more money for everyone. Rural areas would benefit from a portion of the increased wealth.

Chapter 20: A Wish List for Quebec

The genie sat impassively. I looked at him closely, trying to gauge his reaction to my wishes while trying not to appear to be staring. I could not fathom his thoughts or his mood.

"Now I come to my last wish," I said. "Thank you for your patience."

"Your last wish then," he said with no sign of emotion. "Speak."

"Sorry, what I meant to say is 'my last category of wishes'. They are about the Province of Quebec."

"Category?" A flicker of annoyance seemed to cross his face.

"I assure you it is not too long. I will be brief. It will be a simple matter for you, O mighty genie."

"Speak, then!"

A New Revolution

My first wish for Quebec is for a new Quiet Revolution.

Perhaps this is already under way, as "Quebec re-invents itself." The second revolution would be different from the first. I see religion as the glue that held old-stock Québécois together until about the 1950s. Nationalism replaced religion as the binding social force, and the Quiet Revolution of the 1960s was a nationalist revolution. Its focus was fraternity within one race. The Quebec nation would hold together against alien oppressors. The driving thought was: my fraternal compatriot and I pitted against others. The second Quiet Revolution I wish for would be a kind of social revolution. Its focus would be equality.

The equality I am wishing for here is the complete equality of all Quebecers, regardless of origin. The current nomenclature partitioning Quebec society into Québécois *de souche*, anglo, and allo would become obsolete. Everyone would be a Quebecer, not just in words but in the minds of the population and in everyday life. Fraternity would be replaced by equality. The first quiet revolution pitted francophones against the dominant anglos; originally it was necessary and successful. The second one would help francophones collectively move on to another mode of thinking. In this mode, the glue binding them in their new society would be neither religion nor nationalism but an equality that satisfied their individual self-interest and also their self-esteem. During the first Quiet Revolution, nationalism demanded subjugating the interests of the individual to the interests of a transcendental collectivity, or nation. After the second Quiet Revolution, formerly nationalistic francophones would belong to a larger collectivity that stressed self-interest and racial and ethnic equality.

Language Laws and Social Stratification

I also have a wish, O munificent genie, for nationalist politicians and other elites in Quebec to stop the practice of protecting the French language on the backs of the poor.

In all the countries to which I paid a more than just a cursory visit and had the time to carefully observe, I found that a good knowledge of English is a factor in social stratification. In Germany, France, Switzerland, Saudi Arabia, Japan, and elsewhere, those who speak English have a distinct advantage over those who don't. In Egypt, upward mobility in society is more possible today than some decades ago. However, it is still very restricted. A knowledge of Western languages is an absolute requirement among the small upper classes. Members of the huge lower classes are deprived of the opportunity to learn other languages, and poverty is passed on from generation to generation. In the growing middle class, the opportunity to study other languages, most especially English, is a coveted asset and a dream come true. The economic benefits of speaking English are enormous. In Cairo, a secretary who speaks English can make up to four times more than one who does not. I regret that in Quebec I have detected a steady, creeping trend of social stratification based on knowledge of English.

I have not seen statistics linking the knowledge of English among francophone children to the income levels of their parents. As far as I can tell, wealthy and well-educated de souche Quebecers overwhelmingly make sure that their children are fluent in English. That apparently includes nationalist politicians and intellectuals. In Quebec today, there is more than one way money can buy fluency in English. In my cynical and suspicious mind, influenced by what I have seen elsewhere, loopholes in the law are left intact for the benefit of rich and powerful francophones. A way must exist for them to teach their children English without breaking the law. It does not matter to them that making use of the loopholes requires money, which they have. Even if political correctness and social peace eventually require some of these loopholes to be closed, power, prestige, and wealth will ensure that the remaining cracks in the laws are sufficient or that new loopholes are discreetly opened up. It may be years until the new loopholes attract the attention of the general public and come under attack. When that happens, the rich and powerful will find other ways; as always they will be a step ahead of everyone else. In my opinion, it will never be impossible for francophone members of the elite to obtain a first-class English education for their children. The same cannot be said for low-income Quebecers of all ethnicities, except English.

As the understanding and the pressure grows, there will be calls for more and better English education in French schools, thus creating a more democratic and egalitarian educational system. It will be many years before children in French schools in monolingual French neighbourhoods are able to master English in any meaningful way. Unless, of course, their parents are rich. Or unless my genie can do something quickly to resolve this issue.

Many low-income francophone families are hurt by language laws that increase the risk of their children growing up without fluency in English. Perhaps the French language is being protected, or can ultimately be saved in North America, but this is currently being done on the backs of the poor. The rationale for this aggression against the poor is that French is fragile.

I have had conversations with francophones who are keen to protect the French language. In 1996, I met an intelligent businessman, a separatist, who had worked closely with PQ Minister Loise Beaudouin. He was instrumental in introducing the Internet in its early days and explaining its benefits to the government. I asked him why it was that language laws were needed in Quebec to protect the French language.

He said, "Without these laws, waves of francophone families would send their kids to English schools, not to mention immigrants."

"But in this way, francophones are accepting the elimination of their freedom of choice."

"Yes, to protect French."

"If they are that keen to protect French in this way, they would send their kids to French schools anyway, laws or no laws. Their nationalism would prevail whether or not they were allowed into English schools."

He did not respond directly.

I participated in another notable conversation a few years later, in 1999. I discussed the same question with an ardent francophone businessman, originally from Europe. He did not agree that "waves" of francophones would send their children to English schools.

He admitted he had not seen studies or formal estimates and said, "Perhaps a certain number, 5% or 15%, or whatever, would do it." He added, "Such people (francophones who would enroll their kids in English schools if the law allowed it) are like the Mafia: doing something like that for material gain."

That seemed a little extreme. I protested. "The Mafia is known as a criminal organization which, at least according to novels, murders its enemies and terrorizes them by putting horse heads in their beds and such. Those francophones would not be breaking any laws—"

But he stuck to his viewpoint, repeated "like the Mafia," and then added, "The state must use its power to force people in the right direction."

I asked, "Do you have children?"

"Yes."

"Do they speak English?"

"Oh yes, fluently," he said rather proudly.

"What do you say to poor francophone parents who see your fluently bilingual kids and want their own children to be just like them and have the same opportunities? Low-income people may not have the financial means to do whatever you did to give your children perfect English."

He did not answer, just smiled and looked away. I repeated the question and, again, he just smiled.

Perhaps some fanatic and intelligent francophone nationalists suffer from a painful dichotomy, a realization that English is vital for them and their children even as they fear and loathe it. They must live with two incompatible emotions that pull painfully in opposite directions.[1] It is especially difficult for those who cannot mentally disassociate the English language from the English people in the same way that today Arabic numbers and algebra are disassociated from the Arab people. My wish is that the genie speed up the process of understanding and spare as many youngsters as possible.

As they stand today, language laws contribute to class discrimination.

---

1 This is sometimes called "cognitive dissonance" by behavioural scientists.

Piggyback French on English

My next wish, O wise and mighty genie, is for the French language in the Americas not to be dependent for its survival primarily on one ethnic group, which is declining in numbers from year to year.

Francophone immigrants from countries like Algeria and Haiti are valuable but, in my view, insufficient to make a decisive impact on the strength of the French language in the Americas. Notwithstanding the presence of different ethnicities speaking French, the main brunt of the struggle to protect that language is borne by the original Québécois. Every year, there are fewer of them than the year before.

Even my powerful genie could probably not manage to significantly increase the birthrate in Quebec. For this wish to come true, two things must happen. First, Quebec must become very attractive to immigrants so that a great many of them decide to settle here. Second, a very large proportion of those who do settle in Quebec must willingly and happily learn and use French and teach it to their children.

When evaluating the benefits nationalism has on the well-being of French in North America, the negative impact of coercive nationalism on population size and growth must be considered.

We can formulate the problem as a choice between two courses of action:

One: Force French on newcomers. This will increase the proportion of French speakers among immigrants. However, as a result of said coercion, much fewer will come to Quebec.

The population of Quebec will continue to shrink in relative terms. French will decline compared to English, Spanish, and Portuguese.

Two: Attract many more immigrants by offering bilingual edu-cation, thus substantially increasing the number of French speakers on the continent.

Both decisions entail risks. Decision-making theory helps increase the probability that a course of action is chosen to maximize an objective, such as profits, market share, votes, or public image. Faced with two such mutually exclusive possible courses of action, the so-called "opportunity cost" of pursuing each action is defined as the return given up by not pursuing the other.[2] Of course, the net returns from the course of action

---

[2] Actually, in uncertain environments, one does not pursue returns but rather pursues "expected returns." Under conditions of uncertainty, the decision-making process is complicated, taking into account the expected benefits and costs of each course of action and the estimated probability of various events.

selected, must be greater than those that could have been had from the course of action not pursued. Otherwise the decision will be wrong, since the selected course of action would result in a lower net return than another course of action would have produced.

In our case, the first course of action results in a higher percentage of immigrants learning French; however, there would be fewer total newcomers. The second consists of perhaps a slightly lower percentage of immigrants learning French; however, many more would come.

So far, Quebec has chosen the first course of action.

I believe a very serious study is required, to determine the chances that the second course of action would result in more French speakers on this continent.

Linguistically speaking, there is a very large opportunity cost to selecting the current course of action, which forces immigrants in Quebec into a French education, in order to increase the proportion of newcomers in the province who speak French. That is because the number of immigrants who will go elsewhere and are unlikely ever to learn French is also substantially increased.

It is very difficult, or impossible, to measure exactly to what extent the coerced priorities of Quebec discourage immigrants from settling in the province. But the effect is clearly visible.

A simple estimate may help gauge the magnitude of the population loss for Quebec. If the province had been able to maintain the 1971 relative population of 78% of that of Ontario, then according to my rough, conservative estimate, its population in 2000 might have been 8.344 million.[3] Instead it was only 7.372 million. More elaborate calculations yield better results for Quebec.

No one can control where immigrants decide to settle for good, especially those who are skilled or well-educated. The only way to get them is to attract them. There is no doubt in my mind that over the past few decades, there has been an opportunity cost of at least many hundreds of thousands of immigrants who avoided Quebec. Most of these, and their children, are lost forever to the French language and culture.

---

3 The simplified calculation assumes that all population growth in both provinces is due to immigration and that the combined population of both provinces is unchanged in the year 2000: that is, that all additional immigrants who would have come to Quebec went to Ontario instead. It conservatively assumes that total immigration to both provinces would not change if Quebec were more appealing: i.e., that Quebec's gain is Ontario's loss. The estimated population of Quebec would be even greater if we assumed that a proportion of the immigrants who went to the other provinces would also have come to Quebec under the right circumstances.

My genie is faced with a difficult problem regarding the future of French on this continent. If we continue with our current policies, many immigrants will continue to stay away, and the chance to teach them French will be lost, as will the chance to expand use of the language. If we relax the language laws and give freedom of choice to all, many more immigrants will come. However, the province must be clever at making French attractive. My genie must find a way to attract immigrants and also make them voluntarily and happily adopt French. There may be other ways, but I don't see an alternative to a perfectly bilingual educational system. Success would mean that the French language will flourish even as the de souche francophones continue to decline in numbers.

A Genie's Anger

I thanked the genie for his patience: that was the last of my wishes. From reading and hearing the old tales, I am aware that the jinn have no particular affection for humans. Though there is interaction between the two species, it is generally at arm's length, almost as if both sides would rather avoid it. The stories reflect that while humans generally fear the jinn, the latter are, on the whole, uninterested in humans and view them somewhat disdainfully. However, perhaps the particular genie who hears my wishes will be peculiar in that he does like humans. In the tales of The Thousand-and-One Nights, there are cases where genies take human females as mates. Though at times the circumstances or consequences are unhappy, perhaps this particular genie will have a female human mate whom he loves dearly. Perhaps this affection will extend a little to the human race as a whole. After hearing my last wish, this genie says:

"O human! Verily your wishes disappoint me greatly and fill me with a deep sadness! We meet here in what some have called the best country in the world. I see millions of people living in the lap of luxury in peace and prosperity. I see cities among the wealthiest in the world today and more dazzling than Baghdad or Peking at the height of their legendary glory centuries ago. I see security for the people and an abundance of food and material wealth in a place where many of those designated as poor would be called rich and envied in many places in the world. I see rulers that can be removed by the people, a concept I have been able to observe only recently since my appearance in this world a thousand years ago and which I have not yet fully absorbed or indeed understood. Your ordinary people—"

"I think I see your point—" I begin to say.

"Quiet! You see nothing! You have talked a great deal; now it is my turn! Your ordinary people have more and better entertainment than the greatest of your Roman emperors. The most magnificent of all sultans, the incomparable Haroun Al-Rachid himself, did not have access to such splendid and varied options for entertainment and recreation. Even today, billions all over the world are deprived of even a small fraction of what you take for granted or dispose of as waste. There are wretched souls who rely on criminal gangs and risk or lose their lives in an attempt to come and live among you. Yet, with you and your Canadians living in the lap of luxury and in peace and security, you formulate wishes which are shallow and frivolous as the foam shivered playfully by the breeze over the dark and deep ocean of human misery and suffering. Have you asked for a cure for AIDS? No! Yet you are aware of the terrible suffering this disease has caused even right here."

The genie pauses for breath and speaking quickly I say, "I'm very sorry. I can explain. You see, I have been living in Canada for a long time, and having adapted and integrated I have unfortunately lost some of my historical perspective and global overview."

"Silence!" roars the genie. "What about the plight of the Palestinians! Even as we speak they are a captive people. Enemy tanks and bulldozers rampage through their overcrowded and defenseless refugee camps. You did not deign to make a wish for them, even though they are your people!"

"Actually, I am Egyptian," I mutter feebly, "and really I was just going to get around to a wish about relief for the Palestinians..."

"Don't interrupt!" thunders the genie. "If you interrupt me again I shall turn you into a blind beggar in the poorest district of the worst city in the most wretched country in the world. You shall be covered in rags and will wander the filthy streets and alleys on bare feet in search of sustenance. Children will taunt you, hungry and dilapidated thieves will steal the few pathetic coins from your most valued possession, your tin cup. Stray dogs will snap at your heels. Lines of schoolgirls in neat uniforms will pass you by, orderly and prim, with not so much as a glance, completely insensitive to your plight. Tourists will stare at you in horror as their guides rush them past and tell them not to look. The few kindly souls who drop a pittance in your cup will keep their distance and be very careful not to touch you in any way for fear of contracting a disease or infection. As for that specific beggar whom you will replace, I will bring him here to Canada and he will assume your place. He will have a private residence, warm in winter and cool in summer, with all the food he can eat, a universal healthcare system with a highly-trained, conscientious, and professional staff, and a colour TV set, which he had never seen even before he went blind, as well as fine clothes and many other good things. He will have a car like the ones he now occasionally hears going by or which honk at him loudly and contemptuously if he is in the way. Come to think of it, you have made no direct, urgent wish on behalf of the people forced to beg on the streets of your own Canadian cities, sometimes in deadly cold weather."

I take great care not to interrupt again. The genie continues: "It also did not occur to you to make a wish on behalf of all the abused and oppressed women on the planet, many of whom are treated no better than slaves. You are obviously dedicated to your own children, who grew up well-nurtured, educated and nourished. Yet you made not one wish for the children elsewhere who are forced to labour most of their waking hours, are malnourished, and for whom a proper education is beyond even dreaming about. You have not even made a wish on behalf of the children in the world who are literally starving. Due to the persistent drought conditions in Sub-Saharan Africa, entire towns and villages are being emptied of their now-skeletal inhabitants, who have lost all their possessions and means of subsistence and must pray for help from corrupt and greedy unelected rulers. You never thought of a wish for any of the suffering in Africa, whence you originally came."

The genie pauses and I am tempted to gently interject that I was from *North* Africa even though, of course, I was very concerned. However, still in terror of his threat, I make sure to remain silent.

"Your wishes are esoteric whims for a spoiled and pampered population who seem to create pseudo problems to pass the time. Perhaps it is an additional form of entertainment; I do not claim to understand your species fully. In any case, I have decided to depart from ancient, well-established tradition and deny you your wishes. It is a rare occurrence and I may be penalized. Still, I cannot bring myself to respond to such shallow and trivial wishes that reflect what in global terms are the most minor of difficulties in the best country in the world, while there is so much pain, poverty, injustice, oppression, hunger, and misery elsewhere. You Canadians have all the intellect, all the education, and all the resources to solve these simple so-called problems yourselves. My abilities are needed elsewhere. You will get nothing from me. Goodbye!"

"Wait! Wait!" I call in alarm, "What about the money?"

The jinn pauses. "What money?" he asks.

"The money I wished for myself at the very beginning, O sagacious and benevolent genie, before my first wish for Canada. When do I get it? Is it already in my bank account?"

The genie hesitates for a moment and appears to mellow, then his expression hardens again and he snaps, "No! You get nothing!"

With that, he disappears in a puff, leaving behind an elusive scent of myrrh and pomegranates.

Bibliography

Ahmed, Leila. *A Border Passage. From Cairo to America: A Woman's Journey*. New York: Penguin Books, 1999.

Anderson, Roy R., Robert F. Selbert, and Jon G. Wagner. *Politics and Change in the Middle East*, 4th ed. Englewood Cliffs, NJ: Prentice-Hall, 1993.

Anderssen, Erin. "The New Canada, Part 4." *The Globe and Mail*, Saturday, June 14, 2003, Globe Focus section.

Beamish, Paul W., and Patrick C. Woodcock. *Strategic Management*. Whitby, ON: McGraw Hill Ryerson, 1999.

Chomsky, Noam. *Necessary Illusions: Thought Control in Democratic Societies*. Concord: House of Anansi Press, 1991.

------. 9-11. New York: Seven Stories Press, 2002.

Douglass, Joseph D. Jr. *Soviet Military Strategy in Europe*. Pergamon Press, 1980.

Dürrenmatt, Peter. *Schweizer Geschichte*. Zurich: Schweizer Druck und Verlagshaus AG, 1963.

Francis, Diane. *Immigration: The Economic Case*. Toronto: Key Porter Books, 2002.

Hackett, Gen. Sir John. *The Profession of Arms*. New York: Macmillan, 1983.

His, Eduard. *Eine Historische Staatsteilung*. Tübingen: Verlag von J.C.B. Mohr , 1927. Eidgenossische Zentralbibliothek K1927.

Hochschild, Adam. *King Leopold's Ghost*. Boston, Houghton Miffin, 1999.

Ibn Khaldoun, Abdel-Rahman ibn Mohammad al Hadrami. *The Muqaddimah*. Vol. 3. Translated by Franz Rosenthal. Bollingen Series. Princeton NJ:Princeton University Press, 1980.

Jedwab, Jack. "A Profile of Canadian Immigration at Century's End." A National Conference on Canadian Immigration. Association for Canadian Studies, 2000.

King, Joan Wuchter. *Historical Dictionary of Egypt*. Metuchen, NJ: Scarecrow Press, 1984.

Knox, Alan B. *Adult Development and Learning*. San Francisco: Jossey-Bass, 1977.

Lenski, Gerhard E. *Power and Privilege: A Theory of Social Stratification*. Chapel Hill, NC: The University of North Carolina Press, 1989.

Lorenz, Konrad. *On Aggression*. London: Methuen, 1969.

McCrum, Robert, William Cran, and Robert McNeil. *The Story of English*. Viking, NY: Viking Penguin, Elizabeth Sifton Books, 1986.

McGinn, Catriona. "Immigration: The Good, the Bad and the Ugly." *The New Canadian*, May/June 2003.

Morgenthau, Hans. *Politics Among Nations*. New York: Alfred A. Knopf, 1991.

Morris, Desmond. *The Naked Ape*. New York: McGraw Hill, 1967.

Ortega y Gasset, Jose. *The Revolt of the Masses*. London: Unwin, 1963 (Reprint WW Norton, 1994.)

Peters, Ralph. "Constant Conflict." Parameters: *U.S. Army War College Quarterly*, 27, no. 2 (summer 1997): <http://carlisle-www.army.mil/usawc/parameters/97summer/peters.htm>.

Power, Samantha. *A Problem From Hell; America in the Age of Genocide*. New York: HarperCollins (Perennial), 2002.

Reich, Robert B. *The Work of Nations: Preparing Ourselves for 21st Century Capitalism*. New York: Alfred A. Knopf, 1991.

Ridley, Matt. Genome: *The Autobiography of a Species in 23 Chapters*. New York: HarperCollins, 1999.

Smith, Ekuwa, and Andrew Jackson. *Does a Rising Tide Lift All Boats? The Labour Market Experiences and Incomes of Recent Immigrants*. Canadian Council on Social Development. <http://www.ccsd.ca> Feb. 28, 2002.

Storti, Craig. *The Art of Crossing Cultures*. Yarmouth, ME: Intercultural Press, 1990.

Taber, Robert. *The War of the Flea: Guerrilla Warfare, Theory and Practice*. London: Granada, 1970/2002.

Taylor, J. P., and J. M. Roberts. *The 20th Century*, Vol. 3. Milwaukee: Purnell Reference Books, 1979.

Trudel, Marcel. *Initiation à la Nouvelle-France*. Holt, Rinehart and Winston, 1968.

Weber, Karl. *Die Revolution im Kanton Basel*. Liestal: Gebr. Ludin, 1907.

INDEX

A

Adult Development and Learning (Knox), 207n
Afghanistan, 180n, 243
Ahmed, Leila, 56, 56n
Alaily, Amr, 36, 134
Alaily, Sherif, 36, 134
Albania, 69n, 80, 81, 82, 83
Albright, Madeleine, 150
Alexandria, Egypt, 65
al-Farrabi (Abu Nasr), 26
Alfi, Azmeralda, 167
Algeria, 12–13, 48, 227, 255
Al-Ghazzali (Abu Hamid Mohamed), 26
Al Hassan Ibn Haitham, 62
Ali, Mohamed Pasha, 80–81, 81n, 82
Al-Kholi, Nora, 166
Al Khowarismi (Abu Ja'far Mohamed), 62n
Al Maimun (Maimonides), 111
Al-Qa'ida, 217
Al-Razi (Abu Bakr Mohamed), 62
Anderson, Roy R., et al., 54n, 61n
Anderssen, Erin, 99, 99n, 105, 105n
Anstey, Roger, 51n
anti-Semitism, 109, 116, 118, 123
Aquinas, Thomas, 109
Arabic language, 61, 62, 65–66, 68–70, 71, 82, 200
Arabic numerals and numbers, 203–204, 254
Arabs
    and Arabic numerals and numbers, 203, 254
    attitudes towards, 106, 109, 234
    and basis of Western science, 58
    and events preceding Gulf War, 149
    and position of Egyptians on Israel, 124
    treatment of Jews in Arab world, 111
    and U.S. role in Middle East, 163
    voice of in Canada, 117
    and Western imperialism, 51–52. *See also*
      Muslims
Attaturk, Kemal, 65
Australia, 133, 232

B

Baghdad (Iraq), 170n
Barak, Ehud, 124–125, 125n
Basel, Switzerland, 246–249
Beamish (Paul W.), 195n
Beauchesne, Eric, 102n
Beaudoin, Louise, 189, 253
Begin, Menachem, 122, 122n
Beirut, Lebanon, 122
Belgium, 50–51
Bern, Switzerland, 91
Bin Laden, Osama, 149, 157, 165, 166, 217, 243
Black, Conrad, 123
Black North Americans, 40–41, 43, 104
Blanchfield, Mike, 109n
Bloc Québécois, 235
B'nai Brith, 118

Boer War, 171n
A Border Passage (Ahmed), 56n
Boston, Massachusetts, 38, 134, 208, 232
Bouchard, Lucien, 9, 17, 30, 189, 222, 235
Boutros-Ghali, Boutros, 202
Brazil, 180
Breed, George, 45–46
Bremer, Paul, 79n
Britain. *See* Great Britain
Bureau of Islamic and Arabic Education, 167
Bush, George (Sr.), 149
Bush, George W., 151, 157n, 162, 163, 167–168,
    169n

C

Cairo, Egypt
    author's personal experiences in, 42, 83, 128,
      130, 134, 166, 212
    capture of by Napoleon, 56
    languages used in, 69, 252
    multiculturalism of, 61
    nationalism in, 56
    similarities to Montreal, 41. *See also* Egypt
Camp David Accords, 122n, 141n
Campeau, Jean, 232
Canada
    access to information in, 183
    and anti-Semitism, 109
    attitudes and behavior, 88–89, 91–92, 116, 120,
      158, 250
    blackout of August 2003, 243
    Canadian Muslims, 165
    cultural identity in, 26–27, 61
    "domestic terrorists" in, 217
    eating habits, 34
    education standards, 217
    ethnic composition, 54, 238, 242
    gap between rich and poor, 221
    geography and weather, 32
    and immigrants, 1, 231
        Canada as immigrant destination, 134, 229,
          232
        impositions on, 177
        integration of, 233–234
        interests/priorities of, 194, 249
        opposition to, 95–96
        shift in origin of, 241–242
        voting power of, 160
        welcoming of, 26–29
    and Islamic/Muslim values, 110, 166
    Jewish community in, 116
    not "real" country, 16, 17, 25, 27, 29
    population growth rates, 222, 223, 226
    and Quebec, 77, 82
        October Crisis, 86
    reaction to 9-11, 144, 148, 157
    relations with U.S., 127–140, 150, 242–243
        Gulf War, 75n

war in Iraq, 106–107, 145–146. *See also*
  Quebec
CanWest Global, 117
Caplan, Elinor, 31
Carter, Jimmy, 122
Center for Economic and Social Rights, 139n
Charest, Jean, 229
Chechnya, 27, 165
Chile, 141
China, 13, 243
Chomsky, Noam, 50n, 125n, 155, 155n, 156n, 157,
  158, 158n, 182n, 189n
Chrétien, Jean, 23, 127, 159
Christianity, 109–110, 111, 168, 169, 169n. *See also*
  religion
Churchill, Winston, 224
Cicero, Marcus Tullius, 154
Clarkson, Adrienne, 187
Colbert, Jean-Baptiste, 183, 186, 188
Coligny, Admiral Gaspard de, 185
Colombia, 13
colonialism. *See* European colonialism; Western
  imperialism
Company of New France, 184
Concordia University, 107, 117, 207n
Congo, 51
"counterSpin" (CBC), 158
Cressaty, René, 64
Crossing Cultures (Storti), 34n
Cunningham, Jack, 135, 136

D
Dion, Stéphane, 189
Dirlik, André, 57
Dirlik, Raja, 57
Douglass (Joseph D. Jr), 74n
Dresden, Germany, 171
Duffy, Andrew, 31n
Duke University Hospital, 39
Durham, North Carolina, 39, 43
Dürrenmatt, Peter, 247, 247n

E
East India Company, 52
Ecuador, 196
Egypt
  authoritarianism in, 46–48, 144, 198
  author's personal experiences in, 36, 130, 238
  Canadian immigrants from, 228
  class system, 65–68, 217, 221
  colonization of, 50, 53, 54–60, 75n, 79–81, 82,
    129, 175, 219
  and "internalized colonialism," 56–57
  culture/philosophy/society, 19–23, 25–26, 31–32,
    63, 90–91, 133
  discrimination in, 43–44
  education in, 63–65, 68–69
  Egyptian nationalism, 56
  Egyptians living in Kuwait, 18–19
  entry into Palestine, 155–156
  and Israel, 112, 122, 124, 169
    reaction in Canada, 114–115
  languages used in, 61, 62, 63, 252

language laws, 68–70
  linguistic conflict, 64–65
  under Nasser, 36, 130–131, 208
  as "real" country, 18–19, 23
  relations with U.S., 133–134, 138, 152–153, 163,
    169
  struggle for independence, 9, 11
  transition to industrial economy, 211–213
  treatment of Jews, 111. *See also* Cairo, Egypt
El Alamein, Battle of, 55
El-Baz, Ossama, 111n
El-Hakim, Leila, 138
Enawi, Dr. Moustapha, 198
European colonialism, 51–60, 165
  "internalized colonialism," 56. *See also* Western
    imperialism
European Common Market, 14
European Union, 10, 14
expatriates, as distinct from immigrants, 33–35

F
Farouk (king of Egypt), 69, 69n, 111, 156
Fawzi, Sherein, 23–25, 167
Fiji, 57–58
First Nations peoples of Canada, 54n, 59, 60
FLQ. *See* Front de Libération du Québec
Fouad I (king of Egypt), 53
France
  ally of Mysore, 53
  foreign policy of, 243
  former colonies of, 52, 179
    Algerian war of independence, 12–13
    and immigrants to Quebec, 227
    New France, 183–184
  the French ideal, 164
  home of scientific discoveries, 203
  imperialism of, 59
  intervention in Egypt, 54–55, 75n, 129
  and location of Basel, 246
  as nation-state, 231
  and Suez War, 70
  treacherous history of, 81
    French Revolution, 220
    treatment of Huguenots, 184–185
  use of English in, 252. *See also* New France
Francis, Diane, 95n, 95–96, 96n, 97, 98, 99, 99n,
  101, 102
Frederick VII (ruler in Switzerland), 72
Friscolanti, Michael, 109n
Front de Libération du Québec, 83, 85, 217

G
Gawad, Mahmoud, 25
The Gazette (Montreal), 123, 178n
General Electric, 115
Geneva, Switzerland, 132, 226n
Genome (Ridley), 70n
Germany
  attack on Belgium, 50–51
  ban on dual citizenship, 27
  behavior of combatants during World War I,
    170–172
  Canadian sovereignty and, 127

differences between Germany and Canada, 87
and Egypt, 55
emigrants from, 186
foreign policy of, 243
languages used in, 199–200, 252
and location of Basel, 246
nationalism and, 12
treacherous history of, 81
Nazism, 155, 169, 220
The Globe and Mail, 158
Göring, Reichsmarschall Hermann, 75
Great Britain
Canada's links to, 104
class system in, 67
and creation of Kuwait, 150–151
imperialism of, 13, 50, 52–54
former colonies of, 52–53, 179, 185–186
intervention in Egypt, 50, 54–55, 75n, 129, 175, 219
and invasion of Iraq, 142, 157n
invention of concentration camps, 171n
and Suez War, 70
treacherous history of, 81
Greece, 14, 75n, 231–232
Grunau, Ruth, 87
Grunau, Ted, 87
Guevara, Ernesto "Che," 160
Gulf War of 1991, 75n, 138, 148, 151

H
Hackett, General Sir John, 74, 74n
Haiti, 255
Hamburg, Germany, 171
Hapsburg Empire, 15, 132
Harper, Stephen, 160
Heft, Professor Riva, 207n
Henry IV (king of France), 184
hijab, wearing of, 23
Hiroshima, Japan, 171
His, Eduard, 248n
Historical Dictionary of Egypt (King), 80n
Eine Historische Staatsteilung (His), 248n
Hitler, Adolf, 33, 133n, 171, 220
Hochschild (Adam), 51n
Holland, 179, 200
"Hot Type" (CBC), 50n, 158
Huguenots, 184–185, 186
Hunt, Terence, 163n
Hurgada, Egypt, 212
Hussein (king of Jordan), 124
Hussein, Saddam, 118, 139, 141, 142, 148, 149, 150, 163

I
Ibn Khaldoun, 25
Ibn Rushd, 26, 62
Ibn Sina, 62
immigrants to Canada
as distinct from expatriates, 33–35
economic and social role, 31, 101–102
educational considerations, 207–220
family reunification program, 96–97
hostility towards, 95–96

interests/priorities of, 10, 130, 160, 181, 193–195, 215, 249
language issues, 61, 98–99, 197–205
policies in New France, 184
to Quebec, 231
decline of, 222–226, 229
government priorities, 225–226
integration of, 236–237
language issues, 188, 197–201, 205, 228, 236, 255–257
Muslim and Arab, 234
sovereignty issue, 77, 189–190, 231–233
shift in origin of, 241–242
Immigration (Francis), 95n, 97n, 98n, 99n
India, 13, 52–53, 54, 55, 84, 203n, 243
Indonesia, 110
Initiation à la Nouvelle-France (Trudel), 184n
Institute of Cardiology (Quebec City), 45
Institut für Höhere Electrotechnik, 132
Iran, 141, 148–149, 163
Shah of, 139
Iraq
creation of, 50
Gulf War of 1991, 75n, 148–150
Iraqi cause and Muslims abroad, 165
U.S. foreign policy and, 162–164, 243
2003 war in, 50, 126, 137, 139, 141n, 142–143, 151, 157, 157n, 162–164
Canadian position on, 99, 106–107, 127, 145–146
Islam
Crusaders and, 121n
defamation of, 110
essence and values of, 124, 165, 166, 167, 170, 171
Islamic terrorists, 163
and motives for 9-11, 170
in Soviet Union, 168
strength and influence of, 58, 121–122, 168–169
growth in N. America, 100, 166
war on, 106, 121
and War on Terror, 5. *See also* Muslims
Ismail, Dr. Mohamed, 65
Israel
Canadian attitudes towards, 107, 114–115, 117, 119
creation of, 133
European attitudes towards, 123
as nation-state, 78, 78n, 231, 232
and pattern of oppression and revenge, 48
security of, 161
and special interests in the Middle East
events leading to Gulf War, 149, 150
Suez War, 70
U.S. invasion of Iraq, 162–163
wars with Egypt, Syria, 75n, 129, 157
supporters of Sharon and Likud party, 153
U.N. censure of, 141n
U.S. support for, 168–169
influence of American Jews, 152
Zionist movement, 112, 118, 199. *See also* Palestine
Israel Symphony Orchestra, 122

Istanbul, Turkey, 157n
Italy, 18, 52, 81, 223, 236

J
Jackson (Andrew), 102n
Janissaries, 80
Japan
    bombing of Hiroshima and Nagasaki, 171
    Canadian sovereignty and, 127
    declining birthrate in, 222
    high school dropout rate, 178
    interning of Japanese Canadians, 104
    as nation-state, 17–18
    as "real" country, 16
    treacherous history of, 81
    use of English in, 252
Jedwab, Jack, 31n, 106n, 223n, 225, 225n
Jerusalem (Israel), 121n
Jewish General Hospital, 114–115
Jews
    American
        influence of, 152–153
        and invasion of Iraq, 162–163
        relations with Muslims, 167
    Canadian, 119
        and anti-Semitism, 17, 104, 109
        and Quebec separatism, 116
        Montreal Jewish community, 114–116, 231
    historical relationship with Muslims, 111–112
    and Israel, 78n, 111–114, 112, 232
    Nazi war on, 169, 220
    "self-hating," 119–121, 125n, 162
    and war on Islam, 121
Jonas, George, 124, 126
Jordan, creation of, 50
Judaism, 112, 120, 121, 169. *See also* Jews

K
Kashmir, 84
Khusrau Pasha, 79, 79n, 80
King (Joan Wuchter), 80n
King Leopold's Ghost (Hochschild), 51n
Klein, Joe, 162
Knox, Alan, 207n, 207–208
Knox, Paul, 151, 151n
Kuhle, Peter, 131
Kurdish people, 141, 148, 149
Kuwait, 18–19, 97, 149, 150–151

L
Laight, Brandon, 64
Landry, Bernard, 106, 231, 232, 249
language
    as class issue, 65–68, 252–254
    and identity, 61
    languages in decline, 199–202
    languages used in Egypt, 68, 82
    languages used in Switzerland, 202
    languages used in the Americas, 179–180
    and nationalism, 68–70
    in New France, 183, 185
    in Quebec, 252–254
        and immigrants, 98–99, 177, 194, 197–199,

226–227, 228, 255–257
    language laws, 6, 187, 188, 190, 199
    source of violent conflict, 70–76
    universal dominance of English, 197, 199–200,
        201–202, 203–204, 205, 216, 249, 252. *See
        also* Arabic language
Laos, 196
Lawrence, Steven, 98
Lebanon, 122
Leibnitz (Gottfried), 58
Leno, Jay, 141, 161
Lenski, Gerhard, 73n, 153n, 181, 181n, 182, 191n
Lévesque, René, 84
Lewis, Avi, 89
Likud party of Israel, 153
Lisée, Jean-François, 235–236
Lorenz, Konrad, 70, 71n, 73, 73n
Los Angeles, California, 167
Louis XIV (king of France), 183, 185

M
Mahler, Gustav, 122
Mahmoud, Ninette, 83
Mamelukes, 79, 80, 81n, 82
Manufacturing Consent (Chomsky), 182n
Marcel Dassault company, 115
Maslow, Abraham, 190, 191
Maté, Gabor, 120
McCrum (Robert) et al., 202n
McGill University, 116n, 208, 209
McGinn (Catriona), 102n
McVeigh (Timothy), 100
Medici, Catherine de, 185
Michaud, Yves, 17
Middle East, 129
    corruption and oppression in, 143, 144
    historical role of, 245
    immigrants from
        in Canada, 105
        as targets, 3–4, 95
    and influence of American Jews, 152
    international workers in, 97
    and perspective on Jews, 5
    position on U.S. foreign policy, 150
    U.S. interests in, 156–157, 162–164
    Western imperialism and, 50, 54, 130, 165. *See
        also* individual countries
"militant enthusiasm," 70, 71, 76
Mizrahi, Emmanuel Pasha, 111
Montreal, Quebec
    author's personal experiences in, 38, 41, 77, 83,
        177, 208
    demonstrations against war in Iraq, 146
    as immigrant destination, 228
    Jewish community in, 114–116, 231
    and mercantilism in New France, 184
    multilingualism of, 62
    position in Quebec, 6, 249–250
        migration from rural areas, 227
    pro-Israel lobby, 107
    and sovereignty issue, 76
    October Crisis, 85. *See also* Quebec
Morgenthau (Hans), 25, 171

Morin, Dr., 45, 46
Morocco, 227
Morris (Desmond), 73n
Moslem Brotherhood, 56
Mubarak, President (Hosni), 111n
Mulroney, Brian, 109, 160
The Muqaddimah (Ibn Khaldoun), 25, 26, 26n
Musharaff, General Pervez, 89
Muslims
    antagonism towards, 3–4, 95, 100, 106, 110, 142
    and Canada
        limits on immigration, 109
        part of Canadian mosaic, 105
    and capture of Saddam Hussein, 150
    historical relationship with Jews, 111–112
    and invasion of Iraq, 162
    and Islam, 5, 10, 121–122, 159, 169
    and motives for 9-11, 170
    North American, 165–172
    position on Israel, 124
    and Quebec, 116, 234
    secular, 58
    wearing of hijab, 23
    and Western imperialism, 51–52. *See also* Islam
Mysore, destruction of, 52–53

N
Nagasaki, Japan, 171
The Naked Ape (Morris), 73n
Napoleon I (emperor of France), 54, 56, 247
Nasser, Gamal Abdel, 28, 36, 91, 130–131, 133, 142, 198, 208
nationalism
    Algerian, 12–13
    American, 10, 234
    Canadian, 54
    Egyptian, 56, 63
    German, extreme, 12
    and language, 63, 68–70, 200
    and the nation-state, 9, 12
    origins of, 11, 55
    Quebec, 11, 76, 234, 250
        affecting prosperity, 188
        and immigrants, 177, 227, 237
        and language issues, 201, 252, 253–254
        negative impact of, 76, 255
        replacing religion, 251
        xenophobic, 233, 235
    and violent conflict, 70, 71, 72, 76
National Socialist German Workers Party, 155
nation-state
    behavior of, 9–10, 12, 127
    Belgium as, 51
    benign, 14
    and concept of loyalty, 180n
    in the Industrial Age, 216
    Israel as, 78n, 122
    need for group cohesion in, 180
    Norway as, 14
    Quebec aspirations to become, 231
    and religion, 167
    soldiers-of-fortune and, 15
    spread of idea, 55

U.S. as, 137
    and violent conflict, 71
Necessary Illusions (Chomsky), 155n, 189n
Nelson (Lord Horatio), 55
New Brunswick, 180
Newfoundland and Labrador, 225
New France, 179, 181, 183–187, 188, 195–196, 225, 235
Newton (Isaac), 58
Nieves, Evelyn, 139n
Nile, Battle of the, 55
9-11
    and backlash against Muslims and Arabs, 95, 105, 109, 118, 144, 169n, 234
    and Canada, 86, 127, 148, 234
    and Chechen rebels, 27
    effect on immigrants, 151
    and Muslim faith, 5
    perpetrated by Muslims living in U.S., 165
    reasons for/assignment of blame for, 139, 151–152, 156–160, 170, 171
    resulting in changed world, 243
    Third World reaction to, 147
    victims of, 138, 151
    and War on Terror 3–4, 139, 160–161
9-11 (Chomsky), 158n
Noriega (General Manuel), 139
North Korea, 13–14, 106
Norway, 14
Nova Scotia, 225

O
October Crisis, 85–86
Ohl, Paul, 235, 235n
On Aggression (Lorenz), 71n, 73n
Ontario, 222, 224–225, 228, 250, 256
"Operation Desert Storm," 151. *See also* Gulf War of 1991
Opium Wars, 13
Ortega y Gasset, José, 209, 209n

P
Pakistan, 84, 89–90
Palestine
    creation of, 50
    and creation of Jewish state, 111–112
    Egyptian entry into, 155–156
    Nasser's position on, 133
    Palestinian cause, 258
        Canadian lobby, 117
        and Muslims abroad, 165
        and "self-hating Jews," 119
    and U.S., 141, 157, 163. *See also* Israel
Paris, France, 231
Parizeau, Jacques, 233, 249
Parti Québécois, 178, 190, 238
"pasha," title of, 79n
Pearson, Prime Minister (Lester B.), 9
Perle, Richard, 141n
Peters, Ralph, 217, 217n
Plains of Abraham, Battle of the, 186
Politics and Change (Anderson et al.), 54n, 61n
Portugal, 13, 52, 179

Powell, Colin, 162
Power, Samantha, 137, 137n, 158, 164
Power and Privilege (Lenski), 73n, 153n, 181n, 191n
La Presse, 178n
A Problem from Hell (Power), 137n
The Profession of Arms (Hackett), 74n
"Project for a New American Century," 141n
Pyramids, Battle of the, 56

Q
Quebec
  British and French colonialism and, 59
  civil unrest in, 76, 83–86, 217
  class system in, 217, 252–254
  decline in population, 221–230, 255, 256
  high school dropout rates, 177–178
  history of coercion, 187–189
  immigrants to, 5, 6, 175–178, 194, 229, 231
    and "distinct society," 1, 6
    and ethnic tolerance, 116
    and language issue, 35, 197–205, 235–236
    and "real" Quebecers, 231–238
    and sovereignty movement, 6, 28–29, 116, 225,
      228, 229, 231, 232–233, 237, 238
  integrity in, 92
  marriage laws, 41
  as nation, 11, 16–17, 196, 231–232
    Canadian position on separation, 29
    economic issues, 11
    fragility of French language, 201
    referendum, 29
    tolerance on both sides of issue, 87, 92
  political similarities to Egypt, 82–83
  position of Montreal in, 249–250
  Québécois de souche, 43, 43n, 106, 229, 237, 250,
    251, 252, 257
  "Quiet Revolution," 41, 48, 82, 178, 178n, 191,
    222, 234, 251, 252
  racism against Québécois, 43–44, 48
  reaction to criticism, 5
  translation of documents into French, 45–46
  and U.S.-led invasion of Iraq, 106–107
  vast geography of, 33. *See also* language;
    nationalism
Quebec City, Quebec, 184
"Quiet Revolution." *See* under Quebec

R
Rabin, Prime Minister (Itzhak), 125n
racism
  in Canada, 104–106, 107
    against Québécois, 43–44, 48
  false, 102–104
  following 9-11, 234
  and immigration to Quebec, 188
  in Israel, 112
  in New France, 235
  in U.S., 40–41, 43. *See also* anti-Semitism
"real" country, notion of, 16–17, 25, 27, 29, 128
Reich, Robert, 211n, 213, 214, 215, 215n, 216, 217,
  219
religion
  as basis for conflict, 109–110

New France and, 181n, 184, 188, 235
  religious tolerance in English colonies, 186
  replaced by nationalism, 251
  treatment of Huguenots, 184–185. *See also*
    Christianity; Islam; Jews; Judaism; Muslims
The Revolt of the Masses (Ortega y Gasset), 209,
  209n
Die Revolution im Kanton Basel (Weber), 247n
Richelieu, Cardinal (Armand Jean Duplessis), 183,
  184, 188, 235
Ridley (Matt), 70n
Rifaat, Aziz, 23, 28, 83, 213
Rifaat, Cherif, 123
Rifaat, Heidi, 31, 41, 113, 134, 212, 238
Rifaat, Ismail, 19, 193
Rifaat, Karim, 57
Rifaat, Mo (Mohsen), 18–19, 228
Rifaat, Shereen, 57
Rifaat, Tarek, 57
Roberts, J. M., 51n
Rome, Italy, 236
Rommel, Erwin, 55
Rouleau, Alain, 232
Rousseau, Jean-Jacques, 11, 154
Roy, Arundhati, 139n
Russia, 30, 127, 196, 243
  and Chechnya, 27, 165. *See also* Soviet Union

S
Sadat, Anwar, 28, 122, 122n, 124
Saudi Arabia, 97, 149, 252
Saxer, Professor, 202
Schären, Marianne, 28
Schären, Rolf, 28
Schweizer Geschichte (Dürrenmatt), 247n
Sebe, Alec, 115
Sempach, Battle of, 132
Sevunts, Levon, 124
Sharon (Ariel), 153, 163
Smith (Ekuwa), 102n
The Social Contract (Rousseau), 154n
Solomon, Evan, 50n, 137
Somoza (Anastasio), 139
South Africa, 171n
Southam newspaper chain, 117
Soviet Military Strategy in Europe (Douglass), 74n
Soviet Union, 74, 133, 137, 155, 168, 198, 202. *See
  also* Russia
Spain, 52, 111, 171, 179, 187, 223
Storti (Craig), 34n
The Story of English (McCrum et al.), 202n
Strategic Management (Beamish), 195n
Straw, Jack, 157n
Strutt, Professor M. J. O., 132
Stuttgart, Germany, 113
Sudan, 196
Suez crisis, 55, 70, 129
Sweden, 179
Switzerland
  attitude towards foreigners, 208
  author's personal experiences in, 36, 91, 130–132
  languages spoken in, 202, 204, 252
  as nation-state, 14, 15

neutrality of, 145
as not "real" country, 16
social hierarchy in, 132
success and prosperity of, 159
violent history of, 72
weather and geography, 32. *See also* Basel;
  Geneva; Zurich
"symbolic-analytic" work (Reich), 214–215, 217,
  221, 223, 227
Syria, 50, 163

T
Taber (Robert), 142n
Taher, Adel, 79
Taher, Prince Ahmed, 80, 81
Taher, Malak, 79
Taher, Nemat, 79
Taher Pasha, Mohamed, 79n, 79–81, 80n, 82
Taher, Saiid, 79
Taher, Saiid Sr., 79
Taylor, J. P., 51n
Thoreau, Henry David, 182, 183n
Toronto, Ontario, 35–36, 134, 226, 228, 250
Trudeau, Pierre, 238
Trudel, Marcel, 184n
Turkey, 12, 23, 52, 62, 65–66, 75n, 79–81, 200
The 20th Century (Taylor and Roberts), 51n

U
Ukrainian Canadians, 104
Unitarian Church, 41
United Kingdom. *See* Great Britain
United States
  author's personal experiences in, 38–41, 208
  behavior of combatants during World War I, 170
  civilized behavior in, 250
  class system in, 219
  "domestic terrorists" in, 217
  foreign policy, 106, 243–244
    bombing of poor countries, 242
    and Egypt, 50, 75n, 129, 133–134, 152–153
    Gulf War, 148–151
    invasion of Iraq, 141n, 142
    and Middle East, 75n, 162–164, 165
  immigrants to, 95, 194, 231, 232
  and Islam
    power of, 169
    tenets of, 110
  languages used in, 180, 202
  loss of civil liberties in, 143–144
  loss of Spanish colonies to, 179
  as matriarchy, 133
  and Muslim values, 166
  nationalism of, 10, 234
  as not "real" country, 16
  racism in, 40–41
  relations with Canada, 6, 104, 127–140, 242–243
    Canada/Quebec position on invasion of Iraq,
      106–107
    and Canadians of Middle-Eastern origin, 105
  religious/ethnic/racial tolerance in, 27, 152
  ruling elite of, 154–155
  special interests of, 152–153, 156–157

"symbolic-analysts" in, 221
threat of terrorist attacks, 99–100
treatment of Muslims, 166–168
values of, 4–5, 141–143
War of Independence, 11. *See also* 9-11; Gulf
  War of 1991; Vietnam War; War on Terror
U.S.S.R.. *See* Soviet Union

V
Vallières, Pierre, 43n
Venne, Jules-Pascal, 178, 178n, 190
Vietnam War, 129, 134, 138, 141, 170

W
Waltham, Massachusetts, 45
The War of the Flea (Taber), 142n
War on Terror 219
  9-11 and, 3–4
  and Canada
    immigrants to, 3–4
    Muslim Canadians, 104
    relations with U.S., 127
  effectiveness of, 160–162
  and global class war, 156
  hypothetical scenario, 217
  immigrants and, 99–101
  not war against Islam or Muslims, 5, 167
  and patterns of oppression and revenge, 48
  targeting of certain groups, 144
  and U.S. foreign policy, 106. *See also* 9-11;
    United States
Warsaw, Poland, 122
Weber, Karl, 247, 247n
Weberman, Rabbi Mordechi, 120n
Western imperialism, 49–55, 57–59, 58, 144, 147.
  See also European colonialism
White Niggers of America (Vallières), 43, 43n
Wolfowitz, Paul, 162, 163
The Work of Nations (Reich), 211n

Z
Zionist movement, 112, 118, 119
Zurich, Switzerland, 32, 41, 90, 130, 168, 202